A Guide to
European Community Law

AUSTRALIA AND NEW ZEALAND
The Law Book Company Ltd.
Sydney : Melbourne : Perth

CANADA AND U.S.A.
The Carswell Company Ltd.
Agincourt, Ontario

INDIA
N. M. Tripathi Private Ltd.
Bombay
and
Eastern Law House Private Ltd.
Calcutta and Delhi
M.P.P. House
Bangalore

ISRAEL
Steimatzky's Agency Ltd.
Jerusalem : Tel Aviv : Haifa

MALAYSIA : SINGAPORE : BRUNEI
Malayan Law Journal (Pte.) Ltd.
Singapore

PAKISTAN
Pakistan Law House
Karachi

A Guide to
European Community Law

by

P. S. R. F. Mathijsen

*Director-General with the Commission
of the European Communities
Professor of Law, University of Nijmegen*

Fourth Edition

London
Sweet & Maxwell
1985

First Edition 1972
Second Edition 1975
Second Impression 1976
Third Edition 1980
Fourth Edition 1985

Published in Great Britain by
Sweet & Maxwell Ltd.
of 11 New Fetter Lane, London
Computerset by
P.B. Computer Typesetting,
Pickering, N. Yorkshire
Printed and bound in Great Britain by
Hazell Watson and Viney Limited

British Library Cataloguing in Publication Data

Mathijsen, P.S.R.F.
 A guide to European Community law.—4th ed.
 1. Law—European Economic Community countries
 2. European communities
 I. Title
 341'.094 [LAW]

 ISBN 0–421–33930–6

To my daughters Claire
Bénédicte
Stéphanie
Valérie
Olivia
Daphné

ACKNOWLEDGMENT

Let me start by saying how pleasant it is to have the opportunity to express gratitude on the occasion of the publication of a fourth edition! Maybe I have illusions but it gives me the feeling that there are people who think it is all worthwhile.

In the first place, the publishers who asked me to write this "Guide" once again: I imagine they did it because they saw something in it!

Then there are those who passively or actively were of direct assistance. The passive ones, if one dares call them that, are, in the first place, the family: wife and children who accepted that for months practically every evening and every weekend was spent behind my desk. Without their tolerance and acceptance things would have been quite different.

And those who actively participated: in the first place my colleague Professor Wellens, my assistant Mr. Keurentjes who helped with research, reading of the manuscript and good counsel; in this respect I would also like to mention my student-assistants Mrs. M. Dragstra, Miss P. Visch and Mr. B. Leerschool. And in the second place Mrs. Lonero, who by setting the text on a word-processor enormously simplified my writing and the preparation of the "manu"-script.

PREFACE

The first edition of this book covered the development of Community law up to the middle of 1972 and was published shortly before Denmark, Ireland and the United Kingdom joined the European Communities.

The second edition, which consisted mainly in an updating of the first, appeared in June 1975, after the negotiations regarding Britain's continued membership of the European Communities were concluded.

The third edition came out just before the accession of Greece and this one, the fourth, appears once again on the eve of an enlargement, this time with Portugal and Spain.

Basically the structure of the book has been left unchanged: only Chapter 6 concerning the European Economic Community is now divided in three parts to allow for a more systematic and sectoral approach. For instance, the creation of a special section on External Relations should help those who want to single out this particular subject and it also underlines the importance of the Community's role in this field. Two chapters have been added: one on Fisheries to reflect to recent developments and achievements in this domain, and one on industrial and intellectual property rights which play an increasing role both in the field of the free movement of goods and that of competition.

However the main focus points within Part Two on Common Policies of the EEC remain Agriculture, Competition and Regional Policy.

Since we are so close to the enlargement with Portugal and Spain the resulting modifications have been indicated mainly in the institutional framework.

The object of the book has not changed, i.e. to give the reader an overall view of the state of development of Community law. This development has to be placed, necessarily, within the larger context of the progress made by the European Communities as such. In this respect it will be noted that in the past five years they have not merely survived the economic and energy crisis but have continued to develop both internally and externally. The most impressive of the various events which marked the last five years should be briefly mentioned.

The relation between the Community and an imposing number of developing countries was renewed and strengthened once again. In 1975, the first Lomé Convention was signed with 46 African, Caribbean and Pacific States; there were 58 in 1979; with the third Lomé Convention signed in 1984 the number has increased to 63. Once again the Community's responsibilities and influence in the third world were thereby enlarged.

A number of other important events deserve to be underlined most of them concern the finances of the Community. This is not surprising: the recession all the Member States have gone through in the past years have made them particularly attentive on this subject. It was nevertheless possible after protracted negotiations to reach agreement on an increase of the Community's own resources and although this increase is overdue and insufficient, it constitutes an essential step to allow the Community to expand its activities. Closely linked to this development is the decision of the Council (not accepted by the other institutions) on budgetary discipline and the agreement concerning the U.K. contribution.

Disagreement on these subjects caused severe frictions during the past years and blocked progress in several fields; it is to be expected that the way has now been cleared for further developments mainly in the fields of research and development, high technology, the elimination of the non-tariff trade barriers and the reform of the common agricultural policy.

Mention must also be made of the second direct election of the European Parliament and the increased influence of this institution on the activities of the Community.

It seems therefore not exaggerated to refer to a new vitality of a Community which now encompasses most of Europe and has developed strong links with the rest of the world.

May, 1985

P. S. R. F. MATHIJSEN

CONTENTS

x   *Contents*

TABLE OF CASES

COURT OF JUSTICE OF THE EUROPEAN COMMUNITIES

xvi   *Table of Cases*

COMMISSION DECISIONS

TABLE OF EUROPEAN TREATIES

TABLE OF COMMUNITY SECONDARY LEGISLATION

TABLE OF UNITED KINGDOM LEGISLATION

ABBREVIATIONS

A.C.P.

African, Caribbean and Pacific countries, signatories to the Lomé Convention I and II.

Act of Accession

Act concerning the conditions of accession of Denmark, Ireland and the U.K. and the adjustments to the treaties establishing the ECSC, EEC and EAEC, annexed to the Treaty of accession. For texts see *Sweet & Maxwell's European Community Treaties* (1980).

Adaptation Decision

Council Decision of the European Communities of January 1, 1973, adjusting the instruments concerning the accession of Denmark, Ireland and the United Kingdom to the European Communities, O.J. 1973, L.2. These adjustments were necessary because Norway, although a signatory to the Treaty of accession, did not become a member of the European Communities.

Budgetary Treaties

Treaties of April 22, 1970, (and July 22, 1975) amending Certain Budgetary (Financial) Provisions of the Treaties establishing the European Communities and of the Treaty establishing a Single Council and a Single Commission of the European Communities.

Bull.

Bulletin of the European Communities edited by the Secretariat of the Commission; there are 11 issues per year (July–August are published together).

Bull. Suppl.

Supplement to the Bulletin.

C.M.L.R.

Common Market Law Reports.

C.M.L.Rev.

Common Market Law Review.

Competition Report

Report on Competition Policy.

Dec.   Decision.

Dir.   Directive.

E.C.R.   Official reports of cases before the Court of Justice in English.

ECSC   European Coal and Steel Community.

EEC   European Economic Community.

E.L.Rev.   European Law Review.

Euratom   European Community of Atomic Energy.

Gen. Rep.   General Report on the activities of the Communities, published yearly by the Commission. The year mentioned after the word Report refers to the period covered by the Report.

J.O.   *Journal Officiel*: French edition of the *Official Journal of the European Communities.*
                       Remarks
                       1. This Journal was published under the name *Journal Officiel de la Communauté Européenne du Charbon et de l'Acier* from 1952 to April 19, 1958; on April 20, 1958, the first issue of the *Journal Officiel des Communautés Européennes* appeared, without modifying the structure of the Journal itself; this lasted until December 31, 1967.
                       References to publications in the *Journal Officiel* for the period 1952 to July 1, 1967, are made by mentioning the page and the year or vice versa such as J.O. 849/65. Between July 1 and December 31, 1967, each issue is paged separately.
                       2. After January 1, 1968 (see O.J. 1968, L.30), the Journal was divided into two separate editions designated by the letters "L." (legislation) and "C." (communications).
                       Legislative texts are published in the edition marked "L." and are again subdivided in two categories:

J.O.—*cont.*

    I. Acts for which publication is a condition for their application (see EEC, Art. 191);

    II. Acts for which publication is not required.

All other texts appear in the edition marked "C.".

References to publications in the *Journal Officiel* after January 1, 1968, are made by mentioning the letter "L." or "C.", the year, the No. of the issue and the page, *e.g.* J.O. 1970, 31/1.

3. Starting on January 1, 1973, the Journal is also published in the Danish and English languages.

4. In accordance with Article 155 of the Act of Accession, provision was made in Council Regulation 857/72 of April 24, 1972, for Special Editions of the *Official Journal* for the publication *inter alia* of the English text of acts of the institutions of the Communities adopted and published before accession. Consequently an authentic English translation now exists of the most important Community acts.

This special edition was published in November and December 1972 and a subsequent edition was published in 1974 (see O.J. 1972, L.101/1). All references to an O.J. publication prior to January 1, 1973 are necessarily in the Special Edition.

5. The numbering of the pages is the same in the French, English and other language editions.

6. Starting on January 1, 1981, the Official Journal is also published in Greek.

Merger Treaty

Treaty of April 8, 1965, establishing a Single Council and a Single Commission of the European Communities.

O.J.

Official Journal of the European Communities; see J.O. above.

Rec.

Recueil de la Jurisprudence de la Cour, Official Court Reports.

Reg.   Regulation.

Rules   Rules of Procedure of the Court of Justice (O.J. 1975, L.102/1).

CHAPTER 1

THE EUROPEAN COMMUNITIES

When the European Coal and Steel Community was established in 1952, the drafters of the Treaty coined the word "supranational" to indicate the particular character of their creation and the law it embodied. Although it was set up by an international agreement similar to many others concluded between sovereign states, the signatories were conscious of having drafted something that was different from international law, the law of nations. They were not, like so many countries before them, merely creating mutual obligations[1]; they were doing much more: they were limiting their own sovereign rights, transferring them to institutions over which they had no direct control and endowing them with powers they did not always possess themselves. Furthermore they were not only binding the states they represented to assume new rights and obligations, they were also directly including their citizens, who became subjects of the Community.

By contrast with ordinary international treaties, the European treaties have thus created their own legal system to which the term "international" could not apply; the term "supranational" would therefore indicate the difference: the law of the Community is not international law.

On the other hand, the terms and the spirit of the European treaties make it impossible for the Member States, as a corollary, to accord precedence to their national law over a legal system accepted by them on a basis of reciprocity. The executive force of Community law cannot vary from one state to another in deference to domestic laws without jeopardising the attainment of the objectives of the treaties.[2] The law of the European

---

[1] Case 26/62 *Van Gend en Loos* v. *Nederlandse Administratie der Belastingen* [1963] E.C.R. 1 at 12.
[2] Case 6/64 *Costa* v. *ENEL* [1964] E.C.R. 585 at 594.

1

Communities cannot therefore be regarded as national law. It is different and independent, it stands apart, it is not national law; since it is common to 10 nations, it is "supranational." The term has now fallen into disrepute and is no longer used. This does not change the specific nature of the law created by the Treaties; more important, the concept is now universally accepted and expressed by the words "Community law." Community law is to be found mainly in the European Treaties and the secondary legislation. Originally there were the treaties setting up the European Coal and Steel Community (ECSC), the European Atomic Energy Community (Euratom) and the European Economic Community (EEC). The first two can be designated as sectoral Treaties while the third one, the EEC Treaty, covers the economy in general (hereinafter "the Treaty" means the EEC Treaty signed in Rome in 1957). Reference must also be made to the successive texts which implemented and amended the basic texts: the Convention on certain institutions common to the three Communities; the Treaty establishing a single Council and a single Commission, the Decision creating the Communities' own resources, the Treaty amending certain budgetary provisions, the Treaty of accession of Denmark, Ireland and the United Kingdom, the Treaty amending certain financial provisions, the Act concerning direct elections for the European Parliament and, finally, the Treaty concerning Greek accession and the Treaty amending, with regard to Greenland, the Treaties establishing the European Communities.[3] However those only constitute the charter, the point of departure.

Community law has gradually evolved and developed over the past 32 years, from the 100 Articles of the Coal and Steel Treaty, into an impressive body of law comprising thousands of Regulations, Directives, Decisions, Resolutions, Agreements, Programmes and other measures, and above all the case law of the Court of Justice.

It is impressive, not because of its sheer volume but because of its original character and its growth potential. It is worthwhile considering this particular nature of the body of Community law: except for the basic treaties mentioned earlier, none of the Communities' acts find their origin in the traditional institutions, bodies and organs with which lawyers and citizens are familiar and over which they exercise, through democratic elections,

[3] See O.J. 1985, L. 29/1.

some sort of control. Community regulations, directives, decisions, etc., are issued outside most citizens' own country, according to procedures they often cannot grasp and too remote to be controlled; they are nevertheless directly involved. Not only do those measures impose obligations upon them, without the possibility of their national authorities controlling either their implementation or their enforcement, but they confer upon them rights which they in turn can ask their national courts to uphold against fellow-citizens, undertakings and even their own government. And indeed, these rights arise not only where they are expressly granted by the Treaty, but also as a consequence of the obligations which the Treaty, in a clearly defined way, imposes upon individuals as well as upon the Member States and the institutions of the Community.[4] Citizens can also challenge the legality of Community measures in the Community Court, when they are directly and individually concerned.

The apparent aloofness of the European authorities combined with this direct involvement is sometimes bewildering, although the direct election of the members of the European Parliament has made most people in the Member States familiar with at least some of the aspects of Community law. But, if democratic control through directly elected representatives is to become a reality, some knowledge of the basic rules and procedures of the Community is required.

Since all the citizens are concerned, it seems that not only the law student but also the practitioner, the politician and the general public must understand what it is all about. Unless one realises what the objectives are and what means and procedures have been provided to attain them, no participation is possible, no criticism is justified, no suggestion can be pertinent. The objectives are clearly set out in the Treaty: to promote throughout the Community harmonious development of economic activities, a continuous and balanced expansion, an increase in stability, an accelerated raising of the standard of living and closer relations between the Member States.[5] The means provided by the Treaty seem rather limited; there is first the establishment, functioning and development of a common market and second the progressive approximation of the economic policies of the Member States. But while the Treaty provides precise rules and timetables

[4] See n.1, above.
[5] EEC, Art. 2.

for the former, the second is described in very general terms. However, notwithstanding this vagueness, Community activities have penetrated more and more social, economic and related domains, some of which are not explicitly provided for under the Treaty, *e.g.* energy, regional policy, environment, consumer protection and the European Monetary System. Community law is therefore also impressive because of its continuous growth since next to the coal and steel and nuclear sectors, the EEC Treaty aims at integrating the entire economies of the Member States.

The dynamics of the Communities is not the only proof of their vitality; notwithstanding a decade of economic recession and political crises of all kinds, they not only held together but expanded both geographically and politically, which seems to indicate that they fulfill a basic need and respond to a profound aspiration.

CHAPTER 2

HISTORY

Every institution is the product of a series of historical events and at the same time reflects the convictions, hopes and concerns of those who were instrumental in establishing it. The European Communities are no exception to this. For a full understanding and correct interpretation of the European treaties some knowledge of the historical background seems necessary.

Although the expression "United States of Europe" was already used by Victor Hugo in 1849,[1] there is no need to go that far back! The end of the Second World War seems a fair starting point, notwithstanding the existence before that of a very active but not too influential Pan-European Movement inspired by Count Coudenhove-Kalergi.

1. Churchill's speech

The agreement made at Yalta in 1945 by the United Kingdom, the United States and the U.S.S.R. left Europe more divided than ever and the growing antagonism among the victorious "Allies" spelt only more tensions and catastrophies. It was on September 19, 1946, in a speech at Zurich University, that Winston Churchill proposed a "sovereign remedy," *i.e.* to "recreate the European family, or as much of it as we can, and provide it with a structure under which it can dwell in peace, in safety and in freedom. We must build a kind of United States of Europe." And he went on to "say something that will astonish you. The first step in the recreation of the European family must be a partnership between France and Germany"; at that time it needed a lot of courage and foresight to make such a suggestion. As will be seen, it was this (British) idea which also inspired the French Government in 1950 to propose the establishment of the European Coal and Steel Community. Towards the end of his Zurich speech, Churchill

[1] See Henri Brugmans, *L'idée Européenne, 1920–1970* (Bruges, 1970).

5

also proposed to start by setting up a regional structure and to form a Council of Europe.[2]

2. Marshall Plan-OEEC

If Churchill's words were well received, the European states in those days lacked the necessary stamina to proceed with such far-reaching plans, since they were preoccupied with their daily fight for economic survival. Once again the United States came to the rescue. In another famous university speech, at Harvard this time, George Marshall, United States Secretary of State, announced on June 5, 1947, that the United States would do "whatever it is able to do to assist in the return of normal economic health in the world." This offer was accepted by 16 European countries on July 15, 1947, and so the Marshall Plan was born; but more important for the future of European integration was the setting up of the Organisation of European Economic Co-operation (OEEC)[3] in 1948; this was in response to the American request for an agreement among Europeans.

3. Robert Schuman: May 9, 1950

In the meantime, Churchill's words about a partnership between France and Germany had not been forgotten and on May 9, 1950 Robert Schuman, French Foreign Minister, declared that a united Europe was essential for world peace and that a gathering of the European nations required the elimination of the century-old opposition between France and Germany. As a first practical step towards this end he proposed "to place the whole Franco-German coal and steel production under one joint High Authority, in an organization open to the participation of the other countries of Europe." He described this pooling of production as the "first stage of the European Federation." Germany, the Netherlands, Belgium, Luxembourg and Italy accepted in principle and negotiations started at once.

4. European Coal and Steel Community

The negotiations progressed rapidly and were simplified by the

---

[2] The Treaty establishing the Council of Europe was signed in London on May 5, 1949.

[3] In 1961, it became the Organisation for Economic Co-operation and Development (OECD), with the participation of the U.S.A. and Canada.

fact that all the future partners had accepted the proposed principles; the work consisted mainly in giving them legal form. A sense of urgency was probably added to the existing goodwill by the communist invasion in South Korea. The Treaty establishing the European Coal and Steel Community (ECSC) was signed in Paris, on April 18, 1951. Ratification by the national parliaments met with little opposition and on July 25, 1952, the Treaty entered into force.

5. European Defence Community

The following two years were difficult. It has been said that the easing of the international political situation—Stalin died on March 5, 1953 and July 27, 1953 marked the end of the Korean war—diminished the necessity for "closing the ranks." In any case, two additional proposals for close co-operation among the "Six"—in the form of a European Defence Community and a European Political Community—failed miserably.

6. EEC and Euratom

Undaunted by those setbacks, the Benelux countries proposed in 1955, to their partners in the Coal and Steel Community, to take another step towards economic integration by setting up a common market and jointly developing transportation, classical and atomic energy. This led to the conference of Messina in the same year, at which Mr.Spaak was asked to report on the feasibility of those plans. At that time an invitation was issued also to the British Government to join the negotiations of the Six; alas, to no avail.[4]

The "Spaak Report" was ready in 1956, and was discussed in Venice, where the decision was taken to start negotiations for drafting treaties that would establish a "common market" and an Atomic Energy Community. With incredible speed (June 1956– February 1957) these two complex treaties were prepared for signature in Rome on March 25, 1957, and on January 1, 1958, the European Economic Community (EEC) and the European Atomic Energy Community (Euratom) became a reality. In 1961, the British Government decided to apply for negotiations to determine whether satisfactory arrangements could be made to

---

[4] See Hans Joachim Heiser, *British Policy with regard to the unification efforts on the European Continent* (Leyden, 1959), p. 96.

meet the needs of the United Kingdom, of the Commonwealth and of EFTA. The Government were "baulked in their objective, so that it was not possible to determine whether satisfactory conditions of entry could be obtained."[5]

7. Merger Treaty

On April 8, 1965, the institutional set-up of the Communities was simplified by the treaty establishing "a Single Council and a Single Commission of the European Communities," commonly referred to as the "Merger Treaty." This treaty became effective on July 1, 1967; as from that date there was therefore one Council, one European Commission, one European Court and one Assembly for all three Communities.[6]

8. The Customs Union

The Customs Union was fully operative in the EEC on July 1, 1968. It meant that tariff and quota restrictions between Member States had by then been completely abolished and that the replacement of the national external tariff by- the common external tariff had been completed. The Community was 18 months ahead of the schedule laid down in the Treaty.[7]

9. British membership

After a debate in both Houses of Parliament, at the end of which the Government's decision was approved in the Commons by a majority of 426, the British Government applied for membership of the Communities on May 10, 1967. By December of the same year it was clear however that the "Six" could not reach the unanimity necessary under the Community treaties to return a reply to Britain's application. Thus ended the second endeavour of the United Kingdom to enter "Europe." The British Government, however, decided to maintain their application for membership and it was discussed at many meetings of the Council of the Communities in the following two years.

At the meeting of Heads of State or Government, on December 1 and 2, 1969, at The Hague, it was finally agreed to open

---

[5] *The United Kingdom and the European Communities*, 1971 (Cmnd. 4715), para. 6.
[6] See below.
[7] Twelve years, see EEC, Art. 8 and Acceleration Decisions (J.O. 1960, 1217 and J.O. 1962, 1284).

negotiations between the Communities and the states which had applied for membership. Other important decisions taken at this "Summit" concerned the economic and monetary union and the Community's own resources, *i.e.* Community's direct income system.

The Treaty of Brussels relating to the accession of the United Kingdom, Ireland, Norway and Denmark was signed on January 22, 1972; this Treaty entered into force on January 1, 1973, except for Norway which, as a result of a referendum on the subject, did not ratify the Treaty. Consequently, several provisions of this Treaty and of the "Act concerning the conditions of accession and the adjustments to the Treaties" attached thereto were modified by the Council Decision of January 1, 1973, adjusting the documents concerning accession of the new Member States to the European Communities (hereinafter referred to as the "Adaptation Decision").

10. Further enlargement

On June 12, 1975, Greece applied for membership to the European Communities and the Treaty of Accession, together with an Act concerning the conditions of accession and the adjustments to the Treaties were signed at Athens on May 28, 1979[8]; it was ratified by the Greek Parliament on June 28, 1979. On March 28, 1977, Portugal[9] and on July 28, 1977, Spain[10] applied for membership. Formal negotiations with Portugal started on October 16, 1978, and with Spain on February 5, 1979. They were successfully concluded at the European Council of March 29 and 30, 1985 and the third enlargement should become effective on January 1, 1986, bringing the total of Member States to 12.

11. Direct election of Parliament, Declaration on Democracy and fundamental rights

On September 20, 1976, the representatives of the Member States in Council agreed on the conditions for the direct election and signed an Act concerning the Election of the Representatives of the Assembly by Direct Universal Suffrage[11] which was subsequently ratified by the nine national parliaments. The first

[8] O.J. 1979, L. 291/1.
[9] Bull. 3–1977, 8 and Suppl. 5/78.
[10] Bull. 7/8–1977, 6 and Suppl. 9/78.
[11] O.J. 1976, L. 278/1.

elections were held in June 1979,[12] giving the European Communities their democratic legitimacy.

On April 5, 1977 the European Parliament, the Council and the Commission issued a Joint Declaration on Fundamental Rights[13] with which the Heads of State and of Government associated themselves in their Declaration on Democracy in which they confirm their will to ensure that the values of their legal, political and moral order are respected and to safeguard the principles of representative democracy, of the rule of law, of social justice and of respect for human rights. They stated that the application of these principles implies a political system of pluralist democracy.[14]

On June 19, 1983, the ten Heads of State and Government signed the Solemn Declaration on European Union expressing *inter alia* their determination "to achieve a comprehensive and coherent common political approach" and their will to transform the whole complex of relations between their States into a European Union.[15]

12. Secession of Greenland

On February 1, 1985, Greenland ceased to be part of the European Communities to which it had belonged since January 1, 1973, as part of the Kingdom of Denmark. Greenland has enjoyed a special status within the Kingdom since the Home Rule Act of 1979 and the Greenland Government has exclusive competence among others for fishing, agriculture and stock farming.

Greenland's special features, *i.e.* remoteness, climatic conditions and the cultural particularities of its non-European population pleaded in favour of new arrangements after the people of the island had decided in 1982 by referendum to withdraw from the Community and to seek a new type of relationship. The Treaty Provisions applicable to overseas countries and territories provided an appropriate framework for these relations, although additional specific provisions were needed.[16]

[12] See below, European Parliament.
[13] O.J. 1977, C. 103/1.
[14] Bull. 3–1978, 5; in other words a State without pluralistic democracy cannot be a member of the European Communities.
[15] Bull. 6–1983, 24. See also Draft Treaty establishing the European Union, Bull. 2–1984, 7.
[16] See Commission opinion on the status of Greenland (Bull. 1–1983, 13) and text of amending treaty with various Council regulations (O.J. 1985, L. 29/1).

CHAPTER 3

THE INSTITUTIONS AND OTHER ORGANS OF THE COMMUNITY

Among the various bodies established by, or in pursuance of, the European Treaties,[1] four are referred to as "institutions": the Assembly (European Parliament), the Council, the Commission and the Court of Justice.[2] What distinguishes an institution from another community organ is the fact that it is empowered to take decisions binding upon Member States, institutions or person (natural or legal). The other bodies generally speaking act in an advisory capacity only.

Although "each institution shall act within the limits of the powers conferred upon it by this Treaty,"[3] only the Community itself has legal personality and capacity[4]; when it acquires property or is a party to legal proceedings (outside the Court of Justice) it may only be represented by the Commission. On the other hand for the conclusion of agreements between the Community and one or more states or an international organisation the Community is represented by the Council.[5]

---

[1] For bodies set up by the Treaties, see, *e.g.* the Consultative Committee (ECSC, Art. 18); the Scientific and Technical Committee (Euratom, Art. 134); the Economic and Social Committee (Euratom, Arts. 3 and 165, EEC, Arts. 4 and 193); the Court of Auditors (EEC, Art. 4 (3) and Art. 11 of the Treaty amending certain financial provisions); the European Investment Bank (EEC, Arts. 3 (*j*) and 129); the Monetary Committee (EEC, Art. 105 (2)) and the Committee of Permanent Representatives (Merger Treaty, Art. 4). For bodies set up by the institutions in pursuance of the powers conferred upon them by the Treaties, see, *e.g.* the Committee for medium-term economic policy, Dec. 64/247, (J.O. 1964, 1031).

[2] See EEC, Art. 4 (1).

[3] EEC, Art. 4 (1).

[4] EEC, Arts. 210, 211; see joined Cases 43/59 etc. *Lachmüller* v. *Commission* [1960] E.C.R. 463 at 472 and Ruling 1/78 [1978] E.C.R. 2151. However the EIB and Euratom's Agency have legal personality.

[5] EEC, Art. 228 (1).

The first European institutions—the High Authority, the Common Assembly, the Special Council of Ministers and the Court of Justice— were set up by the Treaty of Paris of 1951 establishing the European Coal and Steel Community.[6] Similar institutions—an Assembly, a Council, a Commission and a Court of Justice—were created by the two Treaties of Rome of 1957 for the EEC and Euratom. The result would, therefore, have been three Assemblies, three Councils, three Commissions (High Authority) and three Courts, had not a Convention[7] signed the same day provided for a single Assembly and a single Court of Justice.

Nonetheless this left three Councils and three Commissions (High Authority) beside the one Assembly and one Court: a total of eight institutions. A further rationalisation was introduced by the Merger Treaty of 1965[8] establishing a "Council of the European Communities" and a "Commission of the European Communities," to replace the existing Councils, Commissions and High Authority of the ECSC, EEC and Euratom. It might be interesting to note that according to the preamble of this treaty the creation of single institutions is seen as a step in the direction of the "unification of the three Communities." The four single institutions now exercise the powers and jurisdiction conferred on the institutions they replace, in accordance with the provisions of the relevant treaties.[9]

Neither the Treaty of Brussels of January 22, 1972, concerning the accession of Denmark, Ireland and the United Kingdom nor the Treaty of Athens of May 28, 1979, concerning the accession of Greece have modified this institutional structure; these treaties merely provide for increases in the number of members of each institution in order to accommodate nationals from the new Member States.

I. *The European Parliament* (*Assembly*)

All the European Treaties refer to this institution as the "Assembly"[10] and it was the Assembly which, back in 1962,

---

[6] ECSC, Art. 7.
[7] Convention relating to certain institutions common to the European Communities, of March 25, 1957, annexed to the EEC and Euratom Treaties.
[8] This Treaty came into force on July 1, 1967 (J.O. 1967, 152/2).
[9] Convention of March 25, 1957, Arts. 1–4 and Merger Treaty, Arts. 1 and 9.
[10] Or "Common Assembly," ECSC, Art. 7.

decided to call itself the "European Parliament."[11] All the institutions, except for a while the Council,[12] have adopted that denomination; the acts of the institutions which require prior consultation of the Assembly now refer to "the opinion of the European Parliament."[13] The Court of Justice has also used the terms "Parliamentary Assembly" and "Parliament" since 1959.[14]

Whether the Assembly was well advised in changing its name is questionable, not so much because this institution lacks the powers that are characteristic of democratic parliaments, *i.e.* the powers to legislate and to raise taxes, beside controlling the Administration, but because by calling itself a Parliament it has created the illusion that democratic control already exists within the Communities.

1. Members of Parliament[15]

According to the Treaty, the European Parliament consists "of representatives of the peoples of the states brought together in the Community."

(1) *Direct elections*

Until June 1979—date of the first direct elections for the European Parliament—the members of the Assembly were not "direct" representatives of the citizens of the Community, since the

---

[11] Resolution of March 30, 1962 (J.O. 1962, 1045). On March 20, 1958, the Assembly had decided to call itself "European Parliamentary Assembly" (J.O. 1958, 6).

[12] Answer to question No. 398/77 concerning denomination of the European Parliament in the Communities' official documents: the Council replied that the denomination of any one of the institutions could only be amended by a Treaty amending the existing Treaties (O.J. 1977, C. 270/18) and No. 1085/78 (O.J. 1979, C. 92/22).

[13] See, *e.g.* Reg. 214/79 concerning the European Regional Development Fund (O.J. 1979, L. 35/1).

[14] See Opinion of December 17, 1959 Procedure for amendment of ECSC Treaty [1959] E.C.R. 266.

[15] It will be noted that the EEC Treaty refers to "representatives" in Art. 137 and to "delegates" in Art. 138. The Act concerning the direct election refers only to "representatives" (O.J. 1976, L. 278/1).

Treaty provided[16] that the "Assembly shall consist of delegates who shall be designated from among their members by the respective Parliaments in accordance with the procedure laid down by each Member State."[17] However, this method of designation of the members was intended as a temporary procedure (although it lasted 27 years) and already the ECSC Treaty[18] provided for the Assembly to be elected by direct universal suffrage. Agreement concerning the implementation of this provision was finally reached at the Summit Conference held in Paris in 1974.[19] Parliament then adopted a new draft convention[20] and on September 20, 1976, the representatives of the Member States meeting in Council agreed on the conditions for the elections and on the Act concerning the Election of the Representatives of the Assembly by Direct Universal Suffrage. On July 25, 1978, the Council decided to hold the first elections between June 7 and 10, 1979.[21] On May 24, 1983, the Council fixed the period June 14 to 17, 1984, as the dates for the second election.

Elections by direct universal suffrage must be held "in accordance with a uniform procedure in all Member States,"[22] but agreement on such a procedure could not be reached and the 1979 and 1984 elections were held in accordance with the method of

[16] EEC, Art. 138. Art. 14 of the Act concerning the election provides that EEC, Art. 138 (1) and (2) shall lapse on the date of the first sitting of the first directly elected Assemble (O.J. 1976, L. 278/1).

[17] In the U.K. the delegates came from both Houses. The first resolutions creating the delegation are in 848 H.C. Deb. 1293 and 337 H.L. Deb. 1114. In both Houses the motion was moved by a Minister (see *Encyclopedia of European Community Law* (Sweet & Maxwell, 1974), Vol. B, B 10–314). In the Netherlands, *e.g.* a royal decree of February 11, 1958, provided that the delegates were to be nominated by both Houses, according to a procedure jointly laid down by them.

[18] See ECSC Treaty, Art. 21 (3). This method was used in 1981 for the designation of the Greek members. See Act for Greek Accession, Art. 23 (2).

[19] See Bull. 12–1974, 8 (para. 12 of official communiqué). These "Summit Conferences" became the conference of Heads of State or Government until they were called "European Council" (see below).

[20] Resolution of January 14, 1975 (O.J. 1975, C. 32/15). The first draft convention was adopted by Parliament on May 17, 1960 (J.O. 1960, 834).

[21] O.J. 1976, L. 278/1. The last notification of parliamentary ratification was deposited by France on June 23, 1979. In accordance with Art. 16 of the Act concerning direct election, the latter entered into force on July 1, 1978 (O.J. 1978, L. 173/30) and the date of the election was fixed on July 25, 1978 (O.J. 1978, L. 205/75).

[22] EEC, Art. 138 (3).

voting decided nationally.[23] One of the first tasks of Parliament is to draft a uniform electoral procedure.[24]

The directly elected Parliament is composed of 434 representatives distributed as follows: 81 each for the large Member States (Germany, France, Italy, United Kingdom), 25 for the Netherlands, 24 each for Belgium and for Greece,[25] 16 and 15 for Denmark and Ireland respectively and 6 for Luxembourg.[26]

(2) Mandate

Members of Parliament are elected for a term of five years.[27] Anybody can stand for Parliament,[28] it being understood that upon election the rules concerning incompatibility[29] must be applied. In case an elected candidate does not wish to relinquish an office which is incompatible with that of representative to the European Parliament he will be replaced, pending the entry into force of the uniform electoral procedure, according to procedures laid down by each Member State.[30] Under the old provisions, members of the European Parliament had to be members of a national Parliament; under the present Act it is simply stated that there is no incompatibility between the two offices.[31]

---

[23] Act concerning direct election, Art. 7 (2). The electoral system chosen in the U.K. is laid down in the European Assembly Election Act of 1978 and is for England, Scotland and Wales, simple majority in single-member seats ("first-past-the-post") and in Northern Ireland, single transferable vote in three-member seats. Most other Member States opted for proportional representation via party lists. For the national legal texts concerning electoral procedures see European Parliament doc. PE 54.524, PE 54.757; see also Twelfth General Report (1978), 360. For election results, see Bull. 6–1979, 20 and 6–1984, 13; the names of the representatives are to be found in O.J. 1979, C. 203/6 and European Parliament Bull. 1984–1985, List of Members, Sept. 10, 1984. See Thirteenth General Report (1979), 27. See Council statement in Bull. 5–1983, 78.

[24] Act concerning direct election, Art. 7 (1).

[25] On October 18, 1982, the Greeks went to the polls to elect not only their national Parliament but also their representatives to the European Parliament, thus the Greek representatives were elected like all the other members.

[26] In the U.K. the seats were distributed as follows: England 66, Scotland 8, Wales 4 and Northern Ireland 3. In Belgium: 13 for the Flemings and 11 for the Walloons and in Denmark one of the 16 seats was allocated to Greenland. All other Member States had national lists. After accession Spain will have 60 and Portugal 24 representatives.

[27] See Act concerning direct election, Art. 3 (1).

[28] Included, in the U.K., peers and ministers of religion who are excluded from elections to Westminster.

[29] Act concerning direct election, Art. 6 (1) and (2).

[30] *Ibid.* Art. 12 (1).

[31] *Ibid.* Art. 5.

During the sessions of Parliament, the representatives enjoy the privileges and immunities accorded to members of national parliaments when in their own state and immunity from detention and legal proceedings when on the territory of any other Member State.

2. Tasks and powers of the European Parliament

According to the Treaty, Parliament exercises only "advisory and supervisory" powers; in fact the Treaty of April 22, 1970, amending certain budgetary provisions of the original treaties and of the Merger Treaty, has conferred upon Parliament certain budgetary powers which directly bind the Member States. Nevertheless, Parliament has no real jurisdiction with regard to Community legislation.

The main tasks of the European Parliament are to:

–participate in the legislative procedure;
–put questions to the Commission and the Council;
–in case it disapproves of the activities of the Commission adopt a motion of censure;
–discuss the annual General Report submitted to it by the Commission;
–participate in the budgetary procedure;
–initiate proceedings in the Court of Justice against the Council or the Commission in case they fail to act or intervene in other cases;
–participate in other activities of the Communities.

(1) *Participation in the legislative procedure*

There are 27 instances[32] in the EEC Treaty where consultation of the European Parliament is required as part of the process leading to a formal decision, regulation or directive of the Council. Generally speaking the Treaty provides for consultation on all important matters such as Community policies (agriculture, transport, competition) and association agreements[33]; however,

---

[32] See EEC Treaty, Arts. 7, 14 (7), 43 (2), 54 (1), (2), 56 (2), 57 (1), (2), 63 (1), (2), 75 (1), 87 (1), 100, 126, 127, 201, 212, 228 (1), 235, 236 and 238.

[33] See request of Parliament to be consulted (O.J. 1982, C. 66/50). The Council agreed in 1973 to a greater participation of the Parliament in the conclusion of commercial agreements. Seventh General Report (1973), 64.

there is no consultation provided, for instance, on economic policy, social policy and the admittance of new members to the Community; but, the Council has agreed to, and does in fact, consult Parliament in many cases where this is not specifically required by the Treaty. When the Council enacts decisions, directives and regulations on the basis of proposals submitted to it by the Commission, consultation of Parliament is initiated by the Council on the basis of those proposals. When provided for in the Treaty, consultation constitutes an "essential procedural requirement" and failure to comply with it constitutes a ground for annulment of an act by the Court of Justice.[34]

The opinions of Parliament are given further weight by the fact that "as long as the Council has not acted, the Commission may alter its original proposal, in particular, when the Assembly has been consulted on that proposal,"[35] but the Commission is not bound to do so. Opinions, such as those of Parliament, have no binding force[36] and therefore, although mention must be made in the act of the fact that the Assembly was consulted, the Treaty does not require the Council to mention whether the expressed opinion was positive or negative, or to refute, in case of a negative one, the arguments brought forward by the Assembly.[37] Finally, it should be noted that if the Commission itself does not modify its proposal, the Council can adopt an act constituting an amendment to that proposal, but then only with an unanimous vote.[38]

Parliament's participation in the legislative process is therefore still rather limited,[39] notwithstanding a slight improvement

---

[34] See joined Cases 138 and 139/79 *Roquette Frères* v. *Council* and *Maizena* v. *Council* [1980] E.C.R. 3333 and 3393, where the Court annulled a regulation because the Council, having consulted Parliament, adopted the regulation although no opinion was delivered.

[35] EEC, Art. 149, second para.; see, *e.g.* Information management, Twelfth General Report (1978), 230.

[36] EEC, Art. 189 (5).

[37] See Case 6/54 *Government of the Kingdom of the Netherlands* v. *High Authority* [1954–56] E.C.R. 103 at 111. The Commission undertook, starting with the July 1973 session of Parliament to systematically inform Parliament of action taken on its opinions.

[38] EEC, Art. 149; renewed consultation of the European Parliament in such cases is only required if the modifications introduced by the Council do affect the essence of the proposal; see Case 41/69 *ACF Chemiefarma* v. *Commission* [1970] E.C.R. 661.

[39] See Vedel Report (Bull. Suppl. 4/72).

which was introduced in 1977: the *conciliation procedure* to be used in the event the Council departs from the opinion of Parliament. This procedure was instituted by a Joint Declaration of the European Parliament, the Council and the Commission.[40] The aim is to give Parliament an effective participation in the procedure for preparing and adopting acts of general application which give rise to important expenditure or revenue and therefore to seek an agreement between Parliament and the Council, if the latter intends to depart from Parliament's opinion. The conciliation procedure should normally not take more than three months.

Irrespective of the opinions issued following consultation by the Council, Parliament has always felt free to formulate other resolutions whenever it considered this necessary.[41] The Rules of procedure provide only that such resolutions must concern matters falling within the activities of the Community.

(2) *Parliamentary questions*

The Commission must reply orally or in writing to questions put to it by Parliament or its members.[42] This obligation, originally only provided for the Commission, is an important aspect of the supervisory powers of Parliament. It is difficult to compare the Community's practice with the national parliamentary procedures, since most questions put by members of the European Parliament are in writing, due to the fact that Parliament assembles in Strasbourg and Luxembourg only during a limited number of days every year.[43] This right of Parliament to obtain answers to its questions was extended considerably over the past years and is widely used.[44]

---

[40] O.J. 1975, C. 89/1.
[41] Rules of Procedure, Art. 47 (O.J. 1981, C. 90/49 at 65); in 1984 the European Parliament adopted 308 resolutions of which 146 are embodying opinions. Parliament even made proposals for legislation, see Resolution of May 11, 1979, containing a draft proposal for a regulation on fishfarming (O.J. 1979, C. 140/117).
[42] EEC, Art. 140 (3).
[43] In 1984, 12 part-sessions were held.
[44] In 1984, 3,189 questions (written and oral) were put by members of Parliament. Answering a written question is a cumbersome procedure; the reply is prepared by the staff of the Council or of the Commission, formally accepted by these institutions, translated into 6 other languages, informally discussed with the other institutions and finally sent to the European Parliament and published in the *Official Journal*.

In the first place, although the Treaty only imposes the obligation to answer on the Commission, Parliament itself extended this obligation to the Council[45] in 1958 and the latter agreed. Secondly, in 1962, Parliament introduced the procedure of oral questions followed by a debate[46] which was accepted by the Council and by the Commission with the provision, however, that, where the Council is concerned, the debate may not be concluded by a vote on a resolution concerning the debated question. Thirdly, in 1973, Parliament introduced the question time in which Council and Commission agreed to participate.[47] Here also a distinction is made between those two institutions since only the answers of the Commission can give rise to a debate. This distinction is of great interest since it confirms the essential difference in the relationship between Parliament on the one hand, and the Council and the Commission on the other. The supervisory powers referred to above concern only the Commission which is under the political control of Parliament. This does not apply to the Council whose relationship with Parliament is rather one of political co-operation and partnership and tends to find expression in a dialogue between the two institutions. Once a year Parliament meets with the President of the Council, in the presence of the Commission, to discuss matters of general interest on which the Council has not yet decided—the so-called "colloquies." Similarly, a representative of the Council presents three times a year to Parliament an oral report on the activities of the Council, and the President of the Council makes a statement to Parliament on the outcome of the meetings of the European Council. Similarly a "programme of the Presidency" is presented by the incoming President of the Council every six months, at the beginning of his six months' term, and a survey of significant developments at the end of the Presidency. Finally, the Chairman of the Conference of Foreign Ministers reports once a year on the progress of European political co-operation,[48] this report may be followed by a debate. These addresses, more than any other form of co-operation, give the members of Parliament an

---

[45] Rules, Arts. 44, 45 and 46.
[46] Rules, Art. 47.
[47] *Ibid.* Art. 47 *bis.* At its 257th session on October 15, 1973, the Council agreed to take part (Seventh General Report (1973), 64). The hour originally provided was extended in 1975 to one and a half hours (Ninth General Report (1975), 17).
[48] See Ninth General Report (1975), 17 and, *e.g.* Bull. 10–1979, 129.

opportunity to impress upon the Council their views on the future developments of the Community.

(3) *The motion of censure*

If Parliament disagrees with the activities of the Commission, it may adopt a motion of censure, thereby forcing the members of the Commission to resign as a body.[49] This is by far the most impressive power vested in the Assembly, but although several motions have been tabled in the past,[50] never yet has such a motion been carried. The procedural requirements are cumbersome. In the first place, the Treaty prescribes a "reflection time" of three days between the time the motion is tabled and the actual open vote. Secondly, the Treaty requires that a majority of the representatives cast their vote and that two-thirds of them vote for the motion.[51] Thirdly, the motion must be moved either by a political group or by one-tenth of the members.

It seems, furthermore, that this power is more apparent than real, since it only affects the Commission. The consequences of this are twofold. In the first place, the Council which, as the decision-making institution, bears the ultimate responsibility for the activities of the Community,[52] remains outside the reach of Parliament. In the second place, a motion of censure might very well remain without practical effect. After the members of the Commission have been forced to resign as a body, "they shall continue to deal with current business until they are replaced in accordance with Article 158."[53]

From there on, the decisions are no longer in the hands of Parliament since it has no influence on the choice of the Commissioners; the governments of the Member States could very well reappoint the same members, for instance on national political grounds.

---

[49] EEC, Art. 144.

[50] The first time was in November 1972 and was based on the failure of the Commission to submit proposals concerning the reinforcement of the budgetary powers of Parliament; it was later withdrawn.

[51] EEC, Art. 144 (2).

[52] This is true notwithstanding the fact that in most cases the Council can only act on a proposal from the Commission since the Council may unanimously adopt an act constituting an amendment to that proposal: EEC, Art. 149.

[53] EEC, Art. 144 (2), Merger Treaty, Art. 11 provides that the members of the Commission are appointed by common accord of the Governments of the Member States.

Whatever its ultimate effects, the motion of censure remains the clearest symbol of parliamentary control within the Communities. Furthermore, the real influence of an institution cannot, of course, be judged on the basis of legal provisions alone, it depends in great part on the expertise of its members and their force of persuasion.

(4) The General Report

Each year the Commission must publish a general report on the activities of the Communities, not later than one month before the opening of the session of Parliament.[54] This report is submitted to Parliament which discusses it in open session. There exists an obvious link between the discussion of the annual report on the activities of the Communities and the motion of censure on the activities of the Commission,[55] but Parliament would certainly not wait for the publication of the report to censure the Commission.

The discussion by Parliament of the annual General Report gives rise to a general debate on all the facets of Community activity, since the report covers all the institutions and bodies, although the work of the Council and the European Investment Bank, for instance, is described in detail, in their own annual reports.[56] The General Report is supplemented by an Annual Report on the Agricultural Situation in the Community,[57] a Report on the Development of the Social Situation in the Community,[58] and a Report on Competition Policy.[59] The Commission also presents an annual Report on the Regional Fund,[60] on the State of the Environment[61] and on Consumer Protection and Information Policy.[62]

---

[54] Merger Treaty, Art. 18. According to EEC, Art. 139 (1) Parliament convenes for its annual session on the second Tuesday in March.

[55] In the ECSC Treaty both subjects are provided for in the same Art. 24.

[56] See the Reviews of the Council's work published by the Secretariat-General of the Council and Annual Reports of the EIB.

[57] See Declaration of the System for Fixing Community Farm Prices contained in the Accession Documents of January 22, 1972 (J.O. 1972, L. 73/200).

[58] EEC, Art. 122.

[59] Undertaking given by the Commission to Parliament on June 7, 1971; see Resolution concerning the competition rules (17) (J.O. 1971, C. 66/11).

[60] Reg. 1787/84, Art. 46 (O.J. 1984, L. 169/1).

[61] See First and Second Programmes (O.J. 1973, C. 112/1 and 1977, C 139/1) and First (1977) and Second (1978) Reports. See below.

[62] See Action Programme (O.J. 1975, C. 92/1) and First Report (1977). See below.

All those reports constitute an invaluable source of information on the activities of the Communities, the problems they encounter and the proposed and adopted solutions. They are less important for the supervisory function of Parliament since it is kept well informed by the permanent contacts it maintains with the Commission mainly through the work of the Parliamentary committees in which the Commission always participates.

More important, however, is the programme-address which the President of the Commission presents to Parliament at the beginning of every year and which gives rise to a general debate.

(5) *Participation in the budgetary procedure*

The present budgetary procedure and the role of Parliament can be summarised as follows.[63]

The Commission draws up a preliminary draft budget and sends it to the Council, not later than September 1, for the financial year starting the following January 1. The Council establishes the draft budget and forwards it to Parliament, not later than October 5.

Parliament can then take one of several actions:

(a) approve the draft budget within 45 days; the budget then stands as finally adopted;

(b) refrain from amending it or proposing modifications, within 45 days; the budget then is deemed to be adopted;

(c) adopt amendments and/or propose modifications:

  (i) with regard to expenditure necessarily resulting from the Treaty or from acts adopted in accordance therewith, ("obligatory expenditure"[64]) Parliament, acting by an absolute majority of the votes, may only propose modifications;

  (ii) with regard to other expenditures, Parliament may, acting by a majority of its members, amend the draft budget, but within a maximum rate of increase communicated by the Commission[65];

---

[63] EEC, Art. 203.

[64] Also referred to as "compulsory expenditure." See below, Financing Community Activities.

[65] This maximum rate of increase results from the trend of GNP within the Community, the average variations in the national budgets and the trend of the cost of living; EEC, Art. 203 (9).

and the draft budget together with the amendments and proposed modifications is forwarded to the Council;

The Council then can act under the following conditions:

–with regard to the proposed modifications, the Council may reject them by a qualified majority (generally referred to as "reversed majority");

–with regard to the amendments (expenditures not necessarily resulting from the Treaty or the acts), it may modify them within 15 days by a qualified majority; in the absence of such majority, the amendments stand.

If the Council does not modify the amendments and accepts the proposed modifications, the budget is deemed to be finally adopted and Parliament is informed accordingly. If, on the other hand, one or more amendments have been modified, or proposed modifications rejected or modified, the modified draft budget is returned to Parliament.

At this stage the powers of Parliament are limited to the expenditures other than those necessarily resulting from the Treaty or from acts adopted by the institutions, and for which it has a right of amendment as described above. Parliament may, within 15 days, amend or reject the modifications made by the Council to its amendments, acting by a majority of its members and three-fifths of the votes cast. Parliament then adopts the budget and the President of Parliament declares that the budget has been finally adopted.

However Parliament, acting by a majority of its members and two-thirds of the votes cast, may, if there are important reasons, reject the draft budget.[66]

From this lengthy procedure[67] it follows that Parliament now has the final decision within the limits of the maximum amount of

---

[66] EEC, Art. 203 (8); this happened in 1979, see Bull. 12–1979, 93 and 120, and in 1984, see Bull. 12–1984, 28.

[67] It should be noted however that the provisions of EEC, Art. 203 have been differently interpreted by Parliament and by the Council and this gave rise to considerable difficulties for the adoption of the 1979 budget; see Twelfth Gen. Rep. (1978), 51. See however the Joint Declaration signed by the Presidents of Parliament, the Council and the Commission with a view to ensuring a more effective development of the budgetary procedure (O.J. 1982, C. 194/1 and 238/35 and Bull. 6–1982, 7).

increase, with regard to the non-obligatory expenditures[68] and actually adopts the budget. On December 4, 1984, the Council agreed on conclusions concerning measures necessary to guarantee the effective implementation of the conclusions of the European Council concerning budgetary discipline thereby limiting Parliament's powers to some extent.[68a]

Parliament also exercises control over the implementation of the Community budget; in this task it is assisted by the Court of Auditors. Parliament gives a discharge to the Commission in respect of the implementation of the budget. To this end the Commission submits annually to Parliament and to the Council the accounts of the preceding financial year together with a financial statement of the assets and liabilities of the Communities.[69] The Council and the Assembly in turn examine the accounts and statement together with the annual Report of the Court of Auditors. In giving a discharge to the Commission, Parliament acts on a recommendation from the Council.

(6) *Procedures in the Court of Justice*

Apart from intervening in cases before the Court,[70] instituting third party proceedings to contest a judgment and applying for interpretation of a judgment Parliament may bring an action before the Court of Justice against the Council or the Commission for failure of these institutions to act in infringement of the treaties.[71]

(7) *Participation in other Community activities*

Several agreements of association between the Community and third states provide for a joint Parliamentary Committee. This is

---

[68] The non-obligatory expenditures represented about 73 per cent. in the 1984 Budget, which in total exceeded 27 billion ECU; see Seventeenth Gen.Rep. (1983), 50.

[68a] See Bull. 12–1984, 24.

[69] Treaty amending certain financial provisions, Arts. 14 and 17 or EEC, Arts. 205A and 206 for 1977 (see O.J. 1979, L. 331/1). In 1984, Parliament refused to discharge the Commission with regard to the 1982 budget implementation; see Bull. 11–1984, 67.

[70] See Res.of Dec. 14, 1979 (O.J. 1980, C. 4/52) to intervene in Cases 138/79 *SA Roquette Frères* v. *Council* [1980] E.C.R. 3333 and 139/79 *Maizena* v. *Council* [1980] E.C.R. 3393.

[71] EEC, Art. 175, (1) and (2). See Case 13/83 *Parliament* v. *Council* (O.J. 1983, C. 49/9, Bull. 1–1983, 35).

the case for the EEC-Turkey[72] association; 18 representatives of the European Parliament sit in each one of these committees. Similarly the Lomé ACP-EEC Convention[73] provides for a Consultative Assembly of which 98 representatives of the European Parliament are members. Finally, it should be noted that Parliament holds an annual joint meeting with the Consultative Assembly of the Council of Europe.[74]

3. Internal organisation[75]

The internal organisation of the European Parliament is broadly comparable to that of any national Parliament; it is based on a double structure: the political parties and the parliamentary committees.

(1) *Political groups*

Representatives sit in nine multinational political groups.[76] The Act concerning the elections stipulates that representatives shall vote on an individual and personal basis and that they shall not be bound by any instructions nor receive a binding mandate.[77]

The rules of procedure of Parliament require for the formation of a political group 21 representatives when they belong to one

---

[72] See Art. 27 of the agreement (J.O. 1964, 3687); for the 1978 meeting, see Bull. 10–1978, 71.

[73] Art. 80 of the Convention (O.J. 1976, L. 25/1); for the 1979 annual meeting, see Bull. 10–1979, 81.

[74] See Bull. 1–1978, 74.

[75] See rules of procedure (J.O. 1967, 280 and for the last modification O.J. 1979, C.93/13).

[76] Situation on September 1, 1984 (in brackets the 1979 figures):

Socialists	130	(124)
European People's Party	110	(117)
European Democrats	50	(63)
Communists and Allies	41	(48)
Liberals and Democrats	31	(38)
Allied European Democrats	29	(22)
Rainbow	20	(—)
European Right	16	(—)
Non-attached	7	(10)

[77] Act concerning direct election, Art. 4(1); there are no party whips in the European Parliament.

single Member State, 15 when they come from two Member States and 10 when the number of Member States is three or more.[78]

(2) *Parliamentary committees*

With regard to the parliamentary committees, the rules of procedure provide for standing or temporary, general or special committees, that can be set up by Parliament which determines their task.[79]

Generally speaking the committees prepare the resolutions to be adopted by Parliament in plenary session; when Parliament is consulted by the Council on Commission proposals, these are examined by the relevant committee(s) which reports to Parliament. The latter expresses its opinion in the form of a resolution.[80]

(3) *Bureau*

Parliament elects a president and 12 vice-presidents which together constitute the "Bureau" (*i.e.* the executive body); this Bureau drafts the agenda of the sessions, decides on matters of competence and makes up the preliminary draft of Parliament's budgets.[81] The Rules also provide for an "enlarged Bureau," consisting of the Bureau and the presidents of the political groups; it is this enlarged bureau which *de facto* constitutes the ultimate centre of decision for all internal matters. Parliament has its own staff of about 3,000 grouped in a "secretariat" headed by the Secretary-General.

---

[78] Rules, Art. 36.

[79] In September 1984 Parliament's committees numbered 18: Political Affairs (45 members); Agriculture, Fisheries and Food (45); Budgets (42); Economic and Monetary Affairs and Industrial Policy (42); Energy, Research and Technology (30); External Economic Relations (25); Legal Affairs and Citizens' Rights (25); Social Affairs and Employment (30); Regional Policy and Regional Planning (28); Transport (24); Environment, Public Health and Consumer Protection (31); Youth, Culture, Education, Information and Sport (24); Development and Co-operation (42); Budgetary Control (30); Rules of Procedure and Petitions (25); Institutional Affairs (30); Women's Rights (25); Verification of credentials (9).

[80] Rules, Arts. 37–44.

(4) *Sessions*

Parliament holds annual sessions; it meets without requiring to be convened on the second Tuesday in March.[82] Parliament may also meet in extraordinary session. All meetings are now held in Strasbourg.[83] Members of the European Commission may attend all meetings. The Council has agreed to be represented at all the plenary sessions.

The minutes of the meetings are published in the *Official Journal* ("C" series) and the full debates are published in an Annex to the *Official Journal*. Except for the adoption of the motion of censure, and the budgetary procedure,[84] the Assembly acts by a majority of votes cast. There is a quorum when the majority of the representatives is present.[85]

4. Conclusion

Until June 1979 the European Parliament played a role of increasing importance within the institutional system of the Communities. This was due partly to the quality of its members and partly to the fact that dual membership gave them a real political power base in their own country. In most cases the latter has disappeared with direct elections.

In the second edition of this book it was stated that "election by universal suffrage only has sense if at the same time the formal powers of the Assembly are increased."[86] The only improvement in this respect is to be found in the budgetary and in the

---

[81] Rules, Arts. 5–7, 12 and 50.
[82] Parliament is understood to be "in session" even if not actually sitting, until the session (yearly or extraordinary) is declared closed. See Case 101/63 *Wagner* v. *Fohrmann and Krier* [1964] E.C.R. 195.
[83] Parliament used to meet alternately in Luxembourg and Strasbourg. In 1984, Parliament held 12 plenary sessions at Strasbourg; in 1983 one special session was held exceptionally in Brussels (O.J. 1983, C.135/1). See for other activities Gen. Reps. Concerning the right of Parliament to decide where to hold its sessions see Case 230/81, *Luxembourg* v. *Parliament* [1983] E.C.R. 255 and Case 108/83, *id.* judgment of 10 April, 1984 (not yet published).
[84] For the motion, see EEC, Art. 144 and above under Tasks and Powers of the European Parliament; for the budget, see EEC, Art. 203(6) and (8) and above *ibid.*
[85] Except that under Art. 33(3) of the Rules, votes (except nominal votes) are always valid when the President has not been formally requested, before the vote, to ascertain the number of members present.
[86] *Op. cit.* p. 173.

conciliation procedure, and Parliament has clearly shown it knew how to use the newly acquired influence.[87] But no progress was made in other fields.

II. *The Council of the European Communities*

To attain the objectives assigned to the Community, the Treaty provides two means: the establishment of the Common Market and the progressive approximation of the economic policies of the Member States.[88] The second of the two means is the proper task of the Council: "ensure co-ordination of the general economic policies of the Member States."[89]

The Treaty rules referring to the economic policies are very general and do not impose precise obligations upon the Member States. It is in the course of the elaboration of the necessary policies that more concrete rules are formulated by the Council. The latter somehow continues the fundamental legislative task of the drafters of the Treaties establishing the Communities.

1. Organisational aspects

(1) *Members of the Council*

The Council consists of representatives of the Member States. Each government delegates to it one of its members.[90] Being representatives of their respective countries, the members of the Council act on the basis of instructions or mandates received from their governments. However, they do not constitute a conference of government representatives comparable to those existing in international organisations,[91] neither are they personally designated to fulfil a Community function in the way representatives, commissioners or judges are. They constitute an institution of the Communities and as such they must always act in the Community interest. It is not evident that this is always clearly perceived by all participants at the Council meetings.

---

[87] With regard to the resources of the Regional Found, for example, Parliament was able to override a decision of the European Council.

[88] EEC, Art. 2.

[89] EEC, Art. 145.

[90] Merger Treaty, Art. 2(1).

[91] *e.g.* The Committee of Ministers of the Council of Europe, Statute, Arts. 13 *et seq.* or the Council of the Organisation for Economic Co-operation and Development, Convention, Art. 7.

Community legislation is silent on which member of the national government should attend the Council meetings, but the Treaty provides that it is to be "one" member, which indicates that each Member State normally has one vote.[92] Often two or more members of a given government will attend the same session. Besides the "general" Council, normally attended by the Ministers of Foreign Affairs, "specialised" Council meetings take place to deal with specific subjects such as agriculture, transport or social affairs. Consequently, it is not unusual to have various Council meetings in session at the same moment. When no member of a government can be present at a Council meeting, the Member State in question may send a civil servant[93]; the latter, however, has no vote. But in case of absence, a member may ask another member to vote on his behalf; no member may act on behalf of more than one other member.[94] Acts of the Council on an urgent matter may be adopted by "written procedure."

Neither the Treaty, nor the Rules of procedure[95] of the Council refer to a quorum. However, since the Council can only, in the simplest of cases, act by a "majority" of its members[96] (at present ten), no decision can be taken unless six votes are cast, which means that a minimum of three members must be present.[97]

Council meetings are convened by the President on his own initiative or at the request of one of its members or of the Commission.[98] The office of President is held for a term of six months by each member of the Council in turn.[99] The same rotation applies to all the subordinate bodies such as the

---

[92] See voting procedure, below.
[93] Rules of procedure, Art. 4 (O.J. 1979, L.268/1); usually this is the Permanent Representative, see below, p. 32.
[94] EEC, Art. 150.
[95] The Rules of procedure were adopted by the Council on April 15, 1958; see Merger Treaty, Art. 5 (previously EEC, Art. 151); (O.J. 1979, L.268/1).
[96] EEC, Art. 148(1); for further details, see below, voting procedure, p. 30.
[97] When *unanimity* is required, the quorum obviously becomes five, each member voting also on behalf of one other member. It should be noted, however, that abstention by members present or represented does not prevent the adoption of Acts which require unanimity (EEC, Art. 148(3)).
[98] Merger Treaty, Art. 3.
[99] The office of President is held in the following alphabetical order: Belgium, Denmark, Germany, Greece, France, Ireland, Italy, Luxembourg, Netherlands, United Kingdom, Merger Treaty, Art. 2(2) and Act concerning Greek accession, Art. 11.

Committee of Permanent Representatives[1] and to other meetings of Ministers such as those on political co-operation.[2]

The meetings of the Council are not public; they are attended by the Commission[3] represented by its President and those members more particularly responsible for the items under discussion.

(2) *Voting procedure*

The basic rule is that "the Council shall act by a majority of its members"[4] except where otherwise provided in the Treaty.[5] Since most provisions do provide otherwise, the general rule is in fact the exception. The other voting procedures are:

(a) *Qualified majority when the Council is acting on a proposal from the Commission;* this is the normal case[6]; the votes of the Council members are weighted[7] and at least 45 votes in favour are required; this means, *inter alia*, that the four "large" Member States (France, Germany, Italy and the United Kingdom) cannot impose their will on the "small" ones, but that the latter acting together and also two large Member States can block qualified majority decision;

(b) *Qualified majority when the Council acts without a proposal from the Commission[8];* with the additional condition that the 45 votes should be cast by at least six members; this means, *inter alia*, that at least two of the small countries besides the large ones have to agree with the measure or that a two-thirds majority of the Member States is required.

---

[1] See below, p. 32.
[2] *Ibid.*
[3] Rules of procedures, Art. 4(*a*) (*b*).
[4] Since there are presently (1985) ten members the majority is six.
[5] EEC, Art. 148(1).
[6] See, *e.g.* EEC, Arts. 20, 28, 38(3), 43(2), 44(5), 54(2), 56(2), 57, 63(2), 69, 75(1), 101.
[7] EEC, Art. 148(2): total 63 votes:

Belgium	5	Ireland	3
Denmark	3	Italy	10
Germany	10	Luxembourg	2
Greece	5	Netherlands	5
France	10	United Kingdom	10

After accession, the total becomes 76; Spain will have eight votes and Portugal five; the required minimum votes becomes 54.
[8] See, *e.g.* EEC, Arts. 73(2), 106(2), 108(2) and (3), 109, 111, 113, 114, 154 and 206. After accession 54 votes must be cast by eight members.

(c) *Unanimous vote*; this has become common practice, although it is only required by the Treaty in a limited number of cases[9] and each time the Council wants to amend a Commission proposal.[10]

The present practice stems from the arrangement regarding majority voting adopted by the Council at its meeting of January 28 and 29, 1966,[11] in Luxembourg, improperly referred to as the "Luxembourg Agreement or Accords." This arrangement ended the most serious crisis the Community has known in the following terms:

1. Where, in the case of decisions which may be taken by majority vote on a Commission proposal and very important interests of one or more partners are at stake, the members of the Council will endeavour, within a reasonable time, to reach solutions which can be adopted by all the members of the Council while respecting their mutual interests and those of the Community, in accordance with Article 2 of the EEC Treaty.

2. With regard to the preceding paragraph, the French delegation considers that, where very important interests are at stake, the discussion must be continued until unanimous agreement is reached.

3. The six delegations note that there is a divergence of views on what should be done in the event of failure to reach complete agreement.

There seems to be no disagreement about the fact that following this arrangement the Member States should try to reach unanimity on very important issues. Disagreement, however, persists with regard to the next stage, *i.e.* what happens if, after a reasonable time-limit, unanimity is not reached? For five Member States the rules of the Treaty then apply and decisions can be taken with qualified majority; for France, discussions should

---

[9] In many cases, the Treaty provides for a unanimous vote during a certain period after the entry into force of the Treaty (all these time periods have now elapsed) and qualified majority afterwards, see EEC, Arts. 28, 33, 42–44, 54, 56, 57, 63, 69, 75, 87, 101 and 111–114. Unanimous vote was required from the beginning by EEC, Arts. 14(7), 45(3), 59, 76, 93(2), 136, 188, 200, 223, 227.

[10] EEC, Art. 149.

[11] See Sweet and Maxwell, *European Community Treaties* (4th ed., 1980), at p. 249.

continue until unanimity is reached.[12] It is obvious that this practice has had a disruptive effect on the functioning of the Community. In the communiqué published after the Conference of Heads of State and Government in Paris on December 9 and 10, 1974, it was, therefore, stated that "in order to improve the functioning of the Council of the Community, they consider that it is necessary to renounce the practice which consists of making agreement on all questions conditional on the unanimous consensus of all the Member States, whatever their respective position may be regarding the conclusions reached in Luxembourg on January 28, 1966."[13]

(3) *The Committee of Permanent Representatives*[14]

The creation of the Committee of Permanent Representatives, Coreper, stems from the fact that the Council meets for no more than a few days a month and that with the increase of Community business a more permanent presence seemed required. The Permanent Representatives—national civil servants with the rank of Ambassador—follow the various Community activities practically on a day-by-day basis; however they are not empowered to take decisions. They constitute a subordinate organ of the Council and are not a gathering of deputies of the members of the Council; indeed, the latter (like the other institutions) may not delegate its powers of decision.

Nevertheless, once Coreper has reached agreement, for instance on a proposal from the Commission, the decision of the Council can for all practical purposes be considered as having been taken. This is expressed by the fact that in such a case the matter is put on the agenda of the next Council meeting as an "A

[12] There seems therefore to be an error of interpretation in the statement of the British Government according to which "on a question where a government considers that vital national interests are involved it is established that the decision should be unanimous" (Cmnd. 4715, 29). It might be so that, in the past, questions that were implicitly recognised as being important were always decided by unanimous vote, but is it "established" that it should be so? The statement under para. 70 of the same document is therefore more correct: "... where Member States' vital interests are at stake, it is Community practice to proceed only by unanimity."

[13] Bull. 12–1974, 8, Pt. 6 of the Communiqué; it will be noted that the expression "Luxembourg Agreement" is not used.

[14] Commonly referred to as Coreper (Comité des Représentants Permanents).

point." The practice is that the Council accepts all such points at the beginning of its meeting and thereby transforms them into one of the binding legal acts provided for in the Treaty. However, it must be emphasised that the Council is in no way bound to accept the "A points" and any member is free to ask for a discussion on the subject, in which case it is placed on the agenda of the next meeting, but as a "B point."

When no agreement can be reached on a subject at Coreper level, but it is thought that a solution could be found at ministerial level, or such is explicitly requested by one of the Ambassadors, the subject is placed on the Council agenda as a "B point," *i.e.* a point on which discussion is needed since no ready solution has been found.

Coreper is assisted in its work by a whole series of working groups, which in turn prepare its work and indirectly the work of the Council. These working groups are composed of senior national officials and convene whenever necessary to examine subjects which fall within their competence. When a Commission proposal is sent to the Council, it is examined in the first place by Coreper which decides either to examine it further or to ask one of the working groups to study it and report to the Committee.

Practically all these meetings, Council, Committee and working groups are attended by the Commission. Each one of those meetings is presided over by a national of the Member State whose representative holds the office of President of the Council.[15] The great advantage of these working groups composed of national civil servants is that the national view is clearly expressed in Brussels, while the national administrations are informed through these direct contacts of the opinion of the Commission and the other Member States.

In the same way, it can be said that the Permanent Representative fulfils a double function: he defends the national interest within the Community and at the same time he represents the Community's viewpoint at home; he thus constitutes a precious link between the national administration and the European institutions.

(4) *The European Council*

When important decisions were no longer taken by qualified

---

[15] See Merger Treaty, Art. 2.

majority and when the subjects to be decided upon became more and more vital for the general economic development of the Member States, the decision-making process within the Community practically came to a halt. It became obvious that new impulses had to be given and new methods of decision-making had to be provided. Since the Council is already a gathering of high-level politicians, the solution was sought more and more in the Conferences of Heads of State or Government[16] which would take the necessary decisions at the highest political level.

At the 1974 Summit Meeting the Heads of Government, "recognizing the need for an overall approach to the internal problems involved in achieving European unity and the external problems facing Europe—consider it essential to ensure progress and overall consistency in the activities of the Communities and in the work on political co-operation—[and] have therefore decided to meet, accompanied by the Ministers of Foreign Affairs, three times a year and, whenever necessary, in the Council of the Communities and in the context of political co-operation."[17]

Consequently, since 1975 the Heads of State or Government meet three times a year as the "European Council." It is presided over by the Head of Government whose representative holds the office of President of the Council and the Secretariat is provided by the General Secretariat of the Council.

The European Council has, to date, mainly confined itself to issuing general guidelines which have been acted upon by the Council proper and the Commission.[18] Notwithstanding the fact that "the prospect of regular European Council meetings acted as a catalyst, expediting certain Council work at ministerial level,"[19] it happens that matters are not decided at Council level but left to fill the agenda of the European Council; fortunately, the European Council has nearly always refused to decide on technical matters and confined itself to matters of policy.[20]

---

[16] The first such conference was held at Paris on February 10 and 11, 1961, see communiqué in Bull. 3–1961, 13; and the second at Bonn on July 19, 1961, see communiqué providing *inter alia* for regular meetings, Bull. 7/8–1961, 40.

[17] Eighth General Report (1974), 297(2) and (3).

[18] Ninth General Report (1975), 19.

[19] Ninth General Report (1975), 19.

[20] See however the March (Brussels) and June 1984 (Fontainebleau) meetings where detailed budgetary matters were discussed; see Bulls. 3–1984, 7 and 6–1984, 7.

The European Council also meets in the context of political co-operation and as an informal gathering of top politicians where all major political problems can be freely and privately discussed. One of the characteristics of the European Council is that it is strictly limited to the Heads of Government, their Foreign Ministers and the President and one Vice-President of the Commission. No officials attend the meetings.

At the European Council meeting in London on June 29 and 30, 1977, agreement was reached on a framework for the organisation of the meetings.[21] It was also agreed that "for discussions aimed at reaching decisions or issuing statements there should be a record of conclusions, which should be issued on the authority of the Presidency."[22]

Notwithstanding the existence of some unsolved problems with regard to the relations between the European Council and the other institutions, particularly the European Parliament, this new Community organ has fulfilled a very important role in determining policies, both within the Community and towards third countries.

(5) *Representatives of the Member States in Council*

In accordance with the Treaties, certain decisions must be taken by the Member States acting by "common accord,"[23] in such cases the members of the Council meet as a "conference of representatives of the Governments of the Member States."[24] This conference, and the acts it issues, are to be distinguished from the meetings of the "representatives of the Governments of the Member States meeting within the Council," which are not provided for in the Treaties. The legal character of such meetings *within* the Council (not: *of* the Council), and of its decisions, raises the same problems as the European Council and its "decisions."[25] In practice, meetings within the Council deal with matters for which the Community itself lacks competence, but

---

[21] See Bull. 6–1977, 83.
[22] Those "conclusions" are published in the Bulletin of the European Communities; see, *e.g.* the conclusions of the Presidency released at the end of the European Council which met at Paris on March 12 and 13, 1979, in Bull. 3–1979, 9.
[23] See EEC, Art. 167; Merger Treaty, Art. 11.
[24] See EEC, Art. 236.
[25] See above.

which, directly or indirectly, affect the Community's powers,[26] or are connected with its activities.[27]

2. Tasks and powers of the Council

(1) *Decision-making*

The Council is the central institution of the Communities endowed with the "power to take decisions"[28]; but the balance of power is such that in most cases the Council can only act on the basis of a proposal from the Commission and under the judicial control of the Court of Justice. Particularly important is the right of legislative initiative conferred upon the Commission; when the Council meets to "make regulations, issue directives, take decisions,"[29] it does so on the basis of a draft put before it by the Commission and therefore, one might presume, formulated in a way which furthers the Community interest. If the Council wishes to adopt an act constituting an amendment to that proposal it may only do so acting unanimously. But clearly, this latitude does not extend to adopting an act which bears no resemblance to the original proposal. It seems one must apply here, by analogy, the Court's view on the requirement of renewed consultation of the European Parliament by the Council in case the Council modifies the wording of the draft in such a way that it affects its substance[30]; this means that when the modifications which the Council unilaterally introduces in the original proposal of the Commission affect its substance, the decision of the Council is annulable on the ground of infringement of an essential procedural requirement,[31] since it could not

---

[26] See the Resolution of the Council and the Ministers of Education meeting within the Council, of February 9, 1976, on the action programme in the educational field (O.J. 1976, C.38/1).

[27] As stated in Act of Accession, Art. 3(1) "The new Member States accede by this Act to the decisions and agreements adopted by the Representatives of the Governments of the Member States meeting in Council. They undertake to accede from the date of accession to all other agreements concluded by the original Member States relating to the functioning of the Communities or connected with their activities."

[28] EEC, Art. 145, although the Commission is also endowed with its own power of decision, see below under Commission, p. 47.

[29] EEC, Art. 189(1).

[30] EEC, Art. 149(2). Case 41/69 *ACF Chemiefarma* v. *Commission* [1970] E.C.R. 661 at 662(3).

[31] EEC, Art. 173.

be said that such decision was taken "on a proposal by the Commission."

The provision granting power to the Council to amend a Commission proposal being an exception to a general principle, it must be strictly interpreted.[32]

The Treaty explicitly provides that the Council shall exercise its power to take decisions "in accordance with the provisions of this Treaty,"[33] thereby restating a basic principle underlying the transfer of sovereign powers from the Member States to the Community institutions. This principle can be found at the very beginning of all the European Treaties[34]: "Each institution shall act within the limits of the powers conferred upon it by this Treaty." The Council, therefore, is not endowed with a general regulatory competence, but may only take those decisions which are explicitly provided for by a provision of Community legislation[35]; it only has "conferred powers." There are, however, cases where action by the Council appears necessary to attain one of the objectives of the Community, while the Treaty has not provided the necessary powers; in such a case the Council may, acting unanimously on a proposal from the Commission, and after consulting the European Parliament, take the appropriate measures.[36] This should not be considered as opening unlimited opportunity for the institutions to increase the powers of the Council, although it does constitute a way of supplementing the Treaty provisions without going through the cumbersome procedure of amending the Treaty.[37] Indeed, the appropriate measures may only be taken when action is necessary "to attain one of the objectives of the Community," which clearly indicates that the powers granted by this provision are purely complementary. Also, the required unanimous vote of the Council should provide the necessary guarantee, since the extension of

[32] An analogous question is whether, in order to avoid amendments to its proposal, the Commission may withdraw it. One may not deny the Council the right to amend the proposal within acceptable limits, and withdrawing a proposal each time the Council is going to do this would empty Art. 149(1) of its contents.

[33] EEC, Art. 145.

[34] ECSC, Art. 3; EEC, Art. 4 and Euratom, Art. 3.

[35] See rules of procedure of the Council, Art. 11, which provides that a Council regulation must contain the indication of the provision by virtue of which the regulation is enacted. For further details see below, Chap. 4, Community Acts.

[36] EEC, Art. 235; see also ECSC, Art. 95 and Euratom, Art. 203.

[37] See EEC, Art. 236.

the Community's powers, generally speaking, will reduce the powers of the Member States in the same proportion. Finally, the Commission's proposal and the opinion of Parliament should ensure that the Community's interests are taken into consideration.[38]

Related to this principle of "conferred powers" is the question of *"implied powers."* In several cases the Court of Justice has admitted that "rules established by international agreements or by law are considered to imply those rules without which the first either would have no sense or could not be reasonably or successfully applied."[39] This prudent approach to a very delicate question cannot be considered as opening the door to extensive treaty interpretation in regard to the powers of the Community institutions. The principle of "conferred powers" therefore remains.

The decision-making powers of the Council are provided *inter alia* in the field of legislation, budget and international agreements.

When the Council enacts *legislation* through regulations, directives and decisions, it in fact continues, as was said, the work of the draftsmen of the treaties. This is particularly true for the EEC Treaty which, in many aspects, contains no more than general principles to guide the Community law-makers and the necessary rules of procedure.[40]

---

[38] At the Paris Summit Meeting in October 1972 it was agreed that for the purpose of carrying out the tasks laid down in the different programmes of action "it was desirable to make the widest possible use of all the dispositions of the Treaties, including Art. 235 of the EEC Treaty." (Cmnd. 5109, para. 15). See also Case 8/73 *Hauptzollamt Bremerhaven* v. *Massey-Fergusson* [1973] E.C.R. 897, where the Court found that the authority for Reg. 803/68 on the value of goods for customs purposes was to be found in Art. 235.

[39] Case 8/55 *Fédération Charbonnière de Belgique* v. *High Authority* [1954 to 1956] E.C.R. 245 at 299 and Case 22/70 *Commission* v. *Council* [1971] E.C.R. 263 at 280(72). See also Opinion 1/76 given pursuant to Art. 228(1) [1977] E.C.R. 741 at 755(3) where the Court found that the authority to enter into international agreements may not only arise from an express attribution by the Treaty, but equally may flow implicitly from its provisions.

[40] See, *e.g.* Agricultural Policy: EEC, Art. 39 sets out the "objectives" while Art. 43 provides that "the Council shall on a proposal from the Commission and after consulting the Assembly, acting unanimously . . . make regulations, issue directives, or take decisions"; free movement of labour: EEC, Arts. 48, 49; the right of establishment: EEC, Art. 54; transport: EEC, Art. 75; the rules of competition: EEC, Art. 87; the approximation of laws: EEC, Art. 100. The EEC Treaty is therefore referred to as a "traité-cadre," as opposed to the ECSC Treaty which constitutes a "traité-loi."

The *budgetary* powers have been examined in some detail in the previous section.[41]

As for *international agreements* to be entered into by the Communities, the powers to do so are based upon the fact that the Community was given legal personality[42] and the Treaty provides that agreements between the Community and one or more states or an international organisation shall be negotiated by the Commission and concluded by the Council.[43]

(2) Co-ordination of economic policies

Besides having the power to take decisions in all cases provided for by the treaties in order to ensure that the objectives set out therein are attained, the Council is more specifically entrusted with the task to "ensure co-ordination of the general economic policies of the Member States."[44]

The co-ordination of the general economic policies constitutes a necessary complement to the establishment and functioning of the common market. The task of the Council in this field is by its very nature a question of policy-making rather than law-making; it is not governed by precise timetables set out in the Treaty since it grows and varies with economic and political circumstances. This task is referred to in the EEC Treaty as "economic policy, conjunctural policy, balance of payments and commercial policy."[45] It should be noted that with regard to those fields of activity, the Treaty refers to the "application of procedures" and not to positive action in the form of legislation.[46] This explains the great variety of acts and the number of organs involved in defining these policies: declarations of the Council, resolutions of the Council, resolutions of the Council and of the representatives of the governments of the Member States, work programmes, etc. Out of this ill-defined situation grew, as was mentioned, the necessity to set up an organ with incontestable political power: the meetings of Heads of State or Government, which became later the European Council.[47] It will also be observed that with

---

[41] See under participation in budgetary procedure, p. 22 above.
[42] EEC, Art. 210.
[43] EEC, Art. 228; see below, External Relations, p. 51.
[44] EEC, Art. 145.
[45] EEC, Part 3, Title II.
[46] EEC, Art. 3(g).
[47] See above, p. 33.

regard to the above-mentioned policies, the Treaty either provides that the Member State shall regard them "as a matter of
common concern,"[48] or "pursue the needed economic policies"[49]
or "co-ordinate their economic policies [and] . . . shall provide for
co-operation between their appropriate administrative departments"[50] or, finally, that the Member States shall "proceed by
common action."[51]

Clearly, this task of co-ordinating economic policies is both
essential for the development of the Community and ill-defined
as regards its means and ultimate objectives.[52] Nevertheless the
system works and considerable progress has been made, such as
the setting-up of the European Monetary System for which
neither powers nor procedures have been provided in the Treaty.
This, however, does not mean that the actual situation is
satisfactory, since the absence of procedures means that the
delicate checks and balances of the institutional framework do
not function. When Council decisions are not taken in the form of
"regulations," "directives" or "decisions," there is often no
Commission proposal, no consultation of the European Parliament, and judicial control by the Court of Justice is doubtful. The
same is true when decisions, often of vital importance to the
Community, are taken by the European Council. It seems evident
that some solutions will have to be found, if one wants to
preserve a democratic approach to the exercise of those powers
transferred by the Member States to the European institutions.

(3) *Political co-operation*

In the final communiqué of the Conference of Heads of State or
Government on December 1 and 2, 1969 in The Hague, the
Ministers of Foreign Affairs were instructed to study the best way
of achieving progress in the matter of political unification within

---

[48] EEC, Arts. 103(1) and 107(1).
[49] EEC, Art. 104.
[50] EEC, Art. 105(1).
[51] EEC, Art. 116, first para.
[52] It will remembered that at one point the European Council sought to define the
ultimate objective as "European Union," at the November 1976 meeting in The
Hague. See statement published at that occasion, Bull. 11–1976, 93.

  On June 19, 1983 in Stuttgart the 10 Heads of State and Government signed
the Solemn Declaration on European Union designed to further European
Integration (Bull. 6–1983, 24).

the context of enlargement.[53] At the request of the Ministers, the Davignon Report was submitted[54] and accepted by the Ministers of Foreign Affairs in 1970. The aim is to further political unification by co-operating in the field of foreign affairs.[55] In 1974, the Heads of State or Government adopted a second report on European political co-operation[56] and approved, *inter alia*, the following measures: Foreign Ministers will meet four times a year; if the circumstances are sufficiently grave or the subject matter sufficiently important, a ministerial meeting may be replaced by a conference of Heads of State or Government. The Political Directors of the Foreign Ministries meet in the Political Committee with a view to preparing ministerial meetings and carrying out tasks entrusted to them by the Ministers.[57] The Commission is represented at all the meetings, and twice a year the Ministers meet with the Political Affairs Committee of the European Parliament.

It is important to note that the political co-operation machinery, which deals on the inter-governmental level with problems of international politics, is distinct, and additional to the activities of the institutions of the Community which are based on the commitments undertaken by the Member States in the EEC Treaty, although both sets of machinery have the aim of contributing to the development of European unification.

There exist, therefore, two parallel systems in connection with activities of the European Communities: one is "communautaire," the other is "inter-governmental." Obviously there is a danger of lack of co-ordination, if not of conflict. An attempt to prevent this is undertaken in the form of close contacts with the

---

[53] Third General Report (1969), 489(15).
[54] See Bull. 11–1979.
[55] The objectives of that co-operation are:
   –to ensure by means of regular consultations and exchanges of information, improved mutual understanding as regards the main problems of international relations;
   –to strengthen solidarity between governments by promoting harmonisation of their views, and the alignment of their positions and, whenever it appears possible and desirable, joint action.
[56] See Seventh General Report (1973), 502.
[57] Other measures concern a "group of correspondents" with the task to follow the implementation of the political co-operation, working parties, medium and long term studies, the role of embassies in the ten capitals and in third countries.

institutions of the Community.[58] The Commission thus plays an increasing role and is fully involved in almost all the political co-operation work being carried out. With regard to Parliament, it was agreed to associate it closely with the work of the President's office, *inter alia*, through replies to questions on political co-operation put by members.[59]

At the December 1974 Paris meeting of Heads of State or Government, it was decided that the President of the Council would be the spokesman for the Nine and would set out their views in international diplomacy. The Community is getting more and more involved in several areas of international political co-operation, an area which strictly speaking does not come under the provisions of the European treaties.

III. *The Commission of the European Communities*

Although in many cases the Commission participates, as was seen, in the law-making process of the Community when it exercises its right of initiative through the submission of the required proposals to the Council, the latter must be considered as the Community legislator. The Commission, on the other hand, is responsible for the functioning and development of the Common Market and is the guardian of the Community legislation; it administers the Communities' finances, negotiates the international agreements and represents the Community both within the Community and in the international field; it also has its own powers of decision. In short, it should be seen as the executive branch of the Community. As such, it constitutes the moving power behind the Community's activities and its uninterrupted presence on the Brussels scene, its staff and its worldwide relations constitute the necessary conditions for it to play a major role within the institutional system of the European Communities.

Most important, however, is the fact that it embodies and represents the common or Community interest and is responsible for ensuring that this interest prevails as regards

---

[58] For further details, see Seventh General Report (1973), 508.

[59] See, *e.g.* Thirteenth General Report (1979), 333, where a distinction is made between the Parliamentary questions addressed to the Commission, the Council and the "Conference of Ministers of Foreign Affairs (political co-operation)."

decisions taken by Member States, the Council and natural and legal persons alike.

1. The European Commissioners

The present Commission consists of 14 members.

The requirements for designation as a European Commissioner are very broadly defined: apart from the fact that the members of the Commission must be nationals of one of the Member State[60] and that no more than two members from the same Member State are permitted,[61] the Treaty provides that members "shall be chosen on the grounds of their general competence" and that their "independence" must be "beyond doubt."[62]

This independence—which is the main characteristic of the Commission—is given a concrete meaning by the conditions required for the *performance of duties*.[63] This is particularly important since the Commission represents the Communities' general interest and must be in a position to take a stand against any government which tries to put national interests first. This function can only be accomplished when the members of the Commission are totally independent of national governments, especially their own.

It must be remembered that it is in connection with this independent position that the ECSC Treaty used the term "supranational."[64] Although the word did not reappear in the later European treaties, the substance of the concept remains. With regard to this independence, obligations are imposed both on the members of the Commission[65] and on the Member

---

[60] Merger Treaty, Art. 10(1), third sub-para.; Art. 10 provides also that the Commission must include at least one national of each of the Member States.

[61] Merger Treaty, Art. 10(1), last sub-para. There are presently two members from Germany, France, Italy and the U.K. It would be sensible to reduce these numbers to one member per country as has been proposed several times. This would keep the commission, after enlargement to include Spain and Portugal, within manageable proportions.

[62] Merger Treaty, Art. 10(1), first sub-para.

[63] Merger Treaty, Art. 10(2): "The members of the Commission shall, in the general interest of the Communities, be completely independent in the performance of their duties."

[64] ECSC, Art. 9: "the Members of the High Authority will refrain from any action incompatible with the supranational character of their duties. Each Member State undertakes to respect this supranational character. . . ."

[65] Merger Treaty, Art. 10(2) and (3).

States.[66] If a Commissioner breaches these obligations he may be dismissed by the Court of Justice or, if no longer in office, deprived of his pension rights. It might seem odd, therefore, that the members of the Commission are appointed by the very governments of the Member States in relation to which this independence is so strongly stressed. Other methods of designation have been suggested in the Tindemans report to the European Council on European union[67] and in the Draft Treaty establishing the European Union adopted by Parliament in February 1984.[68]

Members of the Commission are appointed for four years; the appointment is renewable.[69] The President, who is designated six months before taking office, and the five Vice-Presidents on the other hand are appointed from among the members for two years only, also by common consent of the governments of the Member States; these appointments are renewable.[70]

2. The Commission's tasks and powers

The tasks and powers of the Commission are broadly described in EEC, Art. 155 and in more precise form in various treaty provisions.

The main tasks of the Commission are the following:

–to enforce the application of Community law;
–to issue recommendations and opinions;
–to exercise its power of decision;
–to exercise the powers conferred upon it by the Council;
–to participate in the legislative procedure;
–to negotiate international agreements;
–to implement the budget;
–to publish an annual General Report on the activities of the Communities.

(1) *Enforcement of Community law*

As the European treaties and the acts of the institutions under

---

[66] *Ibid.*
[67] Bull. Suppl. 1–76, 31.
[68] Bull. 2–1984, 7.
[69] Merger Treaty, Art. 11. See Arts. 12 and 13 for replacement and compulsory retirement.
[70] Merger Treaty, Art. 14. To date, the President and Vice-Presidents have always been reappointed at mid-term.

these treaties (secondary legislation) impose obligations on the Member States, institutions and natural and legal persons operating within the Community, the Commission was given certain powers with regard to all those who come under the jurisdiction of Community law. These powers concern the gathering of information and the institution of proceedings in case of failure to fulfil an obligation under the Treaty.

The power to gather information is generally provided for by EEC, Article 213 and more specifically by other provisions of the Treaty and of Community acts.[71] The Commission must be in a position to collect any information and carry out any checks required for the performance of the tasks entrusted to it. Although no general implementing provisions have been laid down by the Council, the obligation imposed upon the Member States to "facilitate the achievement of the Community's tasks"[72] should provide the necessary legal ground for the Commission to obtain all the required data.

When the Commission considers that a *Member State* has not fulfilled an obligation under the Community provision:

(a) it shall[73] remind the Government in question of its duties and invite it to take the measures necessary to ensure conformity with Community law or submit its observations, all this within a time-limit of usually two months;

(b) if no action is taken by the Member State or no comments submitted, or if those comments do not convince the Commission, the latter shall deliver a reasoned opinion on the matter which will lay down a time-limit for the Member State to comply;

(c) if the Member State does not comply, the Commission may[74] bring the matter before the Court of Justice;

---

[71] See, *e.g.* EEC, Arts. 72, 73(2), 93(3), 109(2), 111(5) and 213. See, *e.g.* Reg. 17, Arts. 4 and 5, the first Reg. implementing Arts. 85 and 86 (J.O. 1962, 204).

[72] EEC, Art. 5.

[73] EEC, Art. 169. The terms used by this provision indicate that once the Commission has determined that a Member State has not fulfilled an obligation (and with regard to this determination the Commission has discretionary power) there is an obligation for the Commission to act. The existence of this obligation is essential in a system where the plea of *non adimpletus contractus* is not admissible (see Joined Cases 90 and 91/63 *Commission v. Luxembourg and Belgium* [1964] E.C.R. 625 at 631).

[74] At this point the Commission's power is entirely discretionary.

(d) if the Court of Justice finds that the Member State has failed to fulfil its obligation, "the State shall be required to take the necessary steps to comply with the judgment."

Since the EEC Treaty[75] does not provide for legal coercive ways where Member States are concerned, further compliance is left to the Member State. The only other step the Commission can take in case the Member State does not comply with the judgment of the Court, is to start the procedure all over on the ground that by not complying with the judicial decision, the Member State has failed to fulfil an obligation under the Treaty.[76]

On the other hand, the more advanced the economic integration of the Member States, the more difficult it becomes for one of them to break the rules, since each Member State is in some way or other dependant on the goodwill of its partners for implementing the various common policies.

The majority of infringements by Member States concern quantitative restrictions on the free movement of goods, and more particularly, measures having equivalent effect.[77] It should be noted, on the other hand, that violations by Member States are the object of contacts and discussions between the Commission and the government concerned and are often settled outside Court.

With regard to other *institutions*—the only one concerned here is the Council—the Commission can initiate a Court action both when it is of the opinion that an action by the Council violates the Community provisions[78] or when a failure of the Council to act is considered by the Commission as an infringement of Community legislation.[79] No legal recourse exists against the European Parliament since its powers to take binding decisions are extremely limited.[79a]

---

[75] The ECSC Treaty provides for some kind of coercive measures (see Art. 88) but they were never applied.

[76] This happened in the case of Italy, see Case 48/71 *Commission* v. *Italy* [1972] E.C.R. 527, and in the case of France, see Case 232/78 *Commission* v. *France* [1979] E.C.R. 2729.

[77] A list of infringements is to be found since 1968 in the Bull. See also the General Report, *e.g.* Eighteenth General Report (1984), 307.

[78] EEC, Art. 173; this action will be examined in detail below. See, *e.g.* Case 22/70 *AETR* [1971] E.C.R. 263.

[79] EEC, Art. 175. To date, no such actions were undertaken by the Commission against the Council.

[79a] See however ECSC Treaty, Art. 38 and cases referred to in note 83 on p. 27, above.

With regard to *undertakings* (and natural persons) the Commission has been endowed with the power to impose penalties in certain cases, the most important ones being in the field of competition.[80] It should be noted also that decisions of the Commission imposing such fines are enforceable in the Member States.[81]

(2) *Recommendations and opinions*

The Commission shall formulate recommendations and deliver opinions on matters dealt with in the Treaty, if the latter expressly so provides or if the Commission considers it necessary.[82] It should be remembered that recommendations and opinions have no binding force[83] so that in fulfilling this task the Commission exercises a purely advisory task.

The EEC Treaty provides for several cases where a recommendation or opinion from the Commission is required,[84] other cases where it is simply provided as a possibility.[85] According to the Treaty, when the Commission issues recommendations and opinions not expressly provided for it must be "on matters dealt with in this Treaty."

(3) *Exercise of power of decision*

The Treaty does not confer upon the Commission a general power to take decisions: the basic principle of "conferred powers" also applies here,[86] as is made clear by the words "in the manner provided for in this Treaty." Since, as was seen, the Council must be considered as the Community law-maker, the

---

[80] EEC, Art. 87(2), see Reg. 17, Art. 15, first Regulation implementing EEC, Arts. 85 and 86 (J.O. 1962, 204); see also Reg. 11, Art. 18, concerning the abolition of discrimination in transport rates and conditions in implementation of EEC, Art. 79(3) (J.O. 1960, 1121) and Reg. 1017/68, Art. 22, applying rules of competition to transport by rail, road and inland waterway (J.O. 1968, L.175/1).

[81] EEC, Art. 192; see also below, p. 93.

[82] EEC, Art. 155.

[83] EEC, Art. 189.

[84] A Commission recommendation is required by EEC, Art. 111(2) (tariff negotiations with third countries); an opinion is required by EEC, Art. 237 (accession of new Member States).

[85] See, *e.g.* EEC, Art. 93(1) although the term used is "propose," but legally speaking it has the same value as a recommendation.

[86] So does the principle of "implied powers" (see above, Council, pp. 37, 38).

fact that the Commission also has the power of decision might create the impression that the legislative power within the Community is shared by two institutions. However, a distinction must be made between the power of decision in the sense of "legislation" and the power of decision in the sense of "execution." Both the legislator and the executive have the power to make regulations, issue directives and take decisions,[87] but they do not operate quite on the same level, although it must be recognised that no clear-cut distinction exists between the two.[88]

The power of decision directly entrusted by the Treaty to the Commission is mainly situated in the field of the "functioning and development of the common market,"[89] *i.e.* administration of the customs union,[90] the safeguard clauses,[91] the competition rules,[92] the Community budget,[93] and to some extent the external relations.[94] Other, more extensive powers of decision for the Commission have been provided by the Council through Community secondary legislation.[95]

In certain cases, when exercising its right to act, the Commission has a choice as to the form of the measure[96]; in other instances no form is prescribed,[97] sometimes a given act is required.[98]

Decisions of the Commission are taken by the majority of its members[99]; and when at least eight members are present,[1] the

---

[87] See EEC, Art. 189(1), which makes no distinction between Council and Commission.

[88] See, *e.g.* Commission Dir. 80/723 on the transparency of financial relations between Member States and public enterprises (O.J. 1980, L.195/35) and joined Cases 188 to 190/80, *France, Italy and U.K. v. Commission* [1982] E.C.R. 2545.

[89] EEC, Art. 155.

[90] See EEC, Arts. 10(2), 13(2), 22, 33(6) and (7).

[91] See EEC, Arts. 17(4), 25(2) and (3), 26, 37(3), 46, 73(1) and (2), 107(2), 108(3), 115, first and second paras., 226, Act of accession, Art. 135(2).

[92] See EEC, Arts. 89(2), 90(3), 91(2), 93(2), 97(2).

[93] The Commission is responsible for implementing the budget and administering the various Community Funds, such as the Social Fund (EEC, Art. 124).

[94] See below, external relations, p. 51.

[95] In accordance with EEC, Art. 155, last indent.

[96] See EEC, Art. 90(3): the Commission shall address "appropriate directives or decisions."

[97] *e.g.* EEC, Art. 10(2) "the Commission shall determine the methods of administrative co-operation."

[98] *e.g.* EEC, Art. 45(2) " . . . directives issued by the Commission."

[99] Merger Treaty, Art. 17(1). At present the majority is 8 out of 14.

[1] Rules of Procedure, Art. 6 (O.J. 1974 (2nd) vii).

Commission may not delegate its power of decision to any one of its members or to its civil servants[2]; neither can the Commission delegate such powers to autonomous organs.[3]

The rules of Procedure of the Commission, amended several times, have been published in the *Official Journal*.[4]

(4) *Exercise of powers conferred by the Council*

Most of the Commission's decisions are based on powers provided for in the acts of the Council; the Treaty empowers the latter to confer powers on the Commission for the implementation of the rules the Council lays down.[5] The necessity of such delegation was felt very early when the first decisions were taken regarding the common agricultural policy.[6]

In most cases the Commission must consult either the national authorities or a committee.[7] This system allows the Member

---

[2] See, however, Dec. 68/183 authorising certain management measures to be taken within the framework of the common organisation of agricultural markets (J.O. 1968, L.89/13). This decision is based upon Art. 27 of the Rules of Procedure of the Commission. See Case 8/72 *Cementhandelaren* v. *Commission* [1972] E.C.R. 977, concerning the legality of a document signed by a Director-General rather than by a member of the Commission.

[3] See Case 9/56 *Meroni* v. *High Authority* [1957 and 1958] E.C.R. 133.

[4] O.J. 1973, L.7/1, O.J. 1975, L.199/43.

[5] EEC, Art. 155, last indent. See Case 34/78 *Yoshida* v. *Kamer van Koophandel en Fabrieken voor Friesland* [1979] E.C.R. 115.

[6] See, *e.g.* Reg. 2727/75 (O.J. 1975, L.281/1) on the common organisation of the market in cereals, Art. 14(4).

[7] There are three kinds of such committees: advisory, management and regulatory committees.

Advisory committee: see *e.g.* Reg. 724/75 as amended by Reg. 214/79 (see updated version O.J. 1979, C.36/12) establishing a European Regional Development Fund, Art. 5(2)(*a*): consultation of the Regional Policy Committee. Such consultation has no further legal consequence.

Management committee: see *e.g.* Reg. 2727/75 (O.J. 1975, L. 281/1) Arts. 25 and 26. Such committees are composed of representatives of the Member States and presided over by a representative of the Commission. The votes are weighted in accordance with EEC, Art. 148(2). The Committee delivers an opinion by a majority of 45 votes on the draft of the measure to be taken which is submitted to it by the Commission. The Commission adopts measures which apply immediately; if the measures are not in accordance with the opinion they are communicated to the Council, which may take a different decision within one month with a qualified majority; if no decision is taken within that time-limit the Commission is free to decide.

Regulatory or rule-making committee: the procedure is the same as for the management committee except that the Commission may not take the measure if it is not in conformity with the committee's opinion. The Council has three

States to follow closely the implementation of the common policies and puts the Council in a position to decide itself in the event of a disagreement between the Commission and the Committee. This procedure has been used mainly in the field of agriculture.[8]

(5) Participation in the legislative procedure

As was described,[9] the Council in many instances, may act only on a proposal from the Commission; by submitting draft regulations, directives and decisions, the Commission participates, as the Treaty calls it "in the shaping of measures taken by the Council."[10] Whenever such proposals are required by the Treaty,[11] the Commission is granted an exclusive right of initiative in the Community law-making process. There are cases where the Commission is bound to make proposals within a given time limit[12]; there are other cases where the Commission must use its own judgment as to the opportuneness of making a proposal.[13] The Council may, however, request the Commission to submit to it any appropriate proposal.[14]

The Commission's proposal constitutes the basis for the consultation of Parliament by the Council. This proposal may be altered by the Commission for instance to take into account Parliament's opinion, as long as the Council has not acted.[15] It

---

months to adopt another measure after which the Commission is free to act. See, *e.g.* the committee on the origin of goods (Reg. 802/68, J.O. 1968, L.148/1).

    With regard to the implementation and interpretation of the rules governing these committees see Court of Justice, *e.g.* Case 25/70 *Einfuhr-und Vorratsstelle* v. *Köster* [1970] E.C.R. 1161 at 1170, where the Court bases the legality of the "management committee" procedure on Art. 155; Case 35/78 *Schouten* v. *Hoofdproduktschap voor Akkerbouwprodukten* [1978] E.C.R. 2543, where the Court stated that the absence of an opinion by a "management committee" in no way affects the validity of the measures adopted by the Commission.

[8] See also Art. 39, Reg. 1787/84 on the ERDF (O.J. 1984, L.169/1).
[9] See above, pp. 16 and 36.
[10] EEC, Art. 155, third indent.
[11] See list above, p. 30.
[12] *e.g.* EEC, Art. 21(2).
[13] *e.g.* EEC, Art. 94.
[14] EEC, Art. 152.
[15] This could *inter alia* be the case where the Assembly having been consulted has delivered a diverging opinion. EEC, Art. 149(2).

also constitutes of course the basis for the Council's decision, and if the Council wishes to adopt an act constituting an amendment to that proposal, it may only do so unanimously.[16]

When required by the Treaty, the Commission consults the Economic and Social Committee[17] before submitting its proposal to the Council; unlike consultation of the European Parliament, which only the Council can do, consultation of the Economic and Social Committee may also be initiated by the Commission.

In preparing its proposals to be submitted to the Council, the Commission usually consults with representatives of the Member States[18] on an informal basis. The main discussions, however, take place, after the proposal has been received by the Council, either with the Committee of Permanent Representatives or with working groups set up by the latter. Following these discussions the Commission has in several cases modified its original proposal; but it also happens that the Commission insists that, notwithstanding disagreement in the working groups or in the Committee, the proposal be discussed by the Council itself in the hope that an acceptable solution might be found at the political level.

It must be noted that the Commission might be called upon to justify the proposals it makes to the Council, not only before Parliament[19] but also before the Court of Justice, since the latter recognised the right of applicants, in an action concerning the legality of a Council decision to bring proceedings not only against the Council for having legislated, but also against the Commission for having made the proposal.[20] The Commission's proposals are usually published in the *Official Journal*.[21]

(6) *External relations*

The Commission's tasks are not limited to the internal activities of the Community; the Commission is also responsible for maintaining all appropriate relations with all international

---

[16] EEC, Art. 149, first para.; see further above, p. 36.

[17] See below for more details on this Committee, p. 78. An example of prescribed consultation can be found in EEC, Art. 43(2).

[18] See arrangement adopted by the Council on January 28 and 29, 1966, in Luxembourg (Bull. 3–1966, 5), point 1; see above, p. 31.

[19] *e.g.* in answer to parliamentary questions.

[20] Joined Cases 63–69/72 *Werhahn* v. *Council* [1973] E.C.R. 1229 at 1247(8).

[21] In this respect see also point (a) (2) of the Luxembourg Arrangement (Bull. 3–1966, 8). Proposals are published in the "C" series of the O.J.

organisations, in particular with the organs of the United Nations, of its specialised agencies and of the General Agreement on Tariffs and Trade.[22]

The Commission is also in charge of negotiating the agreements to be concluded between the Community and one or more states or an international organisation; since such agreements are concluded by the Council, the Commission must obtain a mandate from the Council before opening such negotiations. The Commission may obtain beforehand the opinion of the Court of Justice as to whether the envisaged agreement is compatable with the provisions of the Treaty.[23]

(7) Implementation of the Community budget

In the budgetary procedure the role of the Commission is limited to drafting its own budget and consolidating the estimates of all the institutions in a preliminary draft budget to be submitted to the Council before September 1[24] and to declare, after consulting the Economic Policy Committee, what the maximum rate of increase is for the "non-compulsory" expenditures,[25] which is determined by the growth in GNP in the Community.

Once the budget is adopted, it falls to the Commission to implement it in accordance with the provisions of the regulations laid down by the Council.[26] Consequently, the Commission must seek discharge in respect of this implementation. To this end the Commission submits annually to the Council and to Parliament the accounts for the preceding financial year together with a financial statement of the assets and liabilities of the Communities.[27] In exercising their powers of control over the implementation of the budget, the Council and Parliament are assisted by the Court of Auditors, which forwards to them an annual

---

[22] EEC, Art. 229. See also point (a) (5) of the Luxembourg Arrangement (Bull. 3–1966, 9).

[23] EEC, Art. 228(1). See, *e.g.* Opinions 1/75 [1975] E.C.R. 1355, 1/76 [1977] E.C.R. 741 and 1/78 [1979] E.C.R. 2871. The right to obtain an opinion of the Court also belongs to the Council and the Member States.

[24] EEC, Art. 203(2) and (3). For more details on the budgetary procedure see above under participation in the budgetary procedure, p. 22.

[25] *Ibid.* at (9).

[26] See, *e.g.* O.J. 1976, L.362/52.

[27] EEC, Art. 205a.

report after the close of each financial year.[28] The Council and Parliament in turn examine the accounts, the financial statement and the report, and discharge is given by Parliament on a recommendation of the Council.[29]

As part of the Community budget financed by the Communities' own resources,[30] the Commission administers the European Agricultural Guidance and Guarantee Fund, the Social Fund and the European Regional Development Fund. The Commission is also responsible for administering the European Development Fund for the African, Caribbean and Pacific States, financed by direct Member State contributions and for the "banking activities" of the European Coal and Steel Community.[31]

The Commission is also empowered to raise loans in order to finance atomic energy projects[32] and to finance industrial and infrastructure projects.[33] The borrowing itself is done by the Commission but it has delegated the administration of these resources to the European Investment Bank.

(8) *Publication of General Report*

The Commission publishes every year in February—*i.e.* one month before the opening of the sessions of Parliament[34]—a general report on the activities of the Communities. This report covers all the activities of all the institutions and organs of the Communities and as such it is an invaluable source of information. However, several activities are covered very summarily because they are the object of separate reports.

3. The Commission's staff

The Treaty provides that the Commission shall adopt its rules of procedure so as to ensure that both it and its departments operate in accordance with the provisions of the treaties.[35] The

---

[28] EEC, Art. 206a (4) last sub. para. For the Court of Auditors see below, p. 77. See Final Report, 1981 (O.J. 1982, C.344/1).

[29] EEC, Art. 206b. In 1984 Parliament refused to give a discharge for the 1982 budget implementation. See Bull. 12–1984, 67.

[30] See below, Financing Community Activities, p. 81.

[31] See ESCS, Arts. 54 and 56, see also below ECSC.

[32] See Euratom, Art. 172(4) and O.J. 1977, L.88/9.

[33] See O.J. 1978, L.298/9; officially known as New Community Instrument.

[34] See above under the General Report, p. 21.

[35] Merger Treaty, Art. 16.

staff is divided into units—Directorates-General, Services or Groups which more or less correspond to the main sub-divisions of three basic European treaties.[36]

As regards the Communities' staff two texts must be mentioned: the *Protocol on the Privileges and Immunities of the European Communities*[37] and the *Staff Regulations of Officials and the Conditions of Employment of other servants of the European Community*.[38] Officials are recruited directly by the various institutions and organs of the Communities; in other words the Communities' staff is not composed of national civil servants seconded by the Administration of the Member States[39]; the obligations concerning the independence of the members of the Commission described above, applies *mutatis mutandis* to the officials.

IV. *The Court of Justice*

The three European Treaties contain an identical provision to describe the task of the Court: it shall ensure that in the

---

[36] At the beginning of 1985 the Commission had the following units: Secretariat-General, Legal Service, Statistical Office, Customs Union Service, DG I—External Relations, DG II—Economic and Financial Affairs, DG III—Internal Market and Industrial Affairs, DG IV—Competition, DG V—Employment, Social Affairs and Education, DG VI—Agriculture, DG VII—Transport, DG VIII—Development, DG IX—Personnel and Administration, DG X—Information, Spokesman's Group, DG XI—Environment, Consumer Protection and Nuclear Safety, DG XII—Science, Research and Development, Joint Research Center, DG XIII—Information Market and Innovation, DG XIV—Fisheries, DG XV—Financial Institutions and Taxation, DG XVI—Regional Policy, DG XVII—Energy, DG XVIII—Credit and Investments, DG XIX—Budget, DG XX—Financial Control; then there are the Euratom Supply Agency, the Security Office and the Office for Official Publications. There is also a Joint Interpreting and Conference Service responsible for interpreting at meetings organised by the Council, the Commission, the Economic and Social Committee and the European Investment Bank.

[37] See Protocol annexed to the Merger Treaty (J.O. 1962, 1461). See Case 28/83, *Forcheri* v. *Commission,* judgment of March 15, 1984, not yet published.

[38] A consolidated version in English was published as a supplement to O.J. 1973, C.12.

[39] It goes without saying that the nationality of the officials must be taken into account and although "no post may be reserved for a given nationality" (Staff Reg., Art. 27) a geographical equilibrium must exist based on the size of the population of the respective Member State. There were about 12,000 officials at the end of 1984, including those working in the research centres located in various Member States (O.J. 1984, L.12/67).

implementation and application of the Treaty the law is observed. This short and sibylline text covers an extremely varied series of activities.

The Court's task is complicated by the fact that Community law is basically economic law which by definition is essentially evolutive and in constant need of adaptation as far as implementation of the general rules is concerned. It was out of the question to try to regulate the economic policies of the Member States in a document of no more than 250 Articles. Furthermore, only part of the EEC Treaty is drafted with some precision.[40]

Consequently, when called upon to state what is Community law in a given field, it is by reference to the objectives of the Community that the Court interprets the existing rules and formulates new ones. The task of the Court is not only to interpret, but also to state what the law is when the existing legislation does not explicitly provide for it. This, of course, is not unique to the Court of Justice: "wherever there are courts, the law grows in the hands of the judges,"[41] but for the reasons just indicated it is particularly appropriate in the case of the European Communities.

This is the main reason why it is so important for the judges to be totally independent,[42] the more so since, as was explained above, the Council tends to act as an intergovernmental conference where every member fights for his country's interests, the European Parliament has none of the powers required for exercising a democratic control and the Commission, which besides its overwhelming administrative task must fulfil a political function, is bound to accept compromises in the implementation of Community legislation by the Member States.

The Court can only express itself in judgments[43] and when called upon to do so; nevertheless, over the years it was able to build up a set of rules which were of prime importance in shaping the evolution of the Communities themselves; this happened mainly through its rulings concerning the interpretation of the

---

[40] The evolutive character of Community law is referred to by the Court with the words "at the present stage in the development of Community law"; *e.g.* Case 27/80, *Fietje* [1980] E.C.R. 3839 at 3853 (8).

[41] Schwarzenberger, *Internal Law*, p. 24.

[42] See EEC, Art. 167: judges shall be chosen from persons whose independence is beyond doubt.

[43] And exceptionally also in "opinions," see EEC, Art. 228(1), last sub-para.

Treaties and Community legislation[44] at the request of national tribunals confronted with questions of interpretation of Community law applicable in cases pending before them.

1. The Members of the Court

The Court consists of eleven judges[45] and is assisted by five Advocates-General[46]; the latter, however, are not "members" of the Court. The Judges and Advocates-General are to be chosen from persons whose independence is beyond doubt and who have the qualifications for appointment to the highest judicial offices in their respective countries[47] or "who are jurisconsults of recognised competence."[48]

Judges and Advocates-General are appointed for a term of six years by common accord of the governments of the Member States[49]; they are eligible for reappointment.

The eleven Judges are grouped in five Chambers of three or five judges each; cases brought before the Court are normally heard by one of the Chambers.[50]

The position of the Advocates-General is a particularly interesting one: their independent position—they do not participate in the discussions that lead to the Court's decision—allows them to carry out their own personal examination of the case and express personal opinions—which the Judges cannot; they are also free to examine any related question even when it was not brought forward by the parties. Although the reasoned submissions they make in open court do not necessarily reflect the Court's views, they often contain precious indications in regard to the reasoning which led to the decisions.

---

[44] See EEC, Art. 177.
[45] EEC, Art. 165(1). See also EEC, Art. 165(4).
[46] See Eighteenth General Report (1984), p. 38.
[47] EEC, Art. 167(1); this means that qualifications are determined in accordance with national law and that, therefore there are no uniform requirements, the more so since certain Member States have different categories in their judicial system including commercial tribunals for which no legal training is required.
[48] EEC, Art. 167(1).
[49] Further provisions concerning the Judges and the Advocates-General are to be found in the Statute of the Court of Justice annexed as a Protocol to the Treaty and in the Rules of Procedure (O.J. 1979, L.238/1 and C.265/8).
[50] EEC, Art. 165.

2. The Court's jurisdiction

As was pointed out at the beginning of this section, the Court fulfils many different tasks: in the order of the Treaty provisions the Court's jurisdiction consists mainly of the following:

–finding whether a Member State has failed to fulfil an obligation under the Treaty; actions can be brought either by the Commission or by another Member State (Articles 169, 170 and 171);

–unlimited jurisdiction with regard to penalties; actions can be brought by natural or legal persons (Article 172);

–review of the legality of an act or a failure to act of the Council and the Commission at the request of Member States, the Council or the Commission and under certain circumstances natural or legal persons (Articles 173–176); in the case of failure to act also at the request of Parliament (Article 175);

–giving a preliminary ruling at the request of a national court or tribunal (Article 177);

–granting compensation for damages caused by the institutions; actions can be brought against the Community by Member States and natural or legal persons (Articles 178 and 215);

–deciding in disputes between the Community and its servants (Article 179).

(1) *The finding of a failure by a Member State to fulfil its treaty obligations*

When the Commission or a Member State considers that a Member State has failed to fulfil an obligation under the Treaty, they may bring the matter before the Court. The possibility of the Commission initiating an action of this kind constitutes the main instrument at its disposal for fulfilling its task as guardian of Community law. The procedure to be followed by the Commission has been explained in some detail above.[51]

As regards the procedure initiated by Member States, the Treaty provides for an intermediate phase corresponding to an internal administrative procedure.[52]

---

[51] See above, enforcement of Community law, p. 44.

[52] EEC, Art. 170. The first time this procedure was used was in 1977, Case 58/77 *Ireland* v. *France* (O.J. 1977, C.142/8). It was later withdrawn.

The Court's jurisdiction in cases brought against a Member State consists merely in "finding"[53] that the State has failed to fulfil an obligation under the Treaty. If such finding is made, the Member State "shall be required to take the necessary measures to comply with the judgment of the Court."[54] With respect to cases brought by a Member State against another State attention must be drawn to the obligation undertaken by the Member States[55] "not to submit a dispute concerning the interpretation or application of the Treaty to any method of settlement other than those provided for therein."[56] The principal method being the Court, this provision guarantees uniformity in the interpretation of Community law.

(2) *Unlimited jurisdiction with regard to penalties*

In order to ensure compliance with the obligations laid down in its regulations, the Council may make provisions for penalties to be imposed on natural or legal persons.[57] The right of those persons to ask the Court to review the legality of a decision taken by an institution under such provision is provided under the general jurisdiction of the Court to review the legality of Community acts.[58] In a case where the Council wants to grant unlimited jurisdiction to the Court this must be explicitly done.[59]

---

[53] EEC, Art. 171. The "finding" must be seen in contradistinction to the "unlimited jurisdiction" in the case for instance of penalties (EEC, Art. 172; see below) and the power to "annul" an act of an institution (EEC, Art. 174; see below).

[54] EEC, Art. 171. It follows that the obligation to take measures results not from a Court order but from Art. 171.

[55] EEC, Art. 219.

[56] Other methods of settlement could have been the International Court of Justice whose compulsory arbitration was accepted by several Member States, or the Benelux Court of Arbitration where Belgium, the Netherlands and Luxembourg are concerned.

[57] Penalties can only be imposed upon natural or legal persons not on Member States. The Council's competence to provide for penalties results from EEC, Art. 79(3) and 87(2). It is debatable whether or not EEC, Art. 172 besides attributing unlimited jurisdiction to the Court also confers upon the Council a general competence to provide for fines in its regulations.

[58] EEC, Art. 173–174.

[59] See Reg. 11, Art. 18 (J.O. 1960, 1121) and Reg. 17, Art. 17 (J.O. 1962, 204).

In such a case not only may the Court suppress the fine but it may decide also to increase or decrease it.[60]

The Court's unlimited jurisdiction also applies in two other areas: claims for damages resulting from non-contractual liability of the Community[61] and disputes between the Community and its servants.

(3) *Review of the legality of an act or failure to act of an institution*

(a) APPEAL FOR ANNULMENT[62]

In supervising the legality of Community acts[63] the Court protects all those who are subject to Community law against arbitrary action of the institutions, but, it also ensures that Community activities remain within the boundaries laid down by the European Treaties and that the institutions respect the balance of powers within the Community.

Who may lodge an appeal for annulment? With regard to the admissibility of court actions, all Member States apply in their national law a general rule well coined in French as "pas d'intérêt, pas d'action"; the same principle applies within the Communities: the Member States[64] and the Council and Com-

---

[60] See, *e.g.* Case 27/76 *United Brands* v. *Commission* [1978] E.C.R. 207 where a fine was reduced from 1,000,000 units of account to 850,000. There are no examples of the Court increasing a penalty.

[61] EEC, Arts. 178 and 215; see below.

[62] EEC, Art. 173. It should be noted that the proceedings for annulment must be instituted within two months of the publication or notification of the measure.

[63] The Treaty refers to "acts of the Council and the Commission other than recommendations or opinions" (EEC, Art. 173(1)); these other acts are mainly the regulations, directives and decisions provided in EEC, Art. 189, but are by no means limited to those. They include also agreement and generally speaking any measures which binds (some of) those who are subject to Community Law. See Case 22/70 *Commission* v. *Council* [1971] E.C.R. 263 at 277(42): "an action for annulment must therefore be available in the case of all measures adopted by the institutions whatever their nature or form, which are intended to have legal effects," Case 60/81 *IBM* v. *Commission* [1981] E.C.R. 2639 at 2651 (9) and Case 108/83 *Luxembourg* v. *Parliament* where the Court annulled a resolution of the latter, judgment of April 10, 1984 (not yet published).

[64] All Member States have at one time or another appealed for annulment of a Commission act; rarer are appeals by Member States against Council acts; see Case 151/73 *Ireland* v. *Council* [1974] E.C.R. 285. Lately the court has also accepted appeals by a Member State for annulment of Acts of Parliament, although this is not provided for under the EEC Treaty. See Cases 230/81 *Luxembourg* v. *Parliament* [1983] E.C.R. 255 (where the court found that such an

mission[65] are considered to have an overall interest in the correct implementation of the Community law and have therefore, subject to a two months time-limit, an unlimited right to initiate proceedings aimed at controlling the legality of Community acts. Natural and legal persons on the other hand must prove their specific and particular interest in such a control.[66] In this respect it is assumed that acts having a general application concern everybody but nobody in particular, and therefore cannot normally be challenged in Court by individuals unless these acts contain provisions which in reality have an "individual"[67] rather than a "general" application. This can be the case notwithstanding the fact that the act in question was taken in the form of a "general" act, *i.e.* a regulation,[68] or of an individual act but addressed to another person.[69]

The interpretation of the Treaty provisions is of course essential in determining the extent of the legal protection enjoyed by individuals within the European Communities; hence the importance of the case law of the Court of Justice in this field: the Court without resorting to "extensive interpretation" has always given the text a meaning which allowed a wide access to review of the

---

action is provided for under the ECSC Treaty, at 281) and 108/83 *Luxembourg* v. *Parliament*, judgment of April 10, 1984 (not yet published).

[65] Appeals by the Council or the Commission for annulment of each other's acts are very rare: see Case 22/70 *Commission* v. *Council* [1971] E.C.R. 263.

[66] Case 77/77 *BP* v. *Commission* [1978] E.C.R. 1513 at 1525 (13).

[67] The Treaty refers to an act which "is of direct and individual concern" to a person; this according to the Court of Justice is the case only "if that decision affects them by reason of certain attributes which are peculiar to them or by reason of circumstances in which they are differentiated from all other persons and by virtue of these factors distinguishes them individually just as in the case of the person addressed" (Case 25/62 *Plaumann* v. *Commission* [1963] E.C.R. 95 at 107). This would not be the case if the plaintiff is affected by the act because he belongs to a category designated abstractly and as a whole (Case 42/71 *Nordgetreide* v. *Commission* [1972] E.C.R. 105 at 110(5)). See also Case 72/74 *Union Syndicale* v. *Council* [1975] E.C.R. 401 at 410(17).

[68] Joined Cases 41 to 44/70 *Fruit Company* v. *Commission*. The Court held that Art. 1 of Reg. 983/70 "is not a provision with a general application but must be analysed as a bundle of individual decisions" [1971] E.C.R. 411 at 422(21). See also Case 138/79 *Roquette Frères* v. *Council* [1980] E.C.R. 3333.

[69] According to the Court of Justice "another person" in EEC, Art. 173(2) can include Member States since no limitation as to the meaning of these words are to be found in the Treaty. Persons can therefore appeal against acts of the institutions addressed to a Member State when they are directly concerned; Case 730/79, *Phillip Morris* v. *Commission* [1980] E.C.R. 2671.

legality of Community acts,[70] although the Court explicitly recognised that the EEC Treaty "lays down more restrictive conditions than the ECSC Treaty for the admissibility of applications for annulment by private individuals."[71]

It follows that the opportunities for private parties to appeal directly for annulment of Community acts are much more limited than for the Member States and the Community institutions. However, other means exist whereby persons and enterprises may obtain a Court ruling, if not on the legality at least on the applicability of Community acts, which for the applicant has identical consequences if the action is well founded.[72]

Grounds for annulment. The European Treaty provides for four grounds for annulment[73] which have their origin in French administrative law.

(i) *Lack of competence*: this is the expression in juridicial terms of the general principle according to which the Community institutions only have the powers that have explicitly been attributed to them by Community law.[74]

(ii) *Infringement of an essential procedural requirement*: as was mentioned before, if the Council were to take a decision without a proposal from the Commission or without consulting the European Parliament (when these are required under the Treaty) it would infringe an essential procedural requirement and therefore an appeal for annulment of the decision in question could be lodged. The same would apply if the Commission were to make a

---

[70] See *e.g.* joined Cases 16 and 17/62 *Producteurs de fruits* v. *Council* [1962] E.C.R. 471 at 479: a measure entitled by its author a Regulation can contain provisions which are capable of being not only of direct but also of individual concern to certain natural or legal persons and Case 101/76 *Koninklijk Scholten Honig* v. *Council and Commission* [1977] E.C.R. 797.

[71] Joined Cases 16 and 17/62, above at 478.

[72] See below, preliminary ruling, compensation for damages and the exception of illegality.

[73] EEC, Art. 173; the same grounds are provided by the ECSC and Euratom Treaties: respectively Arts. 33 and 146.

[74] Since appeals for annulment must be lodged within two months after publication or notification it could happen that a Community act without legal ground continues to be implemented (see however the exception of illegality, below). The question was raised by the French Government in a procedure before the Court. See joined Cases 6 and 11/69 *Commission* v. *France* [1969] E.C.R. 523 at 539 (11–13).

proposal to the Council without requesting the opinion of the Economic and Social Committee, when required by Community law to do so. The absence of sufficient reasons in a Community act must also be considered as a ground for annulment under this heading.[75]

(iii) *Infringement of the Treaty or of any rule of law relating to its application*: it could of course be argued that the two grounds mentioned earlier also constitute infringements of the Treaty and that this ground in fact covers all possible illegalities. However, the Treaty refers to four grounds and accordingly they must be examined here.

In the expression "infringement of the Treaty," the word treaty must be understood as referring also to secondary legislation, *i.e.* the acts of the institutions,[76] the treaties modifying the three basic treaties and the Protocols.[77]

As to the expression "rules of law relating to its application" this refers to international law[78] and to the general principles of law.[79] The latter include, besides the principles universally

---

[75] See below, p. 91.

[76] These acts are not only the regulations, directives and decisions, but also the agreements concluded by the Community with international organisations and third countries. See, *e.g.* Case 181/73 *Haegeman* v. *Belgium* [1974] E.C.R. 449.

[77] See EEC, Art. 239.

[78] See Case 8/55 *Fédération Charbonnière de Belgique* v. *High Authority* [1954 to 1956] E.C.R. 245 at 299; joined Cases 21 to 24/72 *International Fruit Company* v. *Produktschap voor Groenten en Fruit* [1972] E.C.R. 1219 at 1226 (6); see also Case 41/74 *Van Duyn* v. *Home Office* "it is a principle of international law which the EEC Treaty cannot be assumed to disregard" [1974] E.C.R. 1337 at 1351 (22). However in other cases, the Court did not accept arguments based on international law; see, *e.g.* joined Cases 90 and 91/63 *Commission* v. *Belgium and Luxembourg*, [1964] E.C.R. 625 at 631.

[79] See, *e.g.* Case 92/71 *Interfood* v. *Hauptzollamt Hamburg-Ericus* [1972] E.C.R. 231 at 242(6), confirmed by Case 112/77 *Töpfer* v. *Commission* [1978] E.C.R. 1019 at 1033 (19): protection of legitimate expectation.
Other principles of law recognised by the Court are:
–the right to be heard: Case 17/74 *Transocean Marine Paint Association* v. *Commission* [1974] E.C.R. 1063 at 1080(15);
–respect for fundamental rights: Case 36/75 *Rutili* v. *Minister for the Interior* [1975] E.C.R. 1219 at 1232/(32);
–freedom of trade-union activity, Case 175/73 *Union Syndicale* v. *Council* [1974] E.C.R. 917 at 925(9, 14);
–legal certainty: Case 21/81 *Openbaar Ministerie* v. *Bont* [1982] E.C.R. 381 at 390(13);
–equality of treatment; Case 148/73 R *Louwage* v. *Commission* [1974] E.C.R. 81 at 89(12);

recognised, those principles which are particular to the Member States and which the Court formulates on the basis of the wording, the contents and the system of the treaties or also on the basis of a comparative study of the ten legal systems.[80]

(iv) *Misuse of power*[81]: There is misuse of power when a public authority uses its lawful powers to attain an objective for which the powers were not intended. Although this ground has been invoked many times, the Court does not often base an annulment on misuse of power.[82]

Consequences of annulment. When reviewing the legality of a binding Community act the Court limits itself, in case the action is well founded, to declare the act void; after that, it is up to the institution which issued the act to "take the necessary measures to comply with the judgment of the Court of Justice."[83]

Since annulment means that the act in question is to be considered as having never existed—the Court's declaration has effect *ex tunc* and *erga omnes*—the institution must endeavour to recreate the situation which would have existed had the act not been issued. This might be impossible, especially when the nullity affects a regulation; this is the reason why the Treaty provides that in the case of annulment of a regulation, the Court may state which effects shall be considered definitive.[84]

It should also be noted that annulment does not mean that the whole act must be declared void: if the nullity concerns only

---

–contractual certainty: Case 48/72 *Brasserie de Haecht* v. *Wilkin-Janssen* [1973] E.C.R. 77 at 86(9);
–protection of legal expectation: Case 97/76 *Merkur* v. *Commission* [1977] E.C.R. 1063 at 1078(7);
–principle of proportionality between the means employed and the end in view, Case 122/78, *Buitoni* v. *FORMA* [1979] E.C.R. 677 at 684(16).

[80] See EEC, Art. 215(2).

[81] Probably better known by its French equivalent *"détournement de pouvoir."* For more details as to the meaning of *détournement de pouvoir* see the comparative study of the law of the original six Member States made by the Advocate-General in his opinion in Case 3/54 *ASSIDER* v. *High Authority* [1954 to 1956] E.C.R. 63 at 75.

[82] See, *e.g.* Case 92/78 *Simmenthal* v. *Commission* [1979] E.C.R. 777 at 811(106).

[83] EEC, Art. 176. See Case 30/59 *Steenkolenmijnen* v. *High Authority* [1961] E.C.R. 1 at 17.

[84] EEC, Art. 174(2).

certain provisions, the others are not affected as long as they can remain operative independently of those annulled.

(b) APPEAL AGAINST FAILURE TO ACT[85]

In the case of *failure to act*[86] the Court may be called upon to declare that this failure constitutes an infringement of the Treaty; the term "treaty" must be interpreted also as including secondary legislation.[87] Although in the case of the review of the legality of an act the Court may declare the act void while in the case of a failure to act the Court can only declare this to be an infringement, "both provisions merely prescribe one and the same method of recourse."[88]

One important difference with the annulment proceedings is that an action for failure to act can also be brought by the European Parliament.[89]

Actions for failure to act are not limited to cases in which the Council or Commission were supposed to take a binding decision: the Council, the Assembly or a Member State can also bring an action when the Commission, *e.g.* fails to send a proposal to the Council where this is required by the Treaty.

Natural or legal persons may only bring proceedings when an institution fails to issue[90] a binding act of which they would have been the addressee.[91]

---

[85] EEC, Art. 175. Such an appeal is admissible only when the plaintiff has first called upon the institution to act and the latter has not defined its position within two months; the plaintiff then has another two months to bring his action.

[86] To date mainly actions by natural or legal persons have been brought under this provision against the Commission. See, however, below n.89.

[87] Whether in the absence of the words "of any rule of law relating to its application" a failure to act could be challenged in Court for infringement of a general principle of law has not as yet been tested. It seems however that if an act violating such principles is to be considered illegal, the same applies to failures to act.

[88] Case 15/70 *Chevalley* v. *Commission* [1970] E.C.R. 975 at 979(6).

[89] See Case 13/83 *Parliament* v. *Council* (O.J. 1983, C.49/9) for failure to act in the field of transport.

[90] Failure to act must be distinguished from refusal to act; in the latter case such refusal which constitutes a decision, can only be challenged under Art. 173, annulment: see Case 8/71 *Komponistenverband* v. *Commission* [1971] E.C.R. 705 at 710(2). See also joined Cases 10 and 18/68 *Eridania* v. *Commission* [1969] E.C.R. 459 at 483(17).

[91] Case 15/71 *Mackprang* v. *Commission* [1971] E.C.R. 797 at 804(4).

(4) *Preliminary ruling*[92]

The preliminary ruling which pre-supposes direct effect of Community law, (*i.e.* possibility to invoke Community rules before national courts) constitutes with the action for compensation for damages the best means of protection for the citizens of the Community against illegal activities of the institution; it is also the ideal instrument in the hands of the Court to define and develop Community law. When the Court interprets[93] a provision of Community law, this interpretation must be accepted and applied by the national courts[94] when called upon to ensure the

[92] EEC, Art. 177.

[93] With regard to methods of interpretation see *e.g.* Case 75/63 *Hoekstra* v. *Bedrijfsvereniging Detailhandel* [1964] E.C.R. 177 and Case 53/81 *Levin* v. *Staatssecretaris* [1982] E.C.R. 1035 at 1048(9).

[94] See 1972 European Communities Act, s.3(1) and Case 33/76 *Rewe* v. *Landwirtschaftkammer Saarland* [1976] E.C.R. 1989 at 1997 (5) where the Court based this obligation on EEC, Art. 5. With regard to Community law the Treaty provides for "judicial co-operation" between the Court of Justice and the national courts. Joined Cases 110 and 111/78 *Ministére Public and A.S.B.L.* v. *Van Wesemael* [1979] E.C.R. 35 at 51(21). By and large the national courts are responsible for applying community law while the Court of Justice has exclusive competence to interpret its provisions. The respective tasks and powers have been specified by the case-law of the Court:

(a) the Court has no jurisdiction under Art. 177 to apply the Treaty to a specific national case; Case 6/64 *Costa* v. *ENEL* [1964] E.C.R. 585 at 592; nevertheless it may furnish the national court with the interpretative criteria necessary to enable it to dispose of the dispute: Case 106/79 *Vereniging Boekhandels* v. *Eldi Records* [1980] E.C.R. 1137 at 1147(7);

(b) the considerations which may have led a national court or tribunal to its choice of questions as well as the relevance which it attributes to such questions in the context of a case before it are excluded from review by the Court; Case 53/79 *ONPTS* v. *Damiani* [1980] E.C.R. 273 at 281(5);

(c) the Treaty does not prescribe a particular form in which a national court must present its request for a ruling; the Court must derive from the wording of the request the questions which relate exclusively to the interpretation of the Community provision; Case 5/69 *Völk* v. *Vervaecke* [1969] E.C.R. 295 at 301(2/4);

(d) it is not for the Court to appropriate to itself an assessment of the jurisdiction of the national court to refer the question or of the presence of a legal interest requiring protection on the part of the applicant in the main action, Case 65/81 *Reina* v. *Landeskreditbank* [1982] E.C.R. 33;

(e) the Court may not on the basis of Art. 177, give judgment on the interpretation of a provision of national law; Case 152/79 *Lee* v. *Minister for Agriculture* [1980] E.C.R. 1495 at 1507(11);

(f) the Court in applying Art 177 is not competent to decide on the compatibility of a national provision with Community law; Case 10/71 *Ministère public Luxembourgeois* v. *Muller* [1971] E.C.R. 723 at 729(7);

application of said provision. On the other hand, parties will not contest lightly such an interpretation although they remain free to do so. In other words, if the Court's interpretation is limited *de jure* to the case under review, *de facto* it has effect *erga omnes*.[95]

The object of the Court's competence in this field is to ensure uniform interpretation and application, within all the Member States, of the provisions of Community law; such uniformity constitutes an essential requirement for the existence and functioning of a common market.[96]

Requests for preliminary rulings must emanate from national

nevertheless, the Court has the power to provide the national court with criteria of interpretation coming within Community law enabling that court to determine whether such rules are compatible with the Community rule invoked; joined Cases 95 and 96/79 *Kefer and Delmelle* [1980] E.C.R. 103 at 112(5);

(g) the preliminary ruling of the Court is binding on the national court as to the interpretation of the Community provision; Case 52/76 *Benedetti* v. *Munari* [1977] E.C.R. 163 at 184(3) and Case 811/79 *Amministrazione delle Finanze* v. *Ariete* [1980] E.C.R. 2545 at 2553(6);

(h) the jurisdiction of the Court to give rulings on the validity of measures adopted by the institutions extends to all the grounds capable of invalidating those measures, including the fact that they are contrary to a rule of international law; joined Cases 21 to 24/72 *International Fruit Company* v. *Produktschap voor Groenten en Fruit* [1972] E.C.R. 1219 at 1226(6);

(i) a question relating to the application of Art. 215(2) (non-contractual liability of the Community) cannot be determined in proceedings for a preliminary ruling; Case 101/78 *Granaria* v. *Hoofdproduktschap voor Akkerbouwprodukten* [1979] E.C.R. 623 at 638(10);

(j) the Court has jurisdiction to give a ruling only when there is a genuine dispute before the national court; Case 104/79 *Foglia* v. *Novello* [1980] E.C.R. 745 at 760(11);

(k) when the Court declares a regulation void under a procedure ex Art. 177 it may by analogy with Art. 174 state which of the effects of the regulation shall be considered as definitive; Case 145/79 *Roquette Frères* v. *French customs administration* [1980] E.C.R. 2917 at 2946(52).

[95] See Case 66/80 *ICC* v. *Amministrazione delle Finanze* [1981] E.C.R. 1191 at 1215 (13). See however Case 61/79 *Amministrazione delle Finanze* v. *Denkavit* [1980] E.C.R. 1205 at 1223(17).

[96] See Case 6/64 *Costa* v. *ENEL* [1964] E.C.R. 585 at 594. See also Case 28/67 *Molkerei-Zentrale Westfalen* v. *Hauptzollamt Paderborn* [1968] E.C.R. 143 at 153.

courts or tribunals.[97] The national court or tribunal may, or when there is no judicial remedy against its decision *must*, request such a ruling[98] each time it considers that in order to give judgment in a case pending before it, it needs a decision on the question. This can occur when having to apply a Community rule, they find themselves confronted with a question concerning this rule. The national court then suspends the proceedings before it and asks the European Court to solve the question. A distinction must be made between primary Community law in which case only interpretation can be requested, and secondary Community law, in which case the Court also has jurisdiction to give a ruling on the validity.

As to the precise meaning of the words "where such a question is raised," it seems that this condition is fulfilled as soon as a difference of opinion arises concerning the interpretation (and in the case of acts also the validity) of a provision of Community law. "Questions can be raised by the parties to the dispute but also by the national court or tribunal itself."[99] However, the obligation to refer a question only exists when the national judge considers that a decision on the question is necessary to enable him to give judgment; in other words, it is his decision. Furthermore, it is also within the discretionary powers of the national judge to decide whether a question is raised in good faith or whether it is a purely procedural move initiated by a party for

---

[97] Whether or not a national organ which refers a question to the Court of Justice is a court of law must be determined in accordance with national law. See, *e.g.* Case 61/65 *Vaassen* v. *Beamtenfonds Mijnbedrijf* [1966] E.C.R. 261 at 273. The Court can only be requested to give a ruling by a court which is called upon to give judgment in proceedings intended to lead to a decision of a judicial nature; Case 138/80 *Borker* [1980] E.C.R. 1975 at 1977 (4). Arbitrators in disputes between parties to a contract cannot be considered as a "court or tribunal"; Case 102/81 *Nordsee* v. *Reederei Mond* [1982] E.C.R. 1095. On the other hand an appeals Committee set up by a professional body and which may affect the exercise of rights granted by Community law is considered a "court"; Case 246/80 *Broekmeulen* v. *Huisarts registratie Commissie* [1981] E.C.R. 2311.

[98] The obligation to refer a question to the Court does not exist however when it is raised in a summary procedure; joined Cases 35 and 36/82 *Morson and Jhanjan* v. *State of the Netherlands* [1982] E.C.R. 3723. There are situations where the requirement of the third para. of Art. 177 does not apply: (1) the question raised is not relevant, (2) the Community measure has already been interpreted by the Court or (3) the correct application of Community law is so clear (*acte clair*) that there is no room for any reasonable doubt, Case 283/81 *CILFIT* v. *Ministry of Health* [1982] E.C.R. 3415.

[99] Case 126/80 *Salonia* v. *Poidomani and Giglio* [1981] E.C.R. 1563.

instance to delay judgment.[1] There is therefore nothing automatic in the procedure of the preliminary ruling: it lies entirely within the discretionary powers of the national judge and neither the Court,[2] national law[3] nor a Community rule[4] can deprive him of this right.

It should be noted also that the "summary and urgent character of a procedure in the national court does not prevent the Court from regarding itself as validly seized" to give a preliminary ruling.[5] However, a national court or tribunal is not required to refer to the Court, even when no judicial remedy is available against the decision, when the question is raised in interlocutory proceedings for an interim order, provided that each of the parties is entitled to institute proceedings or to require proceedings to be instituted on the substance of the case and that during such proceedings the question provisionally decided in the summary proceedings may be re-examined and may be the subject of a reference to the Court of Justice.[6]

It is clear from the abundance of requests for preliminary rulings that here lies an essential function, not only in regard to the development of Community law, but also as an instrument at the disposal of natural or legal persons confronted with Community measures whose legality they cannot directly challenge in the Court. Indeed when an act is declared by the Court to be invalid in the course of a proceeding for a preliminary ruling, the act becomes inapplicable.

(5) *Compensation for damage caused by institutions*

In case of non-contractual liability, the Community, in accordance with the general principles common to the laws of the

---

[1] See opinion of the Advocate-General in the Case 6/64 *Costa* v. *ENEL* [1964] E.C.R. 585 at 607 where mention is made of a "preliminary inquiry of legality" concerning the relevance of the question to the solution of the dispute.

[2] Case 5/77 *Tedeschi* v. *Denkavit* [1977] E.C.R. 1555 at 1574(17).

[3] Case 166/73 *Rheinmühlen* v. *EVST* [1974] E.C.R. 33 at 38(4).

[4] Case 127/73 *BRT* v. *Sabam* [1974] E.C.R. 51 at 63(23).

[5] Case 107/76 *Hoffman-La Roche* v. *Centrafarm* [1977] E.C.R. 957 at 973.

[6] *Ibid.* 974. In a decision in summary proceeding, the President of the Arrondissementsrechtbank of Utrecht gave an interim order which was subject to the proviso that the plaintiff initiate proceedings in the same court within a period of six weeks so as to request that Court to make a preliminary ruling which indeed was done: Case 36/74 *Walrave* v. *Union Cycliste Internationale* [1974] E.C.R. 1405.

Member States, shall make good any damage caused by its institutions or by its servants in the performance of their duties.[7]

In one of its first judgments concerning a claim for redress, the Court held that an administrative measure which has not been annulled cannot in itself constitute a wrongful act on the part of the administration, inflicting damage upon those whom it affects.[8] In more recent judgments, however, the Court has reversed its position, indicating that actions for annulment and claims for damages were different proceedings and that the Treaty in providing for an appeal for damages introduced an autonomous form of action, with a particular purpose to fulfil within the system of actions, and subject to conditions on its use dictated by its specific nature. Indeed it differs from an application for annulment in that its end is not the abolition of a particular measure, but compensation for damage caused by an institution in the performance of its duties.[9]

However, the Court maintained that non-contractual liability of the Community pre-supposes at the very least the unlawful nature of the act besides actual damage and a causal relationship between act and damage.[10] On the other hand, the unlawful nature does not in itself make the Community responsible for compensation in case of damage.[11] Where legislative action involving measures of economic policy is concerned, the Community does not incur non-contractual liability unless a sufficiently flagrant violation of a superior rule of law for the protection of the damaged party has occurred.[12]

The damage for which compensation is sought must of course be certain and have been assessed or be assessable; the Court has, however, accepted the admissibility of an action in which the Court is asked to declare the Community liable for imminent damage foreseeable with sufficient certainty even if the damage cannot yet be precisely assessed.[13]

---

[7] EEC, Arts. 178 and 215.

[8] Case 25/62 *Plaumann* v. *Commission* [1963] E.C.R. 95 at 108. See also joined Cases 35/62 and 16/63 *Leroy* v. *High Authority* [1963] E.C.R. 197 at 207 and Case 93/63 *Minot* v. *Commission* [1964] E.C.R. 489 at 511.

[9] Case 5/71 *Zuckerfabrik Schöppenstedt* v. *Council* [1971] E.C.R. 975 at 983(3).

[10] Case 51/81 *De Franceschi* v. *Council and Commission* [1982] E.C.R. 117 at 134(9).

[11] Joined Cases 83 and 94/76, 4, 15 and 40/77 *HNL* v. *Council and Commission* [1978] E.C.R. 1209 at 1224 (4).

[12] See joined Cases 197, etc./80 *Ludwigshafener Walzmühle* v. *Council and Commission* [1981] E.C.R. 3211.

[13] See Case 256/81 *Pauls Agriculture* v. *Council and Commission* [1983] E.C.R. 1707.

The Court has stated that it has no jurisdiction in cases in which the application for compensation is in fact directed against measures adopted by the national authorities for the purpose of applying provisions of Community law; but when the damage caused by the national implementing measures finds its origin in the underlying Community rule the latter can incur the liability of the Community.[14]

Actions for compensation are subject to a five-year period of limitation.[15]

When the Court allocates compensation for damages caused by a Community act, the latter becomes virtually inapplicable, in the same way as an act declared invalid in a proceeding for a preliminary ruling. The action for compensation for damage, therefore, constitutes another instrument put at the disposal of natural and legal persons confronted with Community measures whose legality they cannot directly challenge in the Court.

(6) *Other cases within the Court's jurisdiction*

The objection of illegality[16] gives, according to the Court of Justice,[17] "expression to a general principle conferring upon any party to proceedings the right to challenge, for the purpose of obtaining the annulment of a decision of direct and individual concern to that party, the validity of previous acts of the institutions which form the legal basis of the decision which is being attacked, if that party was not entitled under Article 173 of the Treaty to bring a direct action challenging those acts by which it was thus affected without having been in a position to ask that they be declared void." Although the Treaty refers explicitly to "a regulation," the Court refers to "acts" in general.[18] For the Court it is clear from the wording and the general scheme of Article 184 that, although this is not specified, a declaration of inapplicability is only contemplated in proceedings brought before the Court

---

[14] Case 126/76 *Dietz* v. *Commission* [1977] E.C.R. 2431. See Case 101/78 *Granaria* v. *Hoofdproduktschap voor Akkerbouwprodukten* [1979] E.C.R. 623 at 640(3).

[15] Protocol on the Statute of the Court, Art. 43. See Joined Cases 256, etc./80 and 5/81 *Birra Wührer* v. *Council and Commission* [1982] E.C.R. 85.

[16] EEC, Art. 184; ECSC, Art. 36; see Case 258/80 *Rumi* v. *Commission* [1982] E.C.R. 487.

[17] Case 15/57 *Compagnie des Hauts Fourneaux de Chasse* v. *High Authority* [1957 and 1958] E.C.R. 211 and Case 9/56 *Meroni* v. *High Authority* [1957 and 1958] E.C.R. 133.

[18] Case 92/78 *Simmenthal* v. *Commission* [1979] E.C.R. 777 at 800(39).

itself under some other provisions of the Treaty and that the plea may be used only against a regulation which is the basis of the act in dispute. In other words the objection of illegality does not constitute an independent action and may only be sought incidentally.[19]

Disputes between the Community and its servants[20] come under the exclusive jurisdiction of the Court; with some rare exceptions[21] actions brought by Community servants present little interest for Community law as such. Many hundreds of actions have been brought under Article 179 thereby clogging the Court's register. On several occasions it was proposed to create a special tribunal for those disputes giving the Court more time to develop Community law. In such disputes the four institutions including the Court itself appear as defendants; although it is not an institution, the same applies to the Social and Economic Committee[22] and to the Court of Auditors.[23]

Reference must also be made to the possibility provided for in the Treaty of *attributing jurisdiction* to the Court in contracts concluded by or on behalf of the Community whether those contracts are governed by public or private law.[24] An explicit attribution of jurisdiction to the Court is necessary, the more so since the Treaty provides that disputes to which the Community is a party shall not on that ground be excluded from the jurisdiction of the courts or tribunals of the Member States.[25]

In this context the attributions of jurisdiction in the Protocol on the interpretation by the Court of Justice of the Convention on

---

[19] See joined Cases 275/80 and 24/81 *Krupp* v. *Commission* [1981] E.C.R. 2489. A typical case would be when an undertaking fined by the Commission for violation of a regulation which the undertaking considers illegal appeals to the Court for annulment of the decision imposing the fine, alleging that the regulation itself is inapplicable on the basis of one of the four grounds specified in Article 173. This objection of illegality therefore constitutes another way for natural or legal persons to challenge a measure whose illegality they cannot directly ask the Court to review.

[20] EEC, Art. 179 and Staff Regulations, Art. 91, Suppl. to O.J. 1973, c.12.

[21] See, *e.g.* Cases 7/56, 3–7/57 *Algera* v. *Common Assembly* [1957 and 1958] E.C.R. 39 at 55 and Case 6/60 *Humblet* v. *Belgium* [1960] E.C.R. 559, which in fact concerned a dispute between a servant and a Member State.

[22] Art. 1(2) of the Staff Regulations (O.J. 1968/30) assimilates the Committee to the institutions. See, *e.g.* Case 277/82 *Papageorgopoulos* v. *Economic and Social Committee*, [1983] E.C.R. 2897.

[23] See, *e.g.* Cases 257/83 (O.J. 1983, C.339/3) and 40/83 (O.J. 1984, C.80/5).

[24] EEC, Art. 181.

[25] EEC, Art. 183.

Jurisdiction and the enforcement of judgments in civil and commercial matters[26] concluded between the Member States[27] should also be mentioned.

The Court in cases before it may also prescribe the necessary *interim measures* including suspension of application of the contested act and suspension of the enforcement measures.[28] With regard to suspension of application of measures it must be noted that actions brought before the Court do not have suspensory effect.[29] An application to suspend the operation of any measure adopted by an institution shall be admissible only if the applicant is challenging that measure in proceedings before the Court.[30]

It is of great interest to note that the Court can prescribe interim measures applicable to a Member State.[31] There is no limit as to the kind of interim measures the Court may prescribe; besides the suspension of the application of a measure, the Court has ordered parties to start negotiations to agree upon an alternative solution,[32] authorised another to adopt temporary measures with the consent of the Commission,[33] and suspended the application of a measure on condition that a party continues to provide security.[34]

(7) Judicial remedies: a summary

As was pointed out, the Member States, the Council and the Commission have, subject to time-limits, unlimited access to the Court of Justice; the access is rather limited for natural and legal persons, although they have several actions at their disposal.

[26] See the Protocol of June 3, 1971, Art. 3 (O.J. 1975, L.204/28), (as amended by the Convention of Association of October 9, 1978), to the "Judgments" or "Brussels" Convention of September 27, 1968 (O.J. 1978, L.304/77). See, *e.g.* joined Cases 9 and 10/77 *Bavaria Fluggesellschaft and Germanair* v. *Eurocontrol* [1977] E.C.R. 1517.

[27] This Protocol does not constitute a special agreement to submit disputes between Member States to the Court of Justice in the sense of EEC, Art. 182; indeed the Convention does not concern a "subject matter of the Treaty."

[28] EEC, Arts. 185, 186 and 192; Chap. I of Title III of the Rules of Procedure of the Court of Justice (Rules) (O.J. 1974, L.350/1 and O.J. 1975, L.102/24) refers to "suspension of operation or enforcement and other interim measures."

[29] EEC, Art. 185.

[30] Rules, Art. 83(1).

[31] See, *e.g.* Cases 31/77 R and 53/77 R *Commission* v. *U.K.* [1977] E.C.R. 921 at 925.

[32] Case 61/77 R *Commission* v. *Ireland* [1977] E.C.R. 937 at 943(34).

[33] Case 61/77 R *Commission* v. *Ireland* [1977] E.C.R. 1411 at 1415.

[34] Cases 113/77 R and 113/77 R *Int NTN TOYO* v. *Council* [1977] E.C.R. 1721 at 1726.

To summarise, proceedings in the Court of Justice can be initiated by:

–a Member State,	against another Member State for failure to fulfil an obligation;
	against the Council and/or the Commission for annulment, failure to act or give compensation,
	against Parliament for annulment (ECSC);
–the Council,	against the Commission for annulment or failure to act;
–the Commission,	against a Member State for failure to fulfil an obligation;
	against the Council for annulment or failure to act;
–the Assembly,	against the Council for failure to act;
	against the Commission for failure to act;
–a person,	against the Council for annulment, failure to act or give compensation,
	against the Commission for annulment, failure to act or give compensation,

furthermore a person may:

(i) ask a national court to request a preliminary ruling,
(ii) in a case before the Court of Justice, plead inapplicability of underlying regulation

–servants,	against the Council, the Commission, the Assembly, the Court of Justice, the Social and Economic Committee and the Court of Auditors.

3. The procedure

The rules concerning the procedure before the Court of Justice are laid down in a Protocol on the Statute of the Court of Justice of the European Communities annexed to the EEC Treaty and in the Rules of Procedure which the Court adopts after having received the unanimous approval of the Council.[35] These rules contain, apart from those "contemplated" by the Statute, any other

---

[35] EEC, Art. 188.

provisions necessary for applying and, when necessary, for supplementing it.[36]

The procedure before the Court, for which no fees are charged, consists of two parts: written and oral; as for the language of the proceedings, it must be one of the official languages of the Community and is determined by the applicant.[37]

(1) *The written procedure*[38]

This procedure starts with the submission to the Court of a written application addressed to the Registrar. The Statute and the Rules contain various requirements as to form, content and accompanying documents of the application.[39] The Member States and the institutions are represented by an agent appointed for each case; other parties must be represented by a lawyer entitled to practice before a court of a Member State.[40] It is important to note that the application must state the grounds on which it is based, since parties may not in the course of proceedings raise fresh issues, unless these are based on matters of law or of fact which come to light in the course of the written procedure.[41] The time-limit within which the application must be filed is also essential: appeals for annulment must be instituted within two months of the publication of the measure or of its notification to the plaintiff.[42] This time-limit was slightly extended by the Rules of Procedure for all parties living outside Luxembourg.[43]

---

[36] Protocol on the Statute of the Court of Justice attached to the EEC Treaty (Statute), Art. 44. The Court and the Council have given this provision a very extensive interpretation since the last revision (O.J. 1979, L.238/1) allows the Court to let the Chambers adjudicate any cases brought before the Court, although EEC, Art. 165(2), limits the jurisdiction of the Chambers to "particular categories of cases."

[37] Rules, Art. 29(2). At present there are seven official languages: Danish, German, English, French, Greek, Italian and Dutch.

[38] See Statute, Arts. 18 *et seq.* and Rules Title II, Chap. I.

[39] See Statute, Art. 19 and Rules, Arts. 38 *et seq.*

[40] Statute, Art. 17. The application must also state an address for service at the place where the Court has its seat. It shall also give the name of a person who is authorised and has expressed willingness to accept service; Rules, Art. 38(2).

[41] Rules, Art. 42(2). See Case 231/78 *Commission* v. *United Kingdom* [1979] E.C.R. 1447.

[42] EEC, Art. 173(3).

[43] O.J. 1974, L.350/1.

The application is notified by the Court's registrar to the defendant who then has one month to file a *defence*.[44] Plaintiff's *application* and the defendant's *defence* may be supplemented by a *reply* from the applicant and by a *rejoinder* from the defendant. The time-limit within which these pleadings have to be lodged are fixed by the President of the Court. Before formally closing the written part of the procedure, the Court, at the suggestion of the Judge-Rapporteur[45] or the Advocate-General, may decide to prescribe measures of inquiry[46] for the case, *i.e.* interrogation of parties, request for information, hearing of witnesses,[47] etc.

In the case of a preliminary ruling, the parties, the Member States, the Commission and, where appropriate, the Council, shall be entitled to submit statements of case or written observations to the Court.[48] Finally, it should be noted that the Member States and the institutions may always intervene in cases before the Court; other persons have the same right when they establish an interest in the result of a case.[49]

(2) *The oral procedure*

The oral procedure[50] consists of the reading of the report presented by the Judge-Rapporteur, the hearing by the Court of agents, legal advisers or council and of the opinion of the Advocate-General, as well as the hearing, if any, of witnesses and experts. The opinion of the Advocate-General is usually read during a separate Court session which indicates the end of the oral part of the procedure.[51] The judgment[52] is in turn read in open court at a later date.

---

[44] Rules, Art. 40(1).

[45] See Rules, Art. 9(2).

[46] For details see Rules, Arts. 45–54.

[47] The rules contain several provisions concerning witnesses: the Court may impose penalties in case of default (Statute, Art. 24), the Court may have a witness heard by the judicial authorities of the place of his permanent residence (Statute, Art. 26), Member States must treat any violation of an oath by a witness in the same manner as if the offence had been committed before one of its' courts with jurisdiction in civil procedure and prosecute the offender before its competent court at the instance of the Court of Justice (Statute, Art. 27).

[48] Statute, Art. 20.

[49] *Ibid*. Art. 37.

[50] See Statute, Art. 18(4) and Rules, Arts. 55–62.

[51] Rules, Art. 59.

[52] For the prescribed contents of the judgment see Rules, Art. 63; *e.g.* the judgment always contains a decision regarding the costs which are normally paid by the losing party; see Rules, Arts. 69 *et seq.*

(3) Special form of procedure

The Statute and the Rules contain provisions for various special forms of procedure[53] such as *summary procedure* (by which the President of the Court may suspend execution[54] or prescribe interim measures or suspend enforcement), intervention, judgment by default, third party proceedings, interpretation and revision.

Further Reading

IV. *The Court of Justice*

John Usher, "Exercise by the Court of Justice of its jurisdiction to annul competition decisions" (1980) 5 E.L.Rev. 287.

Ami Barav, "Preliminary censorship? The judgment of the European Court in *Foglia* v. *Novello*" (1980) 5 E.L.Rev. 443.

Christopher Harding, "The private interest in challenging community action" (1980) 5 E.L.Rev. 354.

Hjalte Rasmussen, "Why is Article 173 interpreted against private plaintiffs?" (1980) 5 E.L.Rev. 112.

James Flynn, "*Force majeure* pleas in proceedings before the European Court" (1981) 6 E.L.Rev. 102.

Christine Gray, "Advisory opinions and the European Court of Justice" (1983) 8 E.L.Rev. 24.

Anthony M. Arnull, "Article 177 and the retreat from Van Duyn" (1983) 8 E.L.Rev. 365.

David O'Keefe, "Appeals against an Order to Refer under Article 177 of the EEC" (1984) 9 E.L.Rev. 87.

Ulrich Everling, "The Member States of the European Community before their Court of Justice" (1984) 9 E.L.Rev. 215.

Hjalte Rasmussen, "The European Court's *acte clair* strategy in C.I.L.F.I.T." (1984) 9 E.L.Rev. 242.

---

[53] See Statute, Arts. 36 *et seq.* and Rules, Arts. 83 *et seq.*
[54] See, *e.g.* below, p. 183.

V. *Other Bodies of the European Communities*

1. The Court of Auditors

The Court of Auditors was set up by the Treaty amending certain financial provisions of the European Treaties and of the Merger Treaty.[55] Generally speaking, the provisions concerning the members of the Court of Auditors are similar to those concerning the Judges of the Court of Justice.[56] The ten members, however, are appointed by the Council after consulting Parliament.

The Court of Auditors examines the accounts of all revenue and expenditure of the Community and of any body created by the Community,[57] not only to determine whether all revenue has been received and expenditure incurred in a lawful manner, but also whether the financial management has been sound. Since a vast proportion of the Community revenue is collected and made available by the Member States, on-the-spot checks by the Court of Auditors are provided, not only in the institutions of the Community, but also in the Member States.

The Court of Auditors draws up an annual report which is forwarded to all the institutions of the Community and published in the *Official Journal* together with the replies of the institutions to the observations of the Court of Auditors.[58]

The Court of Auditors may also submit observations on specific questions on its own initiative and deliver opinions at the request of one of the institutions.[59]

---

[55] Art. 15 modifying EEC, Art. 206.
The Treaty was signed at Brussels on July 22, 1975, but only entered into force on June 1, 1977 (O.J. 1977, L.359/20).
[56] See EEC, Art. 206(2)–(10).
[57] EEC, Art. 206a(1); *e.g.* the European Centre for the Development of Vocational Training (O.J. 1975, L.39/1) and the European Foundation for the improvement of living and working conditions (O.J. 1975, L. 139/1). An Annex to the Treaty provides that the Court of Auditors also has jurisdiction to audit the European Development Fund. It does not audit the European Investment Bank.
[58] See, *e.g.* Report for the year 1983 (O.J. 1984, C.348/1).
[59] See, *e.g.* Opinion concerning proposed modifications to the Financial Reg. of December 21, 1977 (O.J. 1979, C.225/3) and Special Report (O.J. 1979, C.221/1). See Report submitted at the request of the European Council on the "Conclusions of the European Council" of June 18, 1983 (O.J. 1983, C.287/1) and Special Report on Milk (O.J. 1985, C.91/1).

2. The Economic and Social Committee[60]

The Economic and Social Committee plays a consultative role mainly within the decision-making process of the Community. When consultation is provided for by the Treaty, it must necessarily take place lest decisions can be annulled by the Court for infringement of an essential procedural requirement; the required consultation must also be referred to in the relevant Community act.

The Committee may also be consulted, either by the Council or by the Commission, in all cases in which they consider it appropriate; however, the Heads of State or Government decided at their 1972 Paris Summit meeting to invite "the Community institutions to recognise the right of the Economic and Social Committee in future to advise on its own initiative on all questions affecting the Community."[61]

The Committee is composed of 156 members appointed for four years by the Council in their personal capacity; they may not be bound by mandatory instructions. The members are representatives of the various categories of economic and social activity, in particular producers, farmers, carriers, workers, tradesmen, craftsmen, members of the professions and the general public.[62]

3. The Consultative Committee of the ECSC

The ECSC Treaty provides for the creation of a Consultative Committee[63] attached to the Commission (High Authority) and consisting of between 60 and 84 members made up of an equal number of producers, workers, consumers and dealers. They are appointed for two years in their personal capacity by the Council from lists drawn up by representative organisations also designated by the Council. The functions of the Consultative Committee are comparable in all points to those of the Economic and Social Committee.

---

[60] EEC, Arts. 193–198.
[61] Declaration of the Summit, pt. 15 (Bull. 10–1972, 23).
[62] For further information on the Committee's composition and activities, see its annual report and the accounts published in the Bulletin under "Economic and Social Committee." For the list of present members see O.J. 1982, C.272/1.
[63] ECSC, Arts. 18 and 19. For list of Members see O.J. 1983, C.4/1.

4. The Scientific and Technical Committee of Euratom

This Committee, set up by the Euratom Treaty, is attached to the Commission[64]; it consists of 28 members appointed for five years by the Council after consultation of the Commission. The Committee has a consultative status.

5. The European Investment Bank[65] (EIB)

The Treaty provides for the establishment of a European Investment Bank to facilitate the economic expansion of the Community by opening fresh resources.[66]

The Bank is directed and managed by a Board of Governors, a Board of Directors and a Management Committee.

The *Board of Governors* consists of the ministers of finance of the Member States; it lays down general directives for the credit policy of the Bank; it also decides on possible increases in the subscribed capital, on grants of special interest-bearing loans to the Bank to finance specific projects by Member States and on the granting of loans for investment projects to be carried out entirely or partially outside the European territory of Member States.

The *Board of Directors* consists of 19 directors and 11 alternates nominated by each Member State and the Commission and appointed by the Board of Governors for five years.

The *Management Committee* consists of a president and five vice-presidents appointed by the Board of Governors on a proposal from the Board of Directors.

The EIB has legal personality and its Members are the Member States.[67] Its statute is laid down in a Protocol annexed to the EEC Treaty. The EIB operates on a non-profit making basis; it grants loans and gives guarantees to facilitate the financing of all sectors of the economy. Decisions regarding these loans are taken by the Board of Directors on proposals from the Management Committee. However, before deciding on the financing of a project, the Bank must secure the opinion of the interested Member State and the Commission; when the Commission delivers an

---

[64] Euratom, Art. 134.
[65] EEC. Arts. 129–130 and Protocol on the Statute of the European Investment Bank annexed to the EEC Treaty.
[66] EEC, Art. 3(*j*).
[67] EEC, Art. 129.

unfavourable opinion, the Board of Directors may not grant the loan (or guarantee) unless its decision is unanimous (the director nominated by the Commission abstaining).

The Bank was mainly intended to provide financial resources for the economic development of Southern Italy, the Mezzogiorno. This is still the case, but other regions have been added, first by the enlargements of the Community in 1973 and 1981 and secondly by the economic crisis of the 1970's. More than two thirds of the Bank's loans go to the development regions of the Community.[68]

Besides the loans to finance projects in less developed regions of the Community the Bank provides loans from its own resources for: large industrial projects, or projects of common interest to several Member States when those projects cannot be entirely financed by the means available in the individual Member States. The same kind of projects can also be financed from resources provided by the new borrowing and loan facilities of the Community[69] which are administered by the Bank.

The Bank also provides loans for projects situated outside the territory of Member States either from its own resources[70] or under mandate, for the account and at the risk of individual Member States, the EEC or Euratom; they consist in financial aid provided for under various agreements, financial protocols and decisions concerning Turkey, the African, Carribean and Pacific States, the Overseas Countries and Territories (French), Portugal, Yugoslavia, Lebanon, Spain, Maghreb and Machreck and till 1981 Greece.[71] The Bank also finances operations on special conditions and risks capital operations from the resources of Member States directly (Turkey) or through the intermediary of the European Development Fund.

By the decision of the Board of Governors, the subscribed capital of the Bank was increased to 14.4 billion ECU in 1982. The

---

[68] EEC, Art. 130 provides that the Bank shall grant loans and give guarantees which facilitate the financing of "projects for less developed regions." In 1984 this represented 62 per cent. of the total finances for the Member States: the Mezzogiorno alone attracted 1,557.7 MECU, EIB Annual Report 1984.

[69] This new instrument was set up in October 1978. Dec. 78/870 (O.J. 1978, L.298/9; see also Bull. 10–1978, 21) and is commonly known as NIC.

[70] Between 1958 and 1983, the Bank loaned outside the Community 25,659 MECU from its own resources.

[71] In loans granted in those regions amounted to 1,278.0 MECU from the Bank's own resources.

four larger Member States subscribe about 3.150 each, Belgium and The Netherlands a little more than 829.5 million, Denmark 420.0, Greece 225.0, Ireland 105.0 and Luxembourg 21.0.

Through its sound financial operations both inside and outside the Community the EIB has acquired a world-wide reputation as one of the major financial institutions for economic development.

VI. *Financing Community Activities*

1. Financial contributions of the Member States and the Community's own resources

The Community's own resources were introduced by Council Decision of April 21, 1970[72] while at the same time the Treaty of April 22, 1970 amended certain budgetary provisions of the ECSC, EEC and Euratom treaties and of the Merger Treaty to confer, as a necessary complement to the transfer of resources to the Communities, certain budgetary powers upon the European Parliament.[73]

On July 22, 1975 the budgetary provisions were again amended and complemented by the Treaty amending certain Financial Provisions of the Treaties establishing the Communities and of the Merger Treaty.[74]

(1) *The Decision of April 21, 1970*

The main features of this decision on the Replacement of Financial Contributions from Member States by the Community's own Resources can be summarised as follows:

(a) Although the Treaty only refers to revenue accruing from the Common Customs Tariff, the Decision provides that both the agricultural levies[75] and the Common Customs Tariff duties[76] constitute own resources to be entered in the budget of the Communities.

---

[72] J.O. 1970, L.94/19; O.J. 1970 (I), 224. This decision (70/243) became effective on January 1, 1971 after having been ratified by the six national Parliaments.

[73] The new budgetary powers of the European Parliament are analysed, above. Participation in budgetary procedure. This treaty became effective on January 1, 1971.

[74] O.J. 1977, L.359/1. See below compulsory and non-compulsory expenditure.

[75] Dec. 70/243, Art. 2(*a*).

[76] *Ibid.* Art. 2(*b*).

(b) The decision provides for a system which made it possible to achieve the transfer of revenue from customs duties progressively over a period of four years. From January 1, 1971 onwards, the total budget of the Community was financed, irrespective of other revenue,[77] from the Community's own resources.

(c) Since revenue accruing from the levies and duties is not sufficient to ensure that the budget of the Communities is in balance, additional tax revenue was allocated to the Communities, *i.e.* that accruing from the application of a rate not exceeding 1.4 per cent. of the basis used for assessing the value added tax, determined in a uniform manner for the Member States.[78]

As from 1980, the Community's expenditures are entirely financed by the revenue accruing from agricultural levies, customs duties and a percentage of the VAT collected by the Member States.

In connection with the decision of April 21, 1970, three resolutions recorded in the minutes of the Council meeting should be mentioned. First, the Council undertakes to make no amendments to the estimate of Parliament's expenditure, as long as there is no conflict with any Community rules. Parliament thus gained sole responsibility for its own budget. The second provides for collaboration through a *conciliation procedure*[79] between the Council and the Parliament with the active assistance of the Commission when Community acts of general application are concerned and which have appreciable financial implications. The third resolution concerns co-operation between the Council and the European Parliament in matters of budgetary procedure, the *budgetary conciliation procedure* which unfortunately has had little effect. In 1982 a new effort was made to improve relations in budgetary matters with a Joint Declaration signed by the Presidents of Parliament, the

---

[77] Other revenues are, *e.g.* the fines imposed on undertakings for violation of Community rules and the income-tax levied on the salaries of officials.

[78] Dir. 77/388 (O.J. 1977, L.145/1). See Regs. 2891/71 and 2892/77 implementing Dec. 70/243 of April 21, 1970 (O.J. 1977, L.336/1 and 8). The decision to increase the transfer of VAT from 1 to 1.4 from January 1, 1986 and to 1.6 on January 1, 1988 was taken by the European Council at Fontainebleau in June 1984. See Bull. 6–1984, 11.

[79] O.J. 1975, C.89/1.

Council and the Commission with a view to ensuring a more effective development of the budgetary procedure.[80]

(2) *Community's own Resources Collected in the United Kingdom*

The agricultural levies, customs duties and VAT revenue which constitute the Community's own resources are collected by the Member States and transferred to the Community. The latter refunds to each government 10 per cent. of the amount paid in order to cover expenses incurred in collection.[81]

The United Kingdom's share of customs duties and agricultural levies was, at the end of 1979, particularly high, due, *inter alia*, to the fact that a large share of the United Kingdom imports still come from non-member countries. As the United Kingdom's trade, as a consequence of its membership of the Community, shifts increasingly from third countries to other Member States, the United Kingdom's share of duties and levies transferred to the Community should decrease slightly. It should be remembered, however, that the introduction of the system of own resources implies that the transfer of revenues accruing from levies and duties cannot be considered as national financial contributions.[82] The claim for "broad balance" between these transfers and the Community expenditures in a given country is, therefore, legally, unfounded.[83] This does not mean, however, that a better balance within the Community budget should not exist, *i.e.* that at present the expenditure under the Common Agricultural Policy—from which the United Kingdom is only a minor beneficiary—is much too high and should be proportionally reduced in favour of structural policies and their instruments, such as the Social and Regional Funds.

In pursuance of the Act of Accession[84] the Community's own resources and, where appropriate, the financial contributions

---

[80] O.J. 1982, C.194. See also O.J. 1982 C.238/64 and Bull. 6–1982, 7.

[81] Dec. 70/243, Art. 3(1).

[82] It should be noted for instance that often duties and levies are collected by the authorities of the country where the products first enter the Community although the recipient of those products, *i.e.* those who bear the costs of these duties and levies, are situated in other Member States; since the duties and levies are the same in all the Member States the point of entry for a given product is determined solely on the basis of transport considerations.

[83] See Commission's answer to Parliamentary questions 1020/77, 604/78 and 607/78, O.J. 1979, C.28/1–3 and question 50/79, O.J. 1979, C.164/9–11.

[84] Act of Accession, Arts. 127–132. For Greece, see Act of Accession of May 28, 1979, Arts. 124–127 (O.J. 1979, L.291).

referred to in the Decision of April 21, 1970, were due in full by the new Member States from January 1, 1978, subject, however, to certain conditions[85] the consequences of which are that the United Kingdom, for instance, contributed in full from January 1, 1980, onwards. For Greece the date is January 1, 1986.

In 1976, a "budget correcting mechanism" was introduced to enable payments to be made to Member States which, due to special economic conditions, are considered to bear a disproportionate burden in financing the budget.[86]

At the Council meeting of May 29 and 30, 1980, agreement was reached on the United Kingdom's contribution to the budget: the financial correcting mechanism was modified to allow a reduction in the United Kingdom's net contribution to the budget and supplementary Community expenditures were provided for to help reduce certain regional disparities in the United Kingdom.[87] This involved a reduction of the United Kingdom's net transfers by about two-thirds. Such transitional measures were applied in 1981, 1982 and 1983 pending agreement on a multiannual plan. In 1984 the United Kingdom will receive a lump-sum of one billion ECU and in the following years 66 per cent. of the differences between the United Kingdom VAT transfers and its receipts from the Community will be compensated.[88]

2. The Community budget, revenue and expenditure

All items of revenue and expenditure of the three Communities must be included in estimates to be drawn up for each financial year and be shown in the budget.[89] The revenue and expenditure shown in the budget must balance.[90] The financial year runs from

---

[85] *Ibid.* Art. 131.

[86] Reg. 1172/76, O.J. 1976, L.131/7. This was one of the results of what is sometimes referred to as the "British renegotiation"; see Bull. 3–1975, 6, on the decision of the European Council at Dublin (March 10 to 11, 1975).

[87] Fourteenth General Report (1980), 59; Bull. 5–1980, 7 and Council Reg. 2744/80 (O.J. 1980, L.284/4). The supplementary measures for 1980 amounted to 1,437.584 million ECU, for 1981 and 1982 they amounted to 1,804.212 and 887.561 million ECU respectively.

[88] Bull. 6–1984, 7–8.

[89] One important item not covered by the Community budget is the European Development Fund (the resources destined to finance aid to developing countries); the activities of the European Investment Bank do not appear on the budget either.

[90] EEC, Art. 199 and Art. 20 of the Merger Treaty.

January 1 to December 31.[91] The structure of the general budget and the form in which it is to be presented are determined by Financial Regulations.[92] The budget consists of separate sections dealing with the revenue and expenditure of each institution. The section dealing with the Commission provides for expenditure in the following fields: agriculture, regional, social, research-energy-industry-transport, refunds and reserves and development co-operation besides administrative expenditures. The total appropriations for commitments in the 1984 budget stood at over 27.3 billion ECU.

(1) *Commitment and Payment Appropriations*

The Community budget contains "non differentiated" and "differentiated" appropriations. Under the former, commitments can be made during the financial year and the corresponding payments can be made practically at the same time, *i.e.* during that financial year and the next. The differentiated appropriations consist of both commitments, *i.e.* the maximum which may be committed during the financial year, and payments which correspond to those commitments and may be disbursed during the same financial year or any time thereafter. The system of commitment and payment appropriations is particularly suited for medium and long term operations such as research projects and infrastructure investments. The total amount for the Community's financial participation in such a project can be committed at the start of the project but the payments only have to be made as the work progresses over the years.[93]

(2) *Compulsory and non-compulsory expenditure*

The Treaty of July 22, 1975, amending certain financial provisions of the existing Treaties introduced the concept of "expenditure necessarily resulting from this Treaty or from acts adopted in accordance therewith,"[94] otherwise referred to as "compulsory"

---

[91] EEC, Art. 203(1).

[92] See O.J. 1977, L.356/1, Arts. 15 and 16; for the latest amendment see O.J. 1979, L.160/1.

[93] The commitment and payment appropriations are used mainly for Euratom research and investment appropriations and for the Regional Fund expenditures.

[94] EEC, Art. 203(4).

expenditures. A budgetary item is considered compulsory when the principle and the amount of the expenditure (either a figure or a precise mechanism for arriving at it) are statutorily prescribed in the Treaties, secondary legislation, international conventions or private contracts.[95] A typical example of compulsory expenditure is that of the agricultural fund. Non compulsory expenditures are practically speaking all the others: regional, social, research and staff appropriations. In practice, however, expenditures are classified in one or the other category in a rather pragmatic way, by agreement between Parliament and the Council.[96] As was pointed out before,[97] the distinction is important with regard to the budgetary powers of the European Parliament. The increase of non-compulsory expenditures is limited to a maximum annual rate established by the Commission[98] and the final decision on this category of expenditure belongs to the Parliament.[99]

3. The European Unit of Account (EUA) and the European Currency Unit (ECU)

The establishment of a unit of account is provided for by the Treaty[1] and the Community first used a parity unit of account defined by reference to a given weight of fine gold. On account of the severe disturbances in international monetary relations and the replacement of the systems of fixed parities of the various currencies with regard to the United States dollar by floating exchange rates, the Community decided to introduce the European Unit of Account (EUA) in 1978. The establishment of the European Monetary System in 1979 made it possible to introduce the ECU for the operations of the European Monetary Co-

---

[95] D. Strasser, *The Finances of Europe* (New York 1977), 33. Another definition given by the Council reads: "expenditure in respect of which, by virtue of existing enactments, no budgetary authority, be it the Council or the European Parliament, has the right freely to determine the appropriations." See also the Joint Declaration of Parliament, Council and Commission of June 1982, Bull. 6–1982, 7.

[96] It was agreed for instance that the expenditures for the Regional Fund were to be considereg as "compulsory" in 1975, 1976 and 1977 and as non-compulsory thereafter. For a classification see Joint Declaration of June 30, 1982 (O.J. 1982, C.194/1–3).

[97] See above, p. 22.

[98] EEC, Art. 203(9).

[99] Non-compulsory expenditures amount to roughly 30 per cent. of the budget.

[1] EEC, Art. 207.

operation Fund on March 13, and for the common agricultural policy on April 9, 1979. The ECU is now used in all areas of Community activity without exception.[2] The value of the ECU in the Member State's currencies is determined each day by the Commission on the basis of the official exchange rates notified by the Member State's central banks. The rates are published daily in the *Official Journal*.[3] The Community has thus returned to using a single unit of account after a period of several years during which units of account of very different nature had existed side by side.[4]

---

[2] The old unit of account was until 1979 used in connection with the common agricultural policy.

[3] *Ibid.* 97.

[4] Bull. 3–1979, 132. See also Bull. 9–1979, 102. See Commission report of March 1984 on five years of Monetary cooperation in Europe. Bull. 3–1984, 15.

Chapter 4

COMMUNITY ACTS

The main lines of the decision-making process within the European Community were outlined briefly in respect of the role played by the European Parliament, the Council and the Commission; reference was made also to the various forms which the Community rules can take. As was pointed out, the actual practice does differ from what the Treaty provisions indicate: the tendency is to multiply the forms of the decisions and the bodies issuing them. Besides the "communiqués," "declarations" and "conclusions" of the Summits and the European Council, there are now "programmes," "resolutions," and "declarations." They are issued not only by the Council, but also by the governments of the Member States, the representatives of the Member States in Council and the representatives of the governments. Since, generally speaking they do not create legal rights and obligations, none of the above-mentioned measures constitute acts whose legality the Court can review or for which a Commission proposal is required or the Assembly's opinion requested; nonetheless those measures shape essential Community policies and therefore the future development of the Community itself. It sometimes appears that the more important the decision, the less formal the procedure and the measure.

Nevertheless the binding acts provided for by the Treaty still play an essential role and the conditions laid down for the decision-making process and for the contents of those acts must be seen as so many guarantees for lawfulness and judicial control and protection.

The above-mentioned developments seem to run counter to the Treaty provisions which invest the Council and the Commission with the responsibility to achieve the purposes of the Community and to carry out this task by making regulations, issuing directives, taking decisions, concluding international agreements, making recommendations and delivering opinions, all in accordance with the provisions of the Treaty. Each one of these acts fulfils a specific function in the development of Community law and the Treaty therefore explicitly provides in several cases which kind of act must be adopted. Different procedural rules apply to the various categories and, more important, the extent of legal protection afforded individuals under the treaties varies widely from one category to another.[1]

1. Acts provided in Article 189

A *regulation* has general application, is binding in its entirety and is directly applicable in all Member States. The criterion for the distinction between a regulation and other acts, especially decisions, must be sought in the "general application." Being essentially of a "legislative nature a regulation is applicable not to a limited number of persons, defined or identifiable,[2] but to categories of persons viewed abstractly and in their entirety."[3]

Secondly, a regulation is binding in its entirety; this distinguishes it from a directive which only binds the Member State to which it is addressed to achieve the specified results. The Court has considered that since a regulation is binding in its entirety, it cannot be accepted that a Member State should apply in an incomplete or selective manner provisions of a Community regulation so as "to render abortive certain aspects of Community legislation."[4]

Finally, a regulation is "directly applicable" in all Member States which means that it does not require a national measure to become binding upon the citizens and also that national authorities and national measures cannot prevent its application.[5]

---

[1] It should be noted that it is not the name given to a measure which classifies it in one of the above-mentioned categories, but rather the contents and objective of its provisions; Case 15/70 *Chevalley* v *Commission* [1970] E.C.R. 975 at 980 (10). The Court has also admitted that the same act can contain provisions pertaining to different categories: joined Cases 16 and 17/62 *Producteurs de fruits* v. *Council* [1962] E.C.R. 471 at 479.

[2] See joined Cases 789 and 790/79 *Calpak* v. *Commission* [1980] E.C.R. 1949 at 1961 (9).

[3] Joined Cases 16 and 17/62, above, n.1.

[4] Case 128/78 *Commission* v. *U.K.* [1979] E.C.R. 419 at 428 (9).

[5] See Case 230/78 *Eridania* v. *Ministry of Agriculture* [1979] E.C.R. 2749 at 2772(35). Nevertheless provisions contained in a regulation might need national implementing measures to become applicable, but the regulation itself does not have to be transformed into national law by a national measure.

Direct applicability must not be confused with "direct effect." A Community measure has direct effect when it creates rights for the citizens of the Community which they can invoke in national courts and which the latter must uphold even when they conflict with national measures whether anterior or posterior.

Not all Community provisions have direct effect, but the Court of Justice is of the opinion that a regulation, by reason of its very nature and its function in the system of sources of Community Law, has direct effect, *i.e.* is capable of creating individual rights which national courts must protect.[6]

Directives can be issued by the Council and the Commission and constitute the appropriate measure when existing national legislation must be modified or national provisions must be enacted: the Member States for instance are free to decide whether those provisions will be legislative or administrative in nature.

Although directives are not directly applicable, since they normally require implementing measures, their provisions can nevertheless have direct effect, but in each case it must be ascertained whether by their nature, background and wording the provisions are capable of producing direct effects in the legal relationships between the addressee of the act and third parties.[7]

As for a *decision*, it is binding in its entirety upon those to whom it is addressed. The addressee can be a Member State or a legal or natural person and decisions can be taken by the Council and by the Commission. Decisions are generally of an administrative nature implementing other Community rules, *e.g.* granting of an exception or authorisation or imposition of fines.

There are no requirements as to the form of a decision, so that it can be doubtful whether a given act constitutes a binding

---

[6] It is for the national legal system to determine which court or tribunal has jurisdiction to give this protection and, for this purpose, to decide how the individual position thus protected is to be classified. Case 43/71 *Politi* v. *Italy* [1971] E.C.R. 1039 at 1048 (9). See also Case 93/71 *Leonesio* v. *Italian Ministry of Agriculture and Forestry* [1972] E.C.R. 287 at 295 (22–23).

[7] Case 9/70 *Grad* v. *Finanzamt Traunstein* [1970] E.C.R. 825 at 837 (5). The Court used as an argument the fact that Art. 177 empowers the national courts to refer to the Court of Justice all questions regarding the validity and interpretation of all acts of the institution without distinction, which implies that individuals may invoke such acts before the national courts.
See also Case 51/76 *Nederlandse Ondernemingen* v. *Inspecteur der invoerrechten en*

decision or not. Obviously, the institutions must ensure that a decision is recognisable as a binding act by its very form.[8] Being binding in its entirety a decision can have direct effect.[9]

Finally, the Treaty provides for *recommendations* and *opinions* which have no binding force. Generally speaking, recommendations aim at obtaining a given action or behaviour from the addressee, while the opinions express a point of view, in most cases at the request of a third party. Having no binding effect, the legality of recommendations and opinions cannot be reviewed by the Court, neither submitted for a preliminary ruling concerning their validity or interpretation.

2. Regulations, directives and decisions must be reasoned

Regulations, directives and decisions must state the reasons on which they are based and must refer to the proposals and opinions which were required to be obtained pursuant to the Treaty.[10]

"Reasons" must be understood as referring both to the legal provision which entitles the institution to take the measure and the reasons which motivated the institution to act. The mention of the provision is particularly important since, as was mentioned before, the institutions of the Community can only exercise those powers which are explicitly provided for by Community law.

As for the motives which prompted the institution to act, they must be mentioned in order to make it possible for the interested parties and for the Court to reconstruct the essential elements of the institution's reasoning,[11] thereby permitting the parties to defend their rights, the Court to exercise its control, and the Member States, and in the same way all interested citizens, to know the conditions under which the institution has applied the Treaty.[12]

To attain these objectives it is sufficient for the act to set out, in a concise but clear and relevant manner, the principal issues of law and fact upon which it is based and which are necessary in order

---

accijnzen [1977] E.C.R. 113 at 127 (23). This last decision is referred to in many subsequent judgments.

[8] Case 28/63 *Hoogovens* v. *High Authority* [1963] E.C.R. 231 at 235.

[9] Case 9/70 *Grad* v. *Finanzamt Traunstein* [1970] E.C.R. 825 at 837 (5).

[10] EEC, Art. 190.

[11] Case 14/61 *Hoogovens* v. *High Authority* [1962] E.C.R. 253 at 275.

[12] Case 24/62 *Germany* v. *Commission* [1963] E.C.R. 63 at 69.

that the reasoning which has led the institution to its decision may be understood.[13] The extent of this requirement depends on the nature of the measure in question. The condition can also be considered as fulfilled when reference[14] is made to the reasons developed in an earlier act.[15]

If an act is not sufficiently "reasoned," this constitutes a ground for annulment: infringement of an essential procedural requirement which can be invoked in an action or review of the legality of the act concerned by the Court of Justice. The Court can and must of its own motion take exception to any deficiencies in the reasons which would make such review more difficult.[16]

As for the reference to the required proposals and opinions, a simple mention is considered sufficient; the institutions are not required to indicate whether or not the opinion was favourable[17] still less to refute dissenting opinions expressed by the consultative bodies.[18]

3. Publication and entry into force[19]

Since regulations are of a legislative nature and therefore concern an unidentifiable group to whom they apply, they must be published in the *Official Journal* which is published in the seven official languages[20] of the Community. They enter into force on the day specified in the act or, in the absence thereof, on the twentieth day following their publication.[21]

---

[13] *Ibid.* See also joined Cases 36, 37, 38 and 40/59 *Geitling* v. *High Authority* [1960] E.C.R. 423 at 439.

[14] Case 75/77 *Mollet* v. *Commission* [1978] E.C.R. 897 at 906 (12).

[15] Case 1/69 *Italy* v. *Commission* [1969] E.C.R. 277 at 285 (9). See, however, Case 73/74 *Papiers peints* v. *Commission* [1975] E.C.R. 1491 at 1514 (31).

[16] EEC, Art. 173, Case 18/57 *Nold* v. *High Authority* [1959] E.C.R. 41 at 52 and Case 158/80, *Rewe* v. *Hauptzollamt Kiel* [1981] E.C.R. 1805 at 1834 (27) where Reg. 3023/77 was declared void for not containing a statement of the reasons on which it is based.

[17] This, however, is no secret since both the Commission's proposals and the Parliament's opinions are published in the *Official Journal*.

[18] Case 4/54 *I.S.A.* v. *High Authority* [1954 to 1956] E.C.R. 91 at 100 (6).

[19] EEC, Art. 191.

[20] The official languages of the institutions of the Community are Danish, German, English, French, Greek, Italian and Dutch.

[21] A typical example is Reg. 17 giving effect to the principles of competition: the regulation was adopted by the Council on February 6, 1962, published in the *Official Journal* on February 21, 1962 and, since it did not mention the date of entry into force, it became effective on March 13, 1962. See also Case 98/78 *Racke* v. *Hauptzollamt Mainz* [1979] E.C.R. 69 at 84 (15) and Case 99/78 *Decker* v. *Hauptzollamt Landau* [1979] E.C.R. 101 at 109 (3).

Directives and decisions on the other hand concern only a limited number of persons—Member States or natural or legal persons—and must therefore be notified directly to those to whom they are addressed. However, since the Court may review the legality of decisions at the request of parties which are not addressees of said acts, when the latter are of "direct and individual concern"[22] to them, it is important that they be informed of the contents of all such decisions. The same applies to directives; as was seen, citizens may invoke them in the national courts and request the latter to ask the Court of Justice for a preliminary ruling on their validity or interpretation. Consequently directives are always published in the *Official Journal* as are decisions which may affect the rights of third parties.[23]

4. Enforcement[24]

Decisions of the Council and the Commission which impose a pecuniary obligation[25] on persons other than Member States and judgments of the Court of Justice[26] are enforceable.

Enforcement of Community acts is governed by the rules of civil procedure in force within the Member State where it is carried out. The following steps must be taken. The institution which wants to enforce a decision, presents it for verification of authenticity to the national authority which the Government of each Member State has designated for this purpose[27] and made

---

[22] EEC, Art. 173 (2).

[23] See in this respect joined Cases 73–74/63 *Handelsvereniging Rotterdam* v. *Minister van Landbouw* [1964] E.C.R. 1 at 14 and Case 130/78 *Salumificio* v. *Amministrazione delle Finanze* [1979] E.C.R. 867.

[24] EEC, Art. 192.

[25] For instance decisions of the Commission imposing fines pursuant to Art. 15 of Reg. 17, for violation of the competition rules (O.J. 1959–1962, 87).

[26] EEC, Art. 187.

[27] *The Netherlands*: Law of February 24, 1955, Stb 73, modified by Law of January 13, 1960, Stb 15: Minister of Justice is addressee of request; Griffier of Hoge Raad implements. *Belgium*: Law of August 6, 1967: Greffier en Chef of the Court of Appeal at Brussels. *France*: Décret No. 57/321 of March 13, 1957, *Journal Officiel*, March 19, 1957, 2885, designates (1) persons who have received delegation from the Prime Minister and (2) Secrétariat Général du Comité Interministériel. *Germany*: Bundesgesetzblatt, February 3, 1961, II, 50: Minister of Justice. *Italy*: Decree of December 2, 1960, *Official Gazzetta*, February 21, 1961, No. 46, 738: Minister of Foreign Affairs. *Luxembourg*: Reg. of October 17, 1962, Memorial of October 31, 1962, No. 58, 1028: verification by Minister of Foreign Affairs, and order for enforcement appended by Minister of Justice. *United*

known to the Commission and the Court of Justice. This authority then appends to the decision an order for its enforcement.[28] The institution can then proceed to enforcement in accordance with national law, by bringing the matter directly before the competent national authorities. From that moment on, the national rules of civil procedure apply with the exception that suspension of the enforcement may only be decided by the Court.

An action brought before the Court against the decision which is being enforced has no suspensory effect.[29]

5. Binding acts not provided under Article 189

Community acts are not limited to regulations, directives and decisions. As was pointed out, judgments of the Court are also binding upon the parties and can be enforced. The same applies to agreements concluded by the Community with third countries or international organisations; they are binding upon the institutions of the Community and on the Member States.[30]

The same applies to agreements concluded by the Member States among themselves regarding matters connected with the Treaty.[31] Somewhat different is the position of international agreements concluded by the Member States with third countries: in so far as, under the Treaty, the Community has assumed the powers previously exercised by Member States in the area governed by such international agreement, the provi-

---

Kingdom: European Communities (Enforcement of Community Judgments) Order 1972, S.I. 1972, No. 1590, which provides for the registration in the High Court of England and Northern Ireland and the Court of Session in Scotland of Community judgments and orders to which the Secretary of State has duly appended an order for enforcement. *Ireland*: S.I. 1972, No. 331: enforcement order appended by the Master of the High Court, *Denmark*: by the Minister of Justice; *Greece*: the head of the tribunal of first instance of Athens.

[28] In the United Kingdom "order for enforcement" means an order by or under the authority of the Secretary of State that the Community judgment to which it is appended is to be registered for enforcement in the United Kingdom (S.I. 1972, No. 1590).

[29] When the Commission takes a decision imposing fines on a person, it usually does not seek enforcement in case an appeal has been lodged against the decision. The Court has approved this practice but only on condition that interest is paid in respect of the period of suspension and that a bank guarantee is lodged covering the amount of the fine; see Case 86/82 R *Hasselblad* v. *Commission* [1982] E.C.R. 1555.

[30] EEC, Art. 228 (2).

[31] See, *e.g.* EEC, Arts. 50 and 220.

sions of that agreement have the effect of binding the Community.[32] These agreements can be submitted to the control of legality exercised by the Court when the Community is a party[33] to them and they constitute rules of law relating to the application of the Treaty.[34] with the result that regulations, directives and decisions can be annulled in case of infringement of these rules.

Finally, there are the decisions of the representatives of the governments of the Member States in Council; these cannot be submitted to the Court, since they do not emanate from the Council or the Commission, but they can be binding within the whole Community.[35] However it will have to be established on a case by case basis whether those decisions are binding only for the Member States or also for the institutions of the Community and even for natural or legal persons. Although those "decisions," not provided for under the Treaty, constitute a flexible instrument to solve a number of questions within the scope of the treaties, they are not without danger for the institutional equilibrium provided by the Treaty. Besides immunity from the Court's control, these acts do not require a Commission proposal or an opinion of Parliament. Of course, nothing can prevent the latter from trying to exercise its political control over these acts anyway.

Binding acts not provided for under Article 189 can have "direct effect"; this applies in the first place to international agreements.[36]

---

[32] Joined Cases 21 to 24/72 *International Fruit Company* v. *Produkschap voor Groenten en Fruit* [1972] E.C.R. 1219 at 1227 (18).

[33] See, *e.g.* Case 22/70 *Commission* v. *Council* [1971] E.C.R. 263.

[34] EEC, Art. 173.

[35] See, *e.g.* the "acceleration" decisions by which the Member States agreed to establish the customs union within a shorter time-limit than provided for under the Treaty (J.O. 1960, 1217 and 1962, 1284). These decisions are not to be confused with decisions of the Member States such as the appointment of the Members of the Commission (Merger Treaty, Art. 11) or of the Judges of the Court of Justice (EEC, Art. 167).

[36] See joined Cases 21–24/72 *International Fruit Company* v. *Produktschap voor Groenten en Fruit* [1972] E.C.R. 1219 and joined Cases 290 and 291/81, *Singer and Geigy* v. *Amministrazione delle Finanze* [1983] E.C.R. 847 concerning direct effect of GATT rules.

6. Other forms of Community measures

A form often used is the *resolution,* either of the Council,[37] or of the Council and of the representatives of the governments of the Member States.[38] These resolutions are not to be confused with the decisions of the representatives of the governments of the Member States in Council; in the first place the decisions of the representatives of the Member States are legally binding upon the latter, while resolutions sometimes only constitute a political commitment; secondly, the fact that the Member States act within the institutional framework is intended to indicate that the matter directly concerns the implementation of the Treaty. Resolutions, generally speaking, concern matters directly connected with the Community, but not explicitly provided for therein.

There is also the *programme* or programmes of action, which intend to lay down general principles for future action both by the Member States and by the institutions of the Community. Such programmes are generally adopted by the Council and by the representatives of the governments of the Member States meeting in Council, either by a decision,[39] a *declaration*[40] or a resolution.[41]

Other matters are decided upon by *decisions* which are not formal binding acts[42] in the sense of EEC, Article 189, since they are not provided for under the Treaty; they are used to settle questions related to Community affairs but which do not impose rights or obligations upon the institutions of the Community nor on natural or legal persons.[43] Once again, these "decisions" are not to be confused with the decisions taken by the governments of the Member States in pursuance of the Treaty provisions such

---

[37] See, *e.g.* Council Resolution of February 6, 1979 concerning the guidelines for Community Regional Policy (O.J. 1979, C.36/10) and the conclusions of the Council of December 4, 1984, concerning measures necessary to guarantee the implementation of the conclusions of the European Council concerning budgetary discipline. Bull. 12–1984, 24. In one case, the Court was asked to interpret a Council resolution in a request for a preliminary ruling: Case 9/73 *Schlüter* v. *Hauptzollamt Lörrach* [1973] E.C.R. 1135 at 1162.

[38] See, *e.g.* J.O. 1972, C.38/3.

[39] See, *e.g.* O.J. 1982, L.236/10.

[40] See, *e.g.* O.J. 1973, C.112/1.

[41] See, *e.g.* O.J. 1977, C.139/1.

[42] Other languages such as Dutch and German use a word ("Besluit; Beschlus") which clearly distinguishes this act from an Art. 189 decision ("Beschikking; Entscheidung").

[43] See, *e.g.* O.J. 1973, L.207/46.

as the appointment of the Judges and Advocates-General of the Court of Justice and the members of the Commission. These acts are Community acts, but do not constitute acts of the institutions of the Community and do not therefore come under the jurisdiction of the Court of Justice.

Further Reading

CHAP 4 – COMMUNITY ACTS

John Bridge, "Procedural aspects of the enforcement of European Community Law through the legal systems of the member states" (1984) 9 E.L.Rev. 28.

Nicholas Green, "Directives, equity and the protection of individual rights" (1984) 9 E.L.Rev. 295.

CHAPTER 5

THE SECTORAL TREATIES: ECSC AND EURATOM

I. *The European Coal and Steel Community*

In a White Paper presented to the United Kingdom Parliament in July 1971 it is stated that the Coal and Steel Community "is designed to ensure an orderly supply of coal and steel to the Community, whilst at the same time taking account of the needs of third countries; to promote the orderly expansion and moder- nisation of production; and to provide better conditions of living and employment for the workers in the industries."[1] Even allowing for the brevity of this statement, it hardly does justice to the objectives pursued by the founders of this Community; it fails completely to mention that, as provided by Article 1 of the Paris Treaty, the Coal and Steel Community is "based on a common market, common objectives and common institutions."

1. The common market

The establishment and functioning of this common market for coal and steel products[2] was of essential interest for the six countries, since it gave to their heavy industries a production and distribution basis comparable to that of the United States or the U.S.S.R.; by allowing the European enterprises to lower their production cost through economies of scale, they had a chance of becoming competitive on the world market. The powers attri- buted to the common institutions of the Community must be interpreted in relation to the necessity of setting up and maintain- ing this common market. The general tasks of the Community are set out in Article 3; under the powers granted by the Treaty the most far-reaching are undoubtedly those provided by Article 58

---

[1] Cmnd. 4715, 37–38.
[2] The terms coal and steel are defined in Annex 1 to the Treaty; for instance steel tubes (seamless or welded), cold rolled strips less than 500 mm. in width, are not included.

under which in a period of manifest crisis the High Authority may after consulting the Consultative Community, and with the assent of the Council, establish a system of production quotas and impose fines upon non-complying undertakings.[3] The legal implications of the establishment of the common market are defined in Article 4; this provision specifies which existing measures in the field of trade, administration, finance or commerce are thereby abolished and prohibited within the Community.[4]

First, import and export duties or taxes having equivalent effect[5] are abolished.

Secondly, all measures or practices—whether public or private —which discriminate among producers, buyers or consumers—especially with regard to prices, delivery terms and transport rates—are similarly considered to be "incompatible with the common market for coal and steel and are therefore abolished and prohibited."

In regard to transport, the aim of the ECSC Treaty is to ensure that the transport industry will not jeopardise the fulfilment of the Treaty objectives; it therefore provides for two specific rules: the prohibition of "discriminatory prices, delivery terms and transport rates" (ECSC, Art. 4(2)) and the obligation "to apply to the carriage of coal and steel to and from another country of the Community, the scales, rates and all other tariff rules of every kind which are applicable to the internal carriage of the same goods on the same route" (ECSC, Art. 70). The High Authority may however give a temporary or conditional agreement to the application of special domestic tariff measures in the interest of one or several enterprises.[6]

Article 70 also provides that in order to ensure that comparable[7] price conditions are applied to consumers in comparable positions, the rates, prices and all other tariff rules applied to the carriage of coal and steel within each Member State and between

---

[3] See below, recent developments, p. 102.
[4] This prohibition is similar to that provided by various provisions of the EEC Treaty analysed below, p. 111.
[5] See Case 24/68 *Commission* v. *Italy* [1969] E.C.R. 193 at 201(9).
[6] Joined Cases 27–29/58 *Hauts Fournaux de Givors* v. *High Authority* [1960] E.C.R. 241.
[7] See joined Cases 3, etc./58 *Barbara Erzbergbau* v. *High Authority* [1960] E.C.R. 173 at 191.

the Member States shall be published or brought to the knowledge of the High Authority.[8]

Thirdly, the common market entails the prohibition and abolition of subsidies or state assistance or special charges imposed by the State, in any form whatsoever.[9]

Fourthly, the common market implies the maintenance and the observance of normal conditions of competition.[10] Concentrations of enterprises must be submitted to the High Authority[11] for prior authorisation (Art. 66).[12]

Finally it must be mentioned that within the ECSC common market workers have access to employment in other Member States under the same conditions as nationals of those States (the limitations of ECSC, Article 69 were superseded by EEC, Article 49 and Regulation 1612/68[13]) The ECSC disposes of considerable funds which as stated in the White Paper 1972, "help the development of the industries, provide cheap loans for workers' houses and help finance new employment opportunities and retraining schemes for any coal and steel employees who become redundant. They also provide grants for coal and steel research."[14] Loan funds for financing investments conversion programmes and low-cost housing in the coal and steel industry taken up during 1984, totalled 825.5 million ECU.

2. Common objectives

The main objective of the Coal and Steel Community is to

[8] See Dec. 59/18 (J.O. 1959, 287) and Case 20/59 *Italy* v. *High Authority* [1960] E.C.R. 325; see also Case 25/59 *Netherlands* v. *High Authority* [1960] E.C.R. 355.

[9] See Art. 67 and Case 59/70 *Netherlands* v. *Commission* [1971] E.C.R. 639. Under Art. 95 the Commission decided to allow aids to investment and closure in the steel industry (See Competition Reports 1980 *et seq.*). See Dec. 257/80 establishing Community rules for specific aids to steel industry (O.J. 1980, L.29/5) and Dec. 76/528 concerning aids to the coal industry (O.J. 1976, L.63/1). See also Competition Reports and General Reports.

[10] Art. 65. See Dec. 1–65 (J.O. 1965, 438).

[11] See Dec. 54/24 of the High Authority laying down in implementation of Art. 66(1) of the Treaty a regulation on what constitutes control of an undertaking (J.O. 1954, 345). For Art. 66(3) See O.J. 1978, L.300/21.

[12] Several such authorisations were given: BSC, O.J. 1979, L.245/30 and Sheffield Forgemasters (Bull. 12–1982, 34). See also Joined Cases 160, 161, 170/73 R II *Miles Druce* v. *Commission* [1974] E.C.R. 281.

[13] O.J. 1968, L.257/2.

[14] Cmnd. 4715, 154. For the UK in 1983 alone grants amounted to over 70 million ECU for 69,681 workers. For further details see Eighteenth General Report (1984), p. 224.

"bring about conditions which will of themselves ensure the most rational distribution of production at the highest possible level of productivity" (Art. 2); this means, for instance, the closing down of unproductive coal mines and the concentration of production in those basins which can compete with imported coal.

Other objectives are the expansion of the economy, the development of employment (not necessarily in the coal and steel industries), the improvement of the standard of living, the retraining of workers and the restructuring of the coal and steel industry.

In order to attain those objectives, the institutions of the Community must among others

(a) ensure that the common market is regularly supplied;
(b) assure to all consumers equal access to the sources of production,
(c) seek the establishment of the lowest possible prices while at the same time permitting necessary amortisation and normal returns on investments,
(d) maintain conditions which will encourage enterprises to expand and improve their ability to produce and
(e) promote the regular expansion and the modernisation of production (Art. 3).

Even the Court of Justice has implicitly recognised that some of those objectives are contradictory and may therefore conflict.[15]

The ECSC enjoys wide powers in regard to external relations[16] in so far as required to perform its functions and attain its objectives.

In the *coal* sector the Commission publishes annually a short-term outlook for coal in the Community[17] and various aid systems have been authorised. Although the Council reaffirmed the important role of coal in the Community's energy policy, no agreement could be reached on proposed Community aids for

---

[15] Case 8/57 *Aciéries Belges* v. *High Authority* [1958] E.C.R. 245. *Id.* in Case 276/80 *Padana* v. *Commission* [1982] E.C.R. 517 at 542(21).

[16] ECSC, Art. 6. See *e.g.* agreement with Yugoslavia concerning generalized tariff preference, O.J. 1983, L.237/1.

[17] *e.g.* "The Community coal market in 1982 and forecasts for 1983" (O.J. 1983, C.147/1); for Revised forecasts see O.J. 1983, C.303/3.

financing cyclic stocks of coal[18] or to promote the use of coal for electricity generation.[19]

3. Common institutions

The institutions of the Coal and Steel Community are:

–a High Authority, which was the equivalent of the EEC Commission; it was merged with the latter, together with the Euratom Commission, as of July 1, 1967, under the so-called Merger Treaty;

–a Common Assembly, which was replaced by the Assembly provided for in the Rome Treaties (EEC and Euratom);

–a Special Council of Ministers, which in theory existed until it was merged in 1967 with the EEC and Euratom Councils;

–a Court of Justice, which was replaced in 1958 by the single Court set up for the Economic Community and Euratom (Convention on certain institutions, Arts. 3 and 4).

The institutions are discussed in more detail above: Chap. 3, The Institutions and Other Organs of the Community.

4. Recent developments

The difficulties facing the steel industry led the Commission to decide on December 20, 1976, to implement the first anti-crisis measures of the Community steel policy; they entered into force on January 1, 1977. The measures, known as the "Davignon Plan," were based on voluntary undertakings by steel firms to comply with supply targets on the domestic market for certain products.

In March 1977 guidance prices for rolled products and compulsory minimum prices for certain products were introduced.[20] Towards the end of 1977 it was found that the resulting rise in internal market prices—on which the profitability of steel firms depends—was being compromised by the pressure exerted by imports and an anti-dumping scheme based on the GATT rules was brought into operation on January 1, 1980.[21] In order to

---

[18] O.J. 1977, C.87/6.
[19] O.J. 1977, C.22/4.
[20] O.J. 1977, L.114/1 and C.174/2. See Thirteenth General Report (1979), 85.
[21] O.J. 1977, L.352/8. For further details see Eleventh General Report (1977), 85 *et seq*.

preserve the traditional patterns of trade, agreements were signed with the EFTA countries and a large number of other non-member countries, including certain state-trading countries.[22]

Production quotas. In view of the slump in demand for steel in the third quarter of 1980 both within and outside the Community, the Commission considered, in pursuance of ECSC Article 58(1), that the Community was confronted with a period of manifest crisis. Consequently the Commission, after consulting the Consultative Committee and with the assent of the Council, established a system of production quotas.[23] At the same time the Commission published basic prices for certain iron and steel products.[24] Under Art. 58(4) the Commission had to impose severe fines for non compliance by undertakings.[25]

The situation had an extremely grave impact on jobs. Cyclical factors combined with the effects of the structural crisis reduced employment in the steel industry by almost 41 per cent. since 1974; total employment at the end of 1984 was 446,000.

In 1981 the Commission felt that the manifest crisis situation continued and quotas were fixed once again under ECSC Art. 58.[26] New extensions were decided in 1982,[27] 1983 and 1984.[28] In December 1983 the Council reached agreement on a series of crisis measures including price setting and a system of fines.[29]

Severe problems arose with the United States and the outcome of negotiations between the Community and the United States was an Arrangement limiting Community exports of steel products to the United States. The Arrangement runs to December 31, 1985.[30]

---

[22] See Thirteenth General Report (1979), 226.
[23] Dec. 80/2794 of October 31, 1980 (O.J. 1980, L.291/1). Many of the fixed quotas were contested in the Court, see, *e.g.* Case 119/81 *Klöckner-Werke* v. *Commission* [1982] E.C.R. 2627.
[24] O.J. 1980, L.290/1 and L.291/1.
[25] See, *e.g.* Case 265/82 *Usinor* v. *Commission* [1983] E.C.R. 3105 where the fine was squashed and Case 179/82 *Lucchini* v. *Commission* [1983] E.C.R. 3083 where the fine was reduced.
[26] Dec. 81/1831, O.J. 1981, L.180/1.
[27] Dec. 82/1696, O.J. 1982, L.191/1; Dec. 84/234, O.J. 1984, L.29/1. Eighteenth General Report (1984), 99.
[28] Dec. 83/1809, O.J. 1983, L.177/5.
[29] O.J. 1983, L.373/1; Seventeenth General Report (1983), 95 and (1984), 100.
[30] O.J. 1982, L.307/1; Bull. 10–1982, 13.

II. *The European Atomic Energy Community (Euratom)*

1. Euratom's objective

The essential objective of Euratom is to create "conditions necessary for the speedy establishment and growth of nuclear industries." (Art. 1). After more than 25 years the Community has not quite succeeded in achieving this aim. It might be useful briefly to explain at this point the reasons for this failure. In the first place, the expectations placed in nuclear energy in the fifties were much too high, also the expected need for this supplementary source of energy did not materialise until 1973. On the other hand, the need for joint fundamental research disappeared as soon as the industrial applications appeared to promise rich commercial rewards. Finally, inside the Community itself the disparity between the partners was much too great to make fruitful co-operation possible. The recent oil crisis followed by enormous price increases has renewed the interest in nuclear energy; the question remains, however, whether Euratom can still play a role in this field.

2. Euratom's means

To achieve the above-mentioned objective the Community:

(i) develops research and disseminates the results; this research is carried out either through research contracts[31] with individuals, laboratories, universities or industries or in the Community's Joint Nuclear Research Centre which was set up under Euratom, Article 8. This research centre at present has four branch establishments: Ispra in Italy, Petten in The Netherlands, the Central Nuclear Measurement Bureau at Geel, Belgium, and the European Transuranium Institute at Karlsruhe, Germany. The implementation of the Community's research programme has thus imposed upon the European Commission a great variety of tasks ranging all the way from planning and building reactors and laboratories of the most elaborate kind, the acquisition of great quantities of scientific instrumentation and the training of

---

[31] Thermonuclear fusion constitutes one of the main Community programmes; it includes the construction of a major experimental facility: JET (Joint European Torus) at Culham in the U.K. A four-year research programme was adopted on Dec. 22, 1983 with an expenditure commitment of 700 million ECU (O.J. 1984, L.3/21). See Eighteenth General Report (1984), 217.

personnel in the management of large research establishments to the actual operation of reactors.

The Commission may also "by contract, entrust the carrying out of certain parts of the Community research programme to Member States, persons or undertakings or to third countries, international organisations or nationals of third countries." This has been done on a very large scale.

The technical and scientific information obtained through the implementation of the Community's research programme, is disseminated on a non-discriminatory basis[32];

(ii) has established by directive basic standards for the protection of the health of workers and of the general public from the dangers arising from ionising radiation[33];

(iii) in order to encourage the construction of basic facilities required for the development of nuclear energy has constituted six joint undertakings[34] among which JET at Culham in the United Kingdom.[35] The Commission also expresses its views on all the investment projects in the nuclear field; all projects must therefore be communicated to the Commission (Euratom, Art. 41)[36];

(iv) has constituted a Supply Agency having a right of option on all ores, source materials and special fissile materials produced in the territories of Member States and having the exclusive right of concluding contracts relating to supply of ores, source material and special fissile materials coming from inside or outside the Community (Euratom, Art. 52(2)(*b*)).[37] The statutes of the Agency were laid down by the Council[38] and various regulations

---

[32] See Announcement of the Commission concerning the communication of information to persons and enterprises of the Community (J.O. 1963, 2569).

[33] J.O. 221/59; O.J. 1959–1962, 7—modifications in J.O. 3693/66; O.J. 1965–1966, 265. In 1980 the Council adopted a five-year (1980–1984) biology and health protection programme (O.J. 1980, L.78/19) to which 59 million ECU was allocated.

[34] See J.O. 1173/61, J.O. 1745/63, J.O. 3642/64, J.O. 2681/66 and O.J. 1974, L.165/7.

[35] The Council Dec. was taken in October 1977 (Bull. 10–1977, 64); see also Council Dec. of May 30, 1978 (O.J. 1978, L.151/10 and 1979, L.213/9) relating to its construction and Thirteenth General Report (1979), 191.

[36] Council Reg. No. 4 (J.O. 1958/417); see also Commission Reg. No. 1 (J.O. 1958/511) and Communication of the Commission (J.O. 1959/571).

[37] See Case 7/71 *Commission* v. *France* [1971] E.C.R. 1003. For new developments see Thirteenth General Report (1979), 185.

[38] See J.O. 534/58.

have specified the condition under which nuclear materials can be required, sold and transferred.[39]

The Community also concluded agreements with the United States,[40] Great Britain,[41] Canada,[42] Brazil[43] and Argentina[44] to secure a regular supply of nuclear materials, especially enriched uranium;

(v) guarantees, by appropriate measures of control, that nuclear materials are not diverted for purposes other than those for which they are intended; Euratom in other words does not guarantee peaceful use unless materials have been intended for such purpose by their supplier or consumer.[45] On April 5, 1973 an agreement was signed between Euratom and seven Member States which do not have nuclear weapons and the International Atomic Energy Agency[46] pursuant to the Treaty on the Non-Proliferation of Nuclear Weapons. Consequently, Euratom adapted its safeguards system. Similar agreements were signed between the IAEA on the one hand and Euratom and the United Kingdom[47] and France[48] on the other. Joint teams composed of Euratom and IAEA inspectors operate regularly at 13 major plants;

(vi) has created a common market for specialised materials and equipment[49] and guarantees free movement of capital for nuclear investment (Euratom, Arts. 99, 100) and freedom of employment for specialists within the Community[50];

(vii) enjoys wide powers in the field of external relations (Euratom, Arts. 101–106) to conclude agreements or contracts;

---

[39] See J.O. 777/60; O.J. 1959–1962, 46 (Rules of the Agency determining the manner in which demand is to be balanced against supply); J.O. 116/62 and J.O. 4057/66; O.J. 1965–1966, 297 (regulations of the Commission concerning the implementation of the supply provisions) and J.O. 1460/60 and 240/64 (Communications of the Agency).

[40] See J.O. 312/59, 53/61, 2038/62, 2045/62 and O.J. 1974, L.139/24.

[41] J.O. 331/59.

[42] J.O. 1165/59.

[43] J.O. 1969, L.79/7.

[44] J.O. 2966/63.

[45] See Regs. Nos. 2, 8 and 9 (J.O. 298/59, O.J. 1959–1962, 23; J.O. 651/59, O.J. 1959–1962, 27 and J.O. 482/60, O.J. 1959–1962, 43). See also Commission Reg. O.J. 1976, L.363/1.

[46] Bull. 2–1977, 61. O.J. 1978, L.51/1.

[47] Bull. 7/8–1978, 69.

[48] *Ibid.* 68.

[49] J.O. 406/59 and 410/59.

[50] See Dir. of the Council concerning freedom of access to qualified employment in the nuclear field (J.O. 1650/62; O.J. 1959–1962, 245).

Member States wishing to conclude with a third state, an international organisation or a national of a third state agreements or contracts which concern matters within the purview of the Treaty must communicate the draft to the Commission; if the latter raises objections the Court of Justice can be asked to give a ruling[51];

(viii) Finally, with regard to *nuclear energy*, the Community grants subsidies to undertakings carrying out prospecting programmes for uranium on the territories of the Member States and in 1977 the Council authorised the Commission to borrow up to one billion European units of account on the financial markets in order to grant loans for the construction of nuclear power plants.[52]

This general survey of Euratom's means would not be complete without the mention of the vesting in the Community of property in all special fissionable materials (Euratom, Art. 86). This ownership is limited to materials subject to Euratom's safeguards control; this control does not, according to Euratom, Article 85 extend to "materials intended to meet defence requirements."

3. Euratom's institutions

Two of the institutions of the European Atomic Energy Community were from the beginning institutions common to the three Communities: the Assembly and the Court of Justice.

The Council was merged with the other Councils in 1967.

The Commission, composed of five members only, ceased to exist in 1957 and was replaced, under the Merger Treaty, by the European Commission.

The four institutions were examined in detail above: Chap. 3, The Institutions and Other Organs of the Community.

---

[51] See Ruling 1/78 [1978] E.C.R. 2151.
[52] O.J. 1977, L.88/9. The loans are administered by the E.I.B.

CHAPTER 6

THE EUROPEAN ECONOMIC COMMUNITY (EEC)

The EEC Treaty is by far the most important of the three basic European treaties. While the ECSC and Euratom Treaties provide for "sectoral integration," the EEC Treaty, touching upon most aspects of the economy, constitutes the basis for general economic integration.[1]

The importance of the EEC Treaty also derives from the fact that the full implementation of its objectives requires a common policy of the Member States or even a Community policy[2] in fields not explicitly mentioned in the Treaty itself. This is for instance the case with regional development, industrial policy, energy and environment. Faced with the necessity to organise concerted action in those fields, the institutions of the Community and the Member States had to improvise new procedures and measures. Consequently the role of governments and therefore of politicians has increased at the expense of that of the Community institutions.

The preamble to the EEC Treaty lists very broadly formulated objectives but these do not constitute practical guidelines for Community action; more specific aims are set out in Articles 2 and 3. Article 2 summarises in a few words not only the basic objectives but also the means by which those objectives have to be attained. The objectives are to promote throughout the Community:

---

[1] The EEC Treaty also applies to all the subjects covered by the ECSC and Euratom Treaties in so far as specific rules are not provided by the latter, *e.g.* ECSC competition rules: these constitute *leges speciales* in regard to the EEC Treaty, see EEC, Art. 232.

[2] In the case of *common policies* of the Member States the responsibility and therefore powers of decision lay with the national authorities; in the case of *Community policies*, jurisdiction is transferred to the Community institutions.

–harmonious development of economic activities;
–continuous and balanced expansion[3];
–increase in stability[4];
–accelerated raising of the standard of living[5];
–closer relations between the Member States.[6]

To achieve these objectives the Community institutions have been provided with two means: the establishment of the Common Market and the progressive approximation of the economic policies of the Member States. These two means are rather different in nature, but essentially complementary; they correspond to two major phases in the development of the European Community, *i.e.* the so-called "negative and the positive integration." The first corresponds to the abolition of all obstacles to free movement of goods, persons, services, capital and payments, although that phase is also characterised by the adoption of a common policy in the sphere of agriculture and of transport, the institution of a system ensuring that competition is not distorted and the establishment of special relations with the overseas countries and territories.

The rules provided in the Treaty for this first phase are of a rather legal-technical nature: they constitute a set of more or less specific provisions which apply to industrial and agricultural production and to transport. It is mainly in these areas that the Community institutions have exercised their law-making powers.

The second instrument, *i.e.* progressive "convergence" of national economic policies, corresponds to a more constructive stage, but concerns policy rather than law-making; it is therefore much less defined. If it has been designated as "positive integration," it is nevertheless dependent upon economic and political circumstances, while the development of the first stage is determined by time-limits prescribed by the Treaty itself.

The economic policies referred to in the EEC Treaty are those relating to economic trends, balance of payments, rates of

---

[3] This refers to the necessity to avoid accentuated cyclical ups and downs.
[4] Reference here is made *inter alia* to monetary stability; this objective is at the origin of the European Monetary System; see below, Economic and Monetary Policy, p. 211.
[5] On this aim is based *inter alia* the Community's Social Policy; see below, p. 217.
[6] This relates not only to economic activities, but also to political co-operation; see above, p. 40.

exchange and commercial policy; clearly this list is too limiting, and overall economic and monetary policies including budgetary matters, taxation, regional development and industrial policies have to be included if the co-ordination of economic policies is really to take place. It is clear also that none of those policies will have a chance to succeed if tackled individually; an overall approach is needed. This was attempted in 1971 with the decision concerning the phased establishment of economic and monetary union; it failed due mainly to the deterioration of the overall economic conditions aggravated by the oil crisis. A more modest attempt was made in the form of the European Monetary System.

For the establishment of the above-mentioned policies, the EEC Treaty does not provide the necessary powers. This probably largely explains the emergence of the European Council where the necessary political decisions are taken by the heads of government, leaving it to the Community institution to devise the corresponding complementary legal instruments.

After the broad formulation of the objectives of the EEC in the Preamble and in Article 2, Article 3 provides a more concrete description of the main activities of the Community. To each activity correspond several provisions in Parts Two, Three and Four of the Treaty, which define in more detail their content and the procedures to be followed for enacting the required implementing legislation. The provisions of Article 3 should not be considered as a mere enumeration having no legal force on its own: the Court of Justice rejected that view because it ignores the fact that Article 3 considers the pursuit of the objectives it lays down as indispensable for the achievement of the Community's tasks.[7]

The activities of the Community, including those not mentioned in the Treaty, will be examined below together with the corresponding Community law. They will be grouped in three sections: the Common Market, the Community Policies and External Relations including relations with developing countries.

---

[7] Case 6/72 *Europemballage and Continental Can* v. *Commission* [1973] E.C.R. 215 at 244 (23, 24): the Court rejected the applicant's argument that this provision (*i.e.* EEC, Art. 3(*f*)) merely contains a general programme devoid of legal effect.

PART ONE: THE COMMON MARKET

As was pointed out above the "common market" constitutes with the "approximation of the economic policies of the Member States," the means to achieve the objectives of the EEC.

However, the Treaty does not clearly indicate what is to be understood by the "common market"; no description is given, but its characteristics can be deduced from the provisions of Part Two of the Treaty which refers to the "foundations of the Community." It can therefore be said that the common market is constituted by the so-called basic freedom, *i.e.* the freedom to move goods within the Community, for workers the freedom to move from one Member State to another, the freedom of establishment, the freedom to provide services throughout the Community and the freedom to transfer capital and payments within the EEC. Together with the agricultural policy the existence of these freedoms is necessary to "establish"[8] a common market as provided in EEC Article 2. To allow its proper "functioning and development" much more is needed in the form of accompanying policies in the field of transport, competition, taxation, industrial and regional development, approximation of laws and relations with third countries. Provisions for such policies are to be found mainly in Part Three of the Treaty and in provisions enacted by the Council in pursuance of Article 235.[9]

The most important of the above-mentioned elements is the free movement of goods; all the other activities referred to are in fact required to achieve that single goal.

I. *Free Movement of Goods*

Free movement of goods within the Community[10] is made possible by:

–the establishment of a customs union and
–the elimination of quantitative restrictions on imports and exports.

---

[8] The common market was established progressively during a transitional period of twelve years ending on December 31, 1969. See EEC, Art. 8(1) and (7), and Third General Report (1969) 15.

[9] See above, p. 37.

[10] For a geographical description of the Community see EEC, Art. 227.

1. The Customs Union

The EEC Treaty[11] provides that the customs union shall cover all trade in goods and shall involve (1) the prohibition between Member States of customs duties on imports and exports and of all charges having an equivalent effect and (2) the adoption of a common customs tariff in the relations with third countries. The two are complementary.

The goods covered are both industrial and agricultural products[12] whether originating in the Member States or coming from third countries.[13] For the latter, import formalities must have been complied with in any one Member State and customs duties and charges having equivalent effect must have been levied and not reimbursed.[14] When these conditions are fulfilled these imported products are considered to be "in free circulation in Member States,"[15] *i.e.* assimilated to products originating in the Member States. The customs union among the original six member States was established progressively over a period of ten and a half years, *i.e.* from January 1, 1958 to June 30, 1968, shorter than the twelve years originally estimated.[16] The customs union was similarly extended to Denmark, Ireland and the United Kingdom over a period of a little more than four years from April 1, 1973 to July 1, 1977[17] and is presently in the process of being applied to Greece where the last remaining duties will be abolished on January 1, 1986.[18]

---

[11] EEC, Art. 9(1).

[12] EEC, Art. 38, save as otherwise provided in EEC, Art. 39 to 56.

[13] EEC, Art. 9(2). The inclusion of products originating outside the Community is what differentiates *a customs union* from a *free trade area*. The latter having no common customs tariff only covers products originating within the States belonging to the free trade area; see, *e.g.* EFTA, Art. 4.

[14] EEC, Art. 10(1).

[15] EEC, Art. 9(2).

[16] See EEC, Art. 8 which provides for a transitional period of 12 years in three stages and Arts. 13, 14 and 32. Twice the representatives of the Member States in Council decided, probably on the basis of Art. 15(2) (which is not mentioned in the decisions), to accelerate the establishment of the customs union: Dec. of May 12, 1960 (J.O. 1960, 1217) and Dec. of May 15, 1962 (J.O. 1962, 1284); a final decision abolished all duties on industrial goods as of July 1, 1966 (J.O. 1966, 2971).

[17] Act of accession, Art. 32.

[18] Act of Greek accession, Art. 25 (O.J. 1979, L. 291).

(1) *Elimination of customs duties between Member States*[19]

All existing customs duties were gradually eliminated through successive reduction,[20] but in order to free all trade between Member States, it was also necessary to prevent the introduction of new duties or the increase of existing ones.[21] This explains why the Treaty section on the elimination of customs duties starts with the prohibition to introduce new ones.[22]

The elimination applies both to import and export[23] duties and to customs duties of a fiscal nature.[24]

Of utmost importance are the words "charges having equivalent effect" which are used in conjunction with the words "customs duties."[25] Indeed, without this addition Article 12 would have been less effective.[26] The Treaty therefore prohibits and eliminates not only customs duties but any charge imposed by a Member State at the occasion of a product crossing the border and which, although not formally designated as a customs duty, *i.e.* appearing on a tariff list, does nevertheless have the same impeding effect on imports or exports, unless the charge in question is the consideration for a benefit provided in fact for the exporter or importer and representing an amount proportionate to the said benefit or if it relates to a general system of internal dues applied systematically in accordance with the same criteria to domestic products and imported products alike.[27]

---

[19] EEC, Arts. 12 to 17.

[20] See EEC, Art. 14(2).

[21] See *e.g.* Case 26/62 *Van Gend en Loos* v. *Dutch Fiscal Administration* [1963] E.C.R. 1 at 12.

[22] EEC, Art. 12.

[23] EEC, Arts. 13 and 16. See Case 89/76 *Commission* v. *Netherlands* [1977] E.C.R. 1355.

[24] EEC, Art. 17.

[25] Similar terms are used in Arts. 30 *et seq.*; see below. In Case 46/76 *Bauhuis* v. *Netherlands* [1977] E.C.R. 5 at 14 (10), the Court defined as follows charges having an effect equivalent to that of a customs duty: "any pecuniary charge, whatever its designation and mode of application which is imposed unilaterally on goods by reason of the fact that they cross a frontier and which is not a customs duty in the strict sense."

[26] See joined Cases 2 and 3/62 *Commission* v. *Luxembourg and Belgium* [1962] E.C.R. 425 at 432.

[27] See however Case 89/76, n.23 above where a similar fee levied only upon products intended for export and not on domestic products marketed within the State, was considered not to constitute a charge with equivalent effect.

The expression "charges having equivalent effect" gave rise to abundant case-law of the Court of Justice[28] which also stated that EEC, Art. 12 creates individual rights which national courts must protect.[29]

(2) The Common Customs Tariff (CCT)

The elimination of customs duties between Member States coincided with the setting up of the CCT which determines the duties to be levied on goods entering the Community from third countries; it was gradually introduced over the same period as was needed to eliminate the internal tariffs. The CCT was adopted in its final form, for the original six Member States, as a Council regulation[30]; it replaced the existing customs tariffs of the Benelux, Germany, France and Italy. The community tariffs were established, as a general rule, at a level corresponding to the arithmetical average of the duties applied in the four above-mentioned customs territories on January 1, 1957.[31]

As a consequence of the introduction of the CCT, individual Member States no longer have jurisdiction over the customs tariffs they levy on goods entering their country; neither can they modify them nor interpret them.[32] Furthermore since the entry into force of the Council decision concerning the Communities'

---

[28] See *e.g.* Case 222/78 *ICAP* v. *Beneventi* [1979] E.C.R. 1163: duty falling within a general system of internal taxation can constitute a charge having equivalent effect; Case 30/79 *Land Berlin* v. *Wige*; [1980] E.C.R. 151: charges in trade with non Member States; Case 132/80 *United Food and van den Abeele* v. *Belgium* [1981] E.C.R. 995: incompatibility of duties and charges for health inspection on imported goods with Arts. 9, 12 and 13; Case 132/82, *Commission* v. *Belgium*: storage fee by imports contrary to Art. 12, [1983] E.C.R. 1649.

[29] See Case 26/62, n.21 above.

[30] Reg. 950/68 of June 28, 1968 (J.O. 1968, L.172/1). The customs tariff of the European Communities is published by the Commission and regularly updated: see O.J. 1984, L.320/1.

[31] See EEC, Art. 19. The main exceptions to the rule of the arithmetical average are the products of the lists B, C, D and E for which the Treaty provides a maximum and those of list F for which the duties are fixed therein. These lists constitute Annex I to the EEC Treaty and form part thereof.

[32] See Case 38/75 *Nederlandse Spoorwegen* v. *Inspecteur der invoerrechten en accijnzen* [1975] E.C.R. 1439 at 1449 (14): "the Community authorities alone have jurisdiction to interpret...."

own resources, they must allocate to the Community the revenue accruing from the common customs tariff.[33]

Modifications or suspension of duties in the CCT are an exclusive Community matter and are introduced either autonomously by the Council[34] or as a measure of common commercial policy in its relation with third countries.[35] Important reductions were introduced following multilateral trade negotiations within the General Agreement for Tariffs and Trade (GATT), the so-called Kennedy-round (1964–1967) and Tokyo-round (1973–1979). The effect of the latter was that the level of industrial tariffs were cut by about one third.

In terms of trade, the creation of the customs union has resulted in shifts in the existing trade patterns, since, generally speaking, industrial goods become less expensive for Community consumers when imported from other Member States rather than from outside the Community; consequently internal or interstate trade tends to increase, while trade with third countries is reduced.[36] In the relations with the latter the Community uses the customs union as an instrument to guarantee the effectiveness of its policy.[37]

It must be noted that unification of tariff levels is only a very first step towards the setting up of the CCT: a customs union calls

[33] Dec. of April 21, 1970, on the replacement of financial contributions of Member States by the Communities' own resources (J.O. 1970, L. 94/12; O.J. 1970, 224). The Decision became effective on January 1, 1971. For further details see above, p. 81. Financing Community Activities. See also EEC, Art. 201 which provides for this transfer of resources to the Community.

[34] EEC, Art. 28, see Case 158/80 *Rewe* v. *Hauptzollamt Kiel* [1981] E.C.R. 1805.

[35] See EEC, Arts. 111 and 113 which provide for agreements with third countries. The commercial policy of the Community shall be examined below under External Relations, p. 236.

[36] Between 1959 and 1970, trade within the Community increased by 16 per cent. while exports to non-Community countries grew on average by 9 per cent. The share of intra-Community trade in the total trade of Member States reached 53.6 per cent. in 1979: it has since slightly declined. For the U.K. intra-Community exports as a percentage of total trade grew from 33.1 per cent. in 1973 (year of accession) to 41.2 per cent. in 1981 (see European File, 12/83).

[37] Both for the voluntary restraint agreements concluded with textile exporting country (Eleventh General Report (1977), 88, 220) and for the policy to deal with the crisis in the steel industry, the Community used the technical machinery of the customs union to ensure or monitor implementation: see Twelfth General Report (1978), 100.

for uniform interpretation, continuing administration,[38] while other essential aspects are the harmonisation of customs rules on trade with non-member countries,[39] simplification of customs checks and formalities in intra-Community trade, and the reinforcement of the structure of the customs union.[40]

The consequences of the customs union for countries like the United Kingdom are not to be underestimated, although they cannot always be expressed in financial terms. Britain now forms part of a single market of up to 300 million people stretching from Scotland to Crete and from Ireland to Berlin. Within this vast area, industrial products move freely, at least without tariff and quota restrictions.[41]

The results for the individual firm, are on the one hand, free access to the Community and associated markets, but on the other, of course, stronger competition at home from other Community products: however, as will be seen below, the Treaty provides for a system ensuring that competition in the common market is not distorted and that "dumping" is prevented.

2. Elimination of quantitative restrictions between Member States

Although a customs union is strictly speaking limited to the elimination of internal customs duties and the setting up of a common external tariff, free trade between Member States could be jeopardised if it were possible to limit, one way or another, the quantity of goods crossing the inter-state borders. The EEC Treaty therefore provides for the elimination of "quantitative restrictions on imports and all measures having equivalent effect."[42] What was said about customs duties, *i.e.* elimination of

---

[38] See Thirteenth General Report (1979), 91. Uniform interpretation is guaranteed by the Court of Justice; see Case 158/78 *Biegi* v. *Hauptzollamt Bochum* [1979] E.C.R. 1103 (regulation on tariff classification) and Case 160/78 *Intercontinentale Fleischhandelsgesellschaft* v. *Hauptzollamt München-West* [1979] E.C.R. 2259 (CCT).

[39] The latest version of the CCT came into effect in June 1983, Reg. 3333/83 (O.J. 1983, L. 313/1, see also 1983 L. 351/1 and 24). Many Court cases deal with the nomenclature of the CCT, see Fifteenth General Report (1981), 297.

[40] See Sixteenth General Report (1982), 97 *et seq.*

[41] As was pointed out there still exist, for example, restrictions resulting from differences in internal tax levels. On the other hand simplification of checks and other border formalities remains one of the Communities' fundamental objectives. See Bull. 1985–1, 7.

[42] EEC, Art. 30. The same applies of course to exports, see Art. 34.

existing ones during the transitional period, prohibition on the introduction of new ones, etc., applies *mutatis mutandis* to quantitative restrictions.[43] The words "measures having equivalent effect" are of particular importance in this case also for the functioning of the common market since they cover, as the Court ruled "all trading rules[44] enacted by Member States[45] which are capable of hindering directly or indirectly, actually or potentially, intra-Community trade."[46] This formula is not new: similar words were used by the Court in various judgments concerning the interpretation of the Treaty provisions on competition and more specifically the words "which may affect trade between Member States."[47] This similarity is not surprising since the objective pursued by the provisions of Articles 12 to 36 (the customs union) and 85 to 94 (rules on competition) is the same, *i.e.* to guarantee the free movement of goods.

The formula means, in the first place, that the extreme form of hindrance, *i.e.* actual refusal to admit a product, is not required for the prohibition to apply and, in the second place, actual hindrance itself does not have to be proven: the mere existence of a possibility suffices. More simply stated, Article 30 applies when

---

[43] See EEC, Arts. 30 to 35.

[44] This includes rules of a temporary nature, see Case 82/77 *Openbaar Ministerie of the Netherlands* v. *Van Tiggele* [1978] E.C.R. 25 at 40(20).

[45] The explicit reference to Member States does not exclude the Community itself which is also prohibited from enacting such rules, see joined Cases 80–81/77 *Commissionnaires réunis* v. *Receveur des Douanes* [1978] E.C.R. 927.

[46] Case 8/74 *Procureur du Roi* v. *Dassonville* [1974] E.C.R. 837 at 852 (5). The extreme form of hindrance is of course prohibition of imports; the term "restriction" in EEC, Art. 30 must therefore be understood as being the equivalent of the expression "prohibitions or restrictions on imports" occuring in Art. 36, see Case 34/79 *Regina* v. *Henn and Darby* [1979] E.C.R. 3795 at 3812 (12) and 124/81 *Commission* v. *U.K.* [1983] E.C.R. 203, by prohibiting the import of sterilised milk the U.K. infringed Art. 30.

[47] EEC, Art. 85. (See below, Competition Policy, p. 167). See joined Cases 56 and 58/64 *Consten and Grunding* v. *Commission* [1966] E.C.R. 299 at 341, Case 56/65 *STM* v. *MBU* [1966] E.C.R. 235 at 249 and Case 5/69 *Völk* v. *Vervaecke* [1969] E.C.R. 295 at 302. See also Case 120/78 *Rewe* v. *Bundesmonopolverwaltung für Branntwein* ("Cassis de Dijon") [1979] E.C.R. 649 and Case 31/80 *L'Oreal* v. *De Nieuwe AMCK* [1980] E.C.R. 3775 at 3791 (18). See however joined Cases 177 and 178/82 *Officier van Justitie* v. *De Haan*, judgment of April 5, 1984 (not yet published).

the introduction of a product into a Member State is or can be made unnecessarily[48] difficult.

What is new however is the introduction of the "rule of reason" in the implementation of Article 30. In the so-called *Cassis de Dijon* case[49] the Court confirmed that in the absence of common rules, "obstacles to movement [of goods] within the Community resulting from disparities between the national laws must be accepted in so far as those provisions may be recognised as being necessary in order to satisfy mandatory requirements relating in particular to the effectiveness of fiscal supervision, the protection of public health, the fairness of commercial transaction[50] and the defence of the consumers." In other words, although Article 30 prohibits all possible restrictions by Member States on intra Community trade, some obstacles remain justified, even under Article 30. Indeed, this provision by imposing obligations on the Member States at the same time confers rights upon the beneficiaries of this obligation, *i.e.* natural and legal persons within the Community who acquire the right to trade freely between all the Member States. This right however is not unlimited—no right is—and its limitations result from the necessity to satisfy what the Court calls "mandatory requirements"[51] of the public interest. Since the Member States are the guardians of this public interest they may impose measures required to safeguard it; such measures can constitute obstacles to the free movement of goods. But, as the Court put it, the requirements provided in the law or regulations of a given Member State must be proved to serve a purpose which is in the general interest and such as to take precedence over the requirements of the free movement of goods, which constitutes one of the fundamental rules of the

---

[48] This means that there are cases where imports are hindered out of necessity; see below, p. 119, exceptions to the free movement of goods (EEC Art. 36). See also, *e.g.* Case 6/81 *Industrie Diensten Groep* v. *Beele* [1982] E.C.R. 707 where the Court decided that a rule prohibiting the sale of a given good could be considered as being "necessary" to protect consumers.

[49] See n.47 at 662 (8) and (13). See Commission's letter to the Member States setting out its policy conclusions from the guidance given by the Court (J.O. 1980, C. 256/2). See also Case 788/79 *Gilli and Andres* [1980] E.C.R. 2071 and Case 130/80 *Kelderman* [1981] E.C.R. 527.

[50] See Case 58/80 *Dansk Supermarked* v. *Imerco* [1981] E.C.R. 181 and Case 6/81: see n. 48. unfair competition comes under fairness of commercial transactions and not protection of commercial property (Art. 36).

[51] See however Case 238/82 *Duphar* v. *The Netherlands*, judgment of February 7, 1984, (not yet published) where the court admitted an indirect hindrance without referring to mandatory requirements.

Community. In other judgments the Court simply stated that such laws and regulations should be "reasonable."[52]

In all other cases, therefore, restrictions on inter-state trade resulting from the implementation of national rules do come within the prohibition of Art. 30.[53] Such restrictions exist generally speaking in the case of measures which do not apply equally to domestic and imported products, but even measures which do apply equally can have restrictive effects[54]; in such a case the possible influence on trade will be "indirect."

It is also important to note that "a measure caught by the prohibition provided for by Article 30 of the EEC Treaty does not escape this prohibition simply because the competent authority is empowered to grant exemptions, even if this power is freely applied to imported products."[55]

Finally, mention must be made here of restrictions resulting from discriminations in awarding public supply contracts; in this field also specific Community legislation was enacted to prevent the use of public supply contracts to limit the free movement of goods.[56]

3. Exceptions to the free movement of goods

Every rule has its exceptions and they can be found either in the

---

[52] Case 8/74 *Procureur du Roi* v. *Dassonville* [1974] E.C.R. 837 at 852 (6) and Case 104/75 *De Peijper* [1976] E.C.R. 613 at 636 (18).

[53] In numerous cases the Court was called upon to rule on the compatibility with the common market of national laws concerning, *e.g.* fees charged for veterinary inspection (Case 46/76 *Bauhuis* v. *Netherlands* [1977] E.C.R. 20 (51); pricing (joined Cases 16 to 20/79 *Joseph Danis* [1979] E.C.R. 3327; import certificates (Case 25/78 *Denkavit* [1979] E.C.R. 3369); description of origin (Case 27/80 *Fietje* [1980] E.C.R. 3839); licenses (Case 82/77 *Openbaar Ministerie of the Netherlands* v. *Van Tiggele* [1978] E.C.R. 25); regulating the content of a product (Case 130/80 *Kelderman* [1981] E.C.R. 527); requiring that goods imported from other Member States be marked with or accompanied by an indication of origin (Case 207/83 *Commission* v. *U.K.*, judgment of April 25, 1985. For another typical example see Case 16/83 *PRANTL*, judgment of March 13, 1984, and Case 73/84, O.J. 1985, C.106/4.

[54] See Case 13/77 *INNO-ATAB* [1977] E.C.R. 2115 and more recently Case 27/80 *Fietje* [1980] E.C.R. 3839 and Case 53/80 *Officier van Justitie* v. *Kaasfabriek Eyssen* [1981] E.C.R. 409, where the national measure only applied to products intended for the domestic market and not those intended for export; not prohibited by Arts. 30–36.

[55] Case 27/80 *Fietje* [1980] E.C.R. 3839 at 3854 (14).

[56] Dir. 77/62 (J.O. 1975, L. 13/1 and O.J. 1980, L. 215/1).

provisions of the law laying down the rule or in the interpretation of the rule as given by judges.[57]

From the previous paragraphs it follows that the free movement of goods within the Community is the result of three actions: the elimination of customs duties and assimilated charges, the setting up of the common customs tariff and the prohibition of quantitative restrictions and measures having the same effect: all three combine to ensure free intra-Community trade. Title I of Part Two of the Treaty provides for so-called "escape clauses" to the rules concerning application of the common customs tariff and the quantitative restrictions.[58]

As regards the CCT Art. 25 allows exemptions under specific conditions. If the Commission finds that demand for a particular product cannot be satisfied from within the Community and traditionally depends to a considerable extent on imports from third countries,[59] the Council shall grant a Member State tariff quotas at a reduced rate of duty or duty free. The same exemption will be granted by the Commission when shortage of supply within the Community is such as to entail harmful consequences for the processing industries of a Member State.[60] Finally, with regard to agricultural products[61] the Commission may authorise a Member State to suspend in whole or in part collection of the duties applicable or grant reduced or free rates, provided no serious disturbance of the market of the products concerned results therefrom.[62] In this last case the Commission enjoys a wide discretionary power.[63]

Where *quantitative restrictions* are concerned Article 36 provides for several exceptions, consequently national measures which are capable of hindering intra-Community trade and which

---

[57] Exceptions to the basic freedoms constituting the "common market" are provided in EEC, Art. 36 for the free movement of goods, in Art. 48 (3) for the free movement of workers, in Art. 56 for the freedom of establishment, in Arts. 56 and 66 for the freedom to provide services and in Art. 73 for the free movement of capital.

[58] There are therefore no exceptions whatsoever to the rule prohibiting and eliminating customs tariffs and charges with equivalent effect between the Member States; it is the only absolute rule of the EEC Treaty.

[59] EEC, Art. 25 (1).

[60] EEC, Art. 25 (2).

[61] *i.e.* those mentioned in Annex II to the EEC Treaty.

[62] EEC, Art. 25 (3).

[63] See Case 24/62 *Germany* v. *Commission* (wines) [1963] E.C.R. 63 and Case 34/62 *Germany* v. *Commission* (oranges) [1963] E.C.R. 131.

cannot be considered "reasonable"[64] may nevertheless be considered compatible with the common market. The grounds on which import restrictions may be thus justified[65] are according to this provision: public morality,[66] public policy or public security,[67] the protection of health and the life of humans, animals or plants,[68] the protection of national treasures possessing artistic, historic and archeological value,[69] and finally the protection of industrial and commercial property.[70]

Attention must be drawn to the second sentence of Article 36 which is designed to prevent restrictions on trade provided for under the first sentence from being diverted from their proper purpose, and used in such a way as either to create discrimination in respect of goods originating in other Member States or indirectly to protect certain national products.[71]

A final remark concerns the role of the Community institutions in defining the extent of the derogations provided for in Article 36. In this respect, the Court of Justice considered[72] that Article 36 is not designed to reserve certain matters to the exclusive jurisdiction of Member States, but permits national laws to derogate from the principle of the free movement of goods to the extent to which such derogation is and continues to be justified for the attainment of the objectives referred to in that article. Where, in application of Article 100 of the Treaty, Community directives[73] provide for the harmonisation of the measures

---

[64] See above, elimination of quantitative restrictions, p. 118.

[65] According to the Court "justified" means "necessary for the effective protection of the grounds mentioned in Art. 36"; Case 104/75 *De Peijper* [1976] E.C.R. 613 at 636 (16). This is generally speaking not the case when a product has been lawfully produced and marketed in one of the Member States (Case 120/78, see above note 47, 664 (14)).

[66] See Case 34/79 *Regina* v. *Henn and Darby* [1979] E.C.R. 3795 concerning prohibition on imports of pornographic articles.

[67] See Case 7/78 *Regina* v. *Thompson* [1978] E.C.R. 2247: export ban on silver alloy coins.

[68] The Court considers that "health and the life of humans rank first among the interests protected by Art. 36" (Case 104/75 *De Peijper* [1976] E.C.R. 613 at 635 (15)). This ground has given rise to numerous rulings by the Court: see *e.g.* Case 32/80 *Officier van Justitie* v. *Kortmann* [1981] E.C.R. 251.

[69] See Case 7/68 *Commission* v. *Italy* [1968] E.C.R. 423.

[70] See below, Industrial and Intellectual Property Rights, p. 226. See Case 144/81 *Keurkoop* v. *Nancy Kean Gifts* [1982] E.C.R. 2853.

[71] See *e.g.* Case 40/80 *Commission* v. *United Kingdom* [1982] E.C.R. 2793.

[72] Case 5/77 *Tedeschi* v. *Denkavit* [1977] E.C.R. 1555.

[73] *e.g.* Dir. 70/524 (J.O. 1970, L. 270/1; O.J. 1970 (III), 840) and 74/63 (O.J. 1974, L. 38/31).

necessary to ensure the protection of the interests mentioned in Article 36 and establish Community procedures to check that they are observed, recourse to Article 36 is no longer justified.

In the future therefore, when all the necessary directives have been enacted, recourse to Article 36 will be extremely limited[74] as justification for restrictive measures; from then on practically only the rule of reason will constitute a ground for possible derogation to the free movement of goods.

4. Theory and reality of free movement of goods

The elimination of all customs duties and quantitative restrictions and of measures having equivalent effect between the Member States is not sufficient completely to liberalise inter-state trade within the Community. There still are, twenty years after the completion of the common market, border controls everywhere and long queues of trucks and cars still can be seen at each border crossing![75] It is undoubtedly a disconcerting experience for the European citizen.

What explains this state of affairs? Is everything that was explained in the previous paragraphs pure theory or are there other reasons? The answer is not of course a simple one: on the one hand there have always existed, besides the abolished customs duties, quantitative restrictions and assimilated measures, other national rules whose perfectly legal implementation constitutes an obstacle to the free flow of products across national borders[76] and secondly it has not been possible notwithstanding thirty years of Community activities to eliminate all the differences in certain important fields.[77] The national

---

[74] Since it is excluded that Community directives could satisfactorily regulate all possible cases, some room will be left for national initiatives.

[75] According to the European Parliament the total costs of all crossings of these borders now approaches 12,000 million ECU. (See Doc. COM(83)80 final, para. 18).

[76] According to the Commission the most tangible obstacles appear to have been created by interventions by the public authorities—for example, customs procedures, technical barriers, tax barriers, company law, national preference arrangements and state aid at the microeconomic level, and, for instance, currency movements, diverging inflation and interest rates and energy costs dictated by macroeconomic policies (Doc. COM(83)80 final, para. 33).

[77] It should be noted however that several hundred Directives were issued by the Council to harmonise the laws, regulations and administrative provisions of the Member States. See also Eighteenth General Report (1984).

fiscal policies are a case in point. As it is described in another section[78] the EEC treaty does not prescribe unification of the national tax systems; it only prohibits, generally speaking, discrimination in taxation between domestic products and products of other Member States.[79] And although the Treaty does provide[80] that the Council shall "issue directives for the approximation of such provisions laid down by law, regulation or administrative action in Member States as directly affect the functioning of the common market," not much has been achieved in the field of taxation. Consequently there exist wide differences between the Member States in rates of VAT and therefore products imported from another Member State have to be checked at the border in order to determine whether or not VAT was paid and if so whether the rate was the same as the one which is applied in the importing country, precisely in order to avoid discrimination.

It must however be recognized that not all obstacles to the free movement of goods are legally justified. In a recent report to the Council[81] the Commission noted that "the Community has not yet—to any satisfactory extent—achieved its goals with regard to its internal market"[82] and goes on to examine why, notwithstanding considerable achievements, the Customs Union has not yet become a reality. Among the causes mentioned: bureaucratic inertia, short-term considerations take precedence over medium-term advantages and result in open or disguised protectionist measures and the differences in administrative and legislative traditions.[83]

Although the Commission recognizes that many infringements of the Treaty are the result of bureaucratic negligence rather than attempts at protectionism, too many trade barriers and constraints remain which constitute obstacles for firms or individuals wishing to trade beyond their national markets.

The solution won't be easily found, the more so now that the economic crisis puts extra limits on each government's freedom of action and since, with the increase of the number of Member

---

[78] See below, Tax Provisions and VAT, p. 207.
[79] EEC, Art. 95.
[80] EEC, Art. 100.
[81] Doc. COM(83)80 final; see also Bull. EC 2–1983, 15.
[82] *Ibid.* para. 10.
[83] A typical and very topical example being the problems of standardising technical rules (*ibid.* para. 49).

States, it becomes more and more difficult to find agreement. The way suggested by the Commission to overcome these problems is to restore flexibility to the negotiations within the Council and to simplify decision-making procedures.

Further Reading

General: R. Dauphin, "Les effets socio-économiques de la libre circulation des marchandises, personnes, services et capitaux sur les unités membre et la structure intégrative de la CEE: quelques commentaires (mai 1980) Vol. III Rev. d'Int. Eur. 349.

A. Weber, "Die Bedeutung des Art. 115 EWGV für die Freiheit des Warenverkehrs" (1979) Europa-Recht, 30.

P. Oliver, "Recent tax law on art. 37 EEC" (1980) 17 C.M.L. Rev. 251.

H. Kretscher, "Beschränkungen des innergemeinschaftlichen Warenverkehrs nach der Kommissions entscheidung 80/47 E.W.G." (1981) 1 Eur. Heft 63.

J. Donner, "Articles 30–36 EEC in general" (1982) S.E.W. 362.

H. Jehoram, "Articles 30–36 EEC and intellectual property" (1982) S.E.W. 374.

P. VerLoren van Themaat, "La libre circulation des marchandises après l'arrêt "Cassis de Dijon?" (1982) 2–3 Cah. de Dr. Eur. 123.

R. Barents, "New Developments in measures having equivalent effect" (1981) 18 C.M.L. Rev. 271.

Puifferrat, "Pour un renforcement du marché intérieur" (1983) 266 Rev. du M.C. 190.

Mattera, "Les nouvelles formes du protectionisme économique et les articles 30 et suivants du Traité CEE" (1983) 267 Rev. du M.C. 252.

Martin Moyes, "The Trade Description Act 1972 and Article 30 EEC" (1984) 9 E.L. Rev. 161.

II. *Free Movement of Persons*

It was emphasized over and over again by the Court of Justice that this free movement is one of the fundamental freedoms guaranteed by the Treaty; it follows that the Treaty provisions in this field may not be interpreted restrictively and have direct effect,[84] *i.e.* it confers on individuals rights which the national courts must protect.[85] The Treaty distinguishes between wage-earners ("workers"), *i.e.* anyone who pursues an activity as an employed person, and non-wage earners ("nationals of a Member State"). The free movement of workers[86] is mainly based on the principle of non-discrimination on the ground of national-ity, while the freedom of nationals of the Member States to move within the Community is generally speaking expressed by the right of establishment[87] and the right to provide services.[88]

Mention should be made here of the intention of the Member States to introduce a *European passport* with a uniform format which would greatly facilitate the free movement of persons within the Community beside giving the citizens of the Member States a tangible proof of their European citizenship.[89] On June 7, 1984, the Council and the representatives of the Member States in Council adopted a Resolution concerning the simplification of border-crossing formalities for individuals (Bull. 6–1984, 24).

1. Free movement of workers[90]

The freedom of workers to move within the Community can be jeopardised by discriminatory conditions of work and employ-

---

[84] Case 53/81 *Levin* v. *Staatsecretaris van Justitie* [1982] E.C.R. 1035.

[85] Case 41/74 *Van Duyn* v. *Home Office* [1974] E.C.R. 1337 at 1352 and more clearly in Case 48/75 *Royer* [1976] E.C.R. 497 at 512 (31).

[86] EEC, Arts. 48–51, *i.e.* Chap. 1 of Title III of the Treaty.

[87] EEC, Arts. 52–58, *i.e.* Chap. 2; see below, Freedom of Establishment, p. 133.

[88] EEC, Arts. 59–66, *i.e.* Chap. 3; see below, Freedom to Provide Services, p. 136.

[89] See resolutions of the Representative of the Governments of the Member States meeting in Council (J.O. 1981, C. 241/1; 1982, C. 179/1 and 1984, C. 159/1). The European passport was introduced as of Jan. 1985, in Denmark, Ireland and Luxembourg.

[90] For the definition of "worker" see Art. 1 (*a*) of Reg. 1408/71 (J.O. 1971 (II) L. 149/2; O.J. 1971 (II) L. 149, 416). For previous definition see Case 75/63 *Hoekstra* v. *Bedrijvsvereniging detailhandel* [1964] E.C.R. 177. In Case 44/65 *Hessische Knappschaft* v. *Singer* [1965] E.C.R. 965 at 971, the Court held that it would not be in conformity with the ultimate objective of the Treaty on this point "to limit the concept of 'workers' solely to migrant workers *strictu sensu*." The Court also

ment, by obstacles resulting from laws, regulations or administrative practice and by the lack of harmonisation of the social
security systems of the Member States. The Treaty provides for
remedies in all these cases. Discrimination based on nationality
between workers of the Member States has been abolished,[91] so
have administrative procedures and practices which formed an
obstacle to the free movement of workers[92] and the necessary
measures were adopted in the field of social security.[93] Consequently any worker who is a national of one of the Member States
has the right:

(a) to accept offers of employment actually made in other
    Member States; this does not mean that free entry into a
    Community country could be denied to a worker from
    another Member State who does not have a duly executed
    employment contract: freedom of movement also extends
    to persons who "seriously wish to pursue activities as an
    employed person."[94] Furthermore the employment must
    not necessarily be full-employment: freedom of movement
    for workers also concerns persons who pursue an activity
    on a part-time basis and who by virtue of that fact obtain a
    remuneration lower than the minimum guaranteed wage
    in the sector under consideration.[95] The Court also deter-
    mined that the motives which may have prompted a
    worker to seek employment are of no account and must not
    be taken into consideration.[96] Finally it should be noted
    that the EEC rules in this field only apply to workers from

---

indicated that the activity pursued by the "worker" must be an economic
activity (Case 53/81, see n.84 at 1050 (17)). In the same judgment the Court
stated that the concept "worker" may not be defined by reference to the
national laws of the Member States, but has a Community meaning (*ibid.* at
1049 (11)); neither may it be interpreted restrictively since it defines the field of
application of one of the fundamental freedoms guaranteed by the Treaty (*ibid.*
at 1049 (13)).

[91] EEC, Art. 48 (2). See also EEC, Art. 7.
[92] EEC, Art. 49 (*b*).
[93] EEC, Art. 51.
[94] Case 53/81, see n.84, *ibid.* at 1052 (21).
[95] *Ibid.* at 1050 (16); if part-time employment is covered by the freedom of
movement of workers, it does not include activities on such a small scale as to
be regarded as purely marginal and ancillary, *ibid.* (17). See also Case 96/80
Jenkins v. *Kingsgate* [1981] E.C.R. 911 at 925.
[96] Case 53/81, see n. 84, *ibid.* at 1052 (22).

other Member States and not to a worker who is a national of the State concerned[97];

(b) to move freely within the territory of Member States for this purpose. Article 49 requires the Council, acting on a proposal from the Commission and after consulting the Economic and Social Committee, to issue the necessary directives and regulation to bring about by progressive stages the principles embodied in Article 48[98];

(c) to stay in a Member State for the purpose of employment in accordance with the provisions governing the employment of nationals of that State laid down by law, regulation or administrative action.[99] The right to reside in a Member State is not limited to the worker himself but extends to his direct family.[1] Furthermore this extended right is not limited to residence but encompasses the whole treatment afforded national dependants[2];

(d) to remain in the territory of a Member State after having been employed in that State subject to conditions which shall be embodied in implementing regulations to be drawn up by the Commission.[3] This right must be seen as a

---

[97] See, *e.g.* Case 175/78 *Regina* v. *Saunders* [1979] E.C.R. 1129, where the Court held that Art. 48 does not restrict the power of Member States to lay down restrictions, within their own territory, on the freedom of movement of all persons subject to their jurisdiction (at 1135) and Case 180/83 *Moser* v. *Baden-Württemberg*, judgment of July 28, 1984 (not yet published).

[98] See Reg. 1612/68 (J.O. 1968, L. 257/2; O.J. 1968 (II), 475) and Dir. 68/360 (J.O. 1968, L. 257/13; O.J. 1968 (II), 485). See also Reg. 1251/70 (J.O. 1970, L. 142/24; O.J. 1970 (II), 402) concerning the right to reside after termination of employment; see below n. 3.

[99] See Case 8/77 *Sagulo, Branca and Bakhouche* [1977] E.C.R. 1495 at 1504 (8): the issue of a special residence document provided for in Art. 4 of Dir. 68/360 (see above n. 98) has only a declaratory effect and cannot be assimilated to a residence permit such as is prescribed for aliens in general.

[1] See Reg. 1612/68, Art. 10 (see above n. 98) where the worker's family is defined as (a) his spouse and children under 21 or who are dependants and (b) dependent relatives in the ascending line of the worker and his spouse and Dir. 68/360 (see above n. 98).

[2] See Case 9/74 *Casagrande* v. *Landeshauptstadt München* [1974] E.C.R. 773 at 779 (8) concerning education and training facilities available to nationals: to be extended to children of deceased worker who was employed in Germany; Case 13/76 *Dona* v. *Mantero* [1976] E.C.R. 1333, and Case 807/79 *Gravina* v. *Landesversicherungsanstalt Schwaben* [1980] E.C.R. 2205 concerning orphan's benefits.

[3] See Reg. 1251/70 on the right of workers to remain in the territory of a Member State after having been employed in that State (J.O. 1970, L.142/24; O.J. 1970 (II), 402).

corollary to the freedom of movement; it applies both to the worker himself and to his family.

Finally, the Treaty provides that the principle of non-discrimination towards workers from other Member States does not apply to employment in public service, *i.e.* Member States may restrict "admission" to certain activities; discriminatory measures against a worker once he has been admitted cannot be justified on the basis of this provision.[4]

Notwithstanding all the provisions and measures mentioned above, freedom of movement for workers could nonetheless be illusory if by moving from one Member State to another the worker would lose the rights acquired under social security regulations; this applies particularly to pension rights both for the worker and for his family. The Treaty has therefore provided in the adoption of a system ensuring that:

(a) all periods taken into account under the laws of the several countries where the beneficiary has worked will be added together for the calculation of the amount of his benefits;

(b) these benefits will be paid to the beneficiary in whichever Member State he resides.[5]

These Treaty provisions were worked out in two basic Council Regulations[6] which gave rise to numerous judgments in which

---

[4] EEC, Art. 48 (4). See Case 152/73 *Sotgiu* v. *Deutsche Bundespost* [1974] E.C.R. 153 and 149/79 *Commission* v. *Belgium* [1980] E.C.R. 3881 and [1982] 1845.

[5] EEC, Art. 51. During the year 1982 alone the Court of Justice delivered 15 judgments on the interpretation or validity of certain provisions enacted under Art. 51 (Fourteenth General Report (1980) 136).

[6] Reg. 1408/71 (J.O. 1971, L. 149/2; O.J. 1971 (II), 416) amended by Reg. 1390/81 (O.J. 1981, L. 143/1) on the application of Social Security Schemes to employed persons, to self-employed persons and to their families moving within the Community, lastly amended by Reg. 2793/81 (O.J. 1981, L. 275/1). The main provisions concern a broad definition of the persons covered (Arts. 1 and 2): it includes, *e.g.* employed and self-employed persons, stateless persons or refugees residing within the EEC, members of their families and their survivors. The Regulation covers the following branches of social security: sickness and maternity (see *e.g.* Case 41/77 *Regina* v. *Warraj* [1977] E.C.R. 2085 (sickness) and Case 69/79 *Jordans-Voster* v. *Bedrijfsverenignig* [1980] E.C.R. 75 (maternity)), invalidity (see Case 2/72 *Murru* v. *Caisse Régionale d'Assurance Maladie de Paris* [1972] E.C.R. 333), old age (see Case 1/72 *Frilli* v. *Belgium* [1972] E.C.R. 457), survivors (see family benefits), unemployment (see Case 76/76 *Di Paolo* v. *Office National de l'Emploi* [1977] E.C.R. 315), family benefits (see Case 65/81 *Reina* v. *Landeskreditbank Baden-Württemberg* [1982] E.C.R. 33), benefits in respect of

the Court of Justice gave an interpretation which reflects the objectives of freedom of movement for persons. The essential object of these regulations is to ensure that social security schemes governing workers moving within the Community are applied in each Member State in accordance with uniform Community criteria.

On July 1, 1982, several regulations came into effect extending the application of social security schemes to self-employed persons and their families moving within the Community, thereby facilitating the exercise of the right of establishment and freedom to provide services by ensuring that self-employed workers who so wish benefit from the same social protection as non-migrant workers.[7]

The Administrative Commission and the Advisory Committee on Social Security for Migrant Workers were set up by Reg. 1408/71[8] to help the Commission and the Member States with the implementation of the regulations adopted within the framework of the provisions of Article 51.

Exception to the free movement of workers

Article 43(3) which lays down the basic principles determining the free movement of workers contains the words "subject to limitations justified on grounds of public policy, public security or public health." Thus national authorities may invoke these grounds to refuse entry into or residence within their territory and to expel[9] workers who are nationals of other Member

---

accidents at work and occupational diseases (see Case 268/78 *Pennartz* v. *Caisse Primaire d'Assurance Maladie des Alpes-Maritimes* [1979] E.C.R. 2411) and death grants (see Case 22/813 *Regina* v. *Social Security Commissioner (Browning)* [1981] E.C.R. 3357). See also Reg. 574/72 fixing the procedure for implementing Reg. 1408/71 (J.O. 1972, L. 74/1; O.J. 1972 (I), 159), amended several times, lastly by Reg. 2474/82 (O.J. 1982, L. 266/1).

[7] Reg. 1390/81 (see above n. 6).

[8] J.O. 1971, L. 149/2; O.J. 1971, 416, Arts. 80–81 and 82–83 respectively.

[9] See Case 98/80 *Romano* v. *Inami* [1981] E.C.R. 1241. In Case 98/79 *Pecastaing* v. *Belgian State* [1980] E.C.R. 691 the Court declared however that a person against whom an expulsion order has been issued may exercise all the remedies available to nationals in respect of acts of the administration. The remedies have suspensory effect. See also Case 131/79 *Regina* v. *Secretary of State for Home Affairs* [1980] E.C.R. 1585: a recommendation for deportation made under British legislation by a criminal court at the time of conviction may constitute an opinion under Art. 9 of Dir. 64/221.

States.[10] A first attempt to determine the scope of these grounds was made by the Council[11] and further clarifications resulted from the abundant case law of the Court.[12]

2. Freedom of movement of non-wage earners

The Treaty provisions concerning free movement of non-wage earners are to be found under the headings "Right of establishment"[13] and "Services."[14] The right of establishment, in so far as it concerns individuals, includes the right to take up and pursue activities as a self-employed person in another country; it implies that this person moves to another Member State. The right to provide services, on the other hand, concerns nationals of Member States who are established in a State other than the one of the person for whom the services are intended. There is great similarity between the two cases: as in the case of free movement of workers, the Treaty only provides that persons from Member States establishing themselves in another Member State to pursue an economic activity or to provide services therein shall be treated like nationals of that State,[15] *i.e.* application of the

---

[10] See Case 41/74 *Van Duyn* v. *Home Office* [1974] E.C.R. 1337 where the Court upheld the right of the Home Office to refuse leave to enter the U.K. and Case 157/79 *Regina* v. *Pieck* [1980] E.C.R. 2171.

[11] Dir. 64/221 (J.O. 1964, 850; O.J. 1963–1964, 117) on the co-ordination of special measures concerning the movement and residence of foreign nationals which are justified on grounds of public policy, public security or public health. Concerning the direct effect of this Directive see, *e.g.* Case 41/74 *Van Duyn* v. *Home Office* [1974] E.C.R. 1337.

[12] See Case 30/77 *Regina* v. *Bouchereau* [1977] E.C.R. 1999 referring to Dir. 64/221: the Court held that previous criminal convictions do not in themselves constitute grounds for the imposition of restrictions on the free movement provided by Art. 48, unless the personal conduct constitutes a present threat to the requirements of public policy. *Id.* in Case 131/79 (see n. 9 above).

[13] EEC, Part Two "Foundations of the Community," Title III, "Free movement of persons, services and capital," Chap. 2, Arts. 52–58.

[14] *Ibid.* at Chap. 3, Arts. 59–66.

[15] EEC, Arts. 52 (2) and 60. It is interesting to note that in Case 115/78 *Knoors* v. *Secretary of State for Economic Affairs* [1979] E.C.R. 399, the Court determined that the reference to "nationals of Member States" in Art. 52 cannot be interpreted in such a way as to exclude from the benefit of Community law own nationals who want to "establish" themselves in their own country after having resided in another Member State and acquired there trade qualifications which are recognized by Community law; see also Case 246/80 *Broekmeulen* v. *Huisarts Registratie Commissie* [1981] E.C.R. 2311. In regard to the free movement of workers the Court, on the other hand, held that the EEC rules only apply to workers from other Member States; see Case 175/78 *Regina* v. *Saunders* [1979] E.C.R. 1129.

principle of non discrimination between nationals of Member States. Both rights also apply to undertakings, companies and firms although special rules are provided for services in the field of transport, banking and insurance.[16]

Also for both "establishment" and "services" the Treaty provides for the Council, acting on a proposal from the Commission and after consulting the Economic and Social Committee and the Assembly, to draw up a general programme for the abolition of existing restrictions.[17]

Liberal professions present a particular problem because of the required diplomas, certificates and other evidence of formal qualification. The Treaty therefore provides that the Council, on a proposal from the Commission and after consulting the Assembly, shall issue directives for the mutual recognition of such diplomas, certificates and other evidence and issue directives for the co-ordination of the provisions laid down by law, regulation or administrative action in Member States concerning the taking up and pursuit of activities as self-employed persons.[18] The implementation of the Treaty provisions and the

---

[16] EEC, Art. 61. See below, Freedom of Establishment, p. 133 and Freedom to Provide Services, p. 136.

[17] EEC, Arts. 54(1) and 63(1): the two programmes were adopted: for "Establishment" see J.O. 36/62; O.J. Sp. ed. (2nd) IX, 7 and for "Services" see J.O. 32/62; O.J. Sp. ed. (2nd) IX, 3.

[18] Both kinds of Directives (mutual recognition and coordination) are grouped below.

Doctors: Dir. 75/362 (Arts. 3, 5(2), 5(3) and 7(2), amended by Act of accession of Greece: O.J. 1979, L. 291/91) and Dir. 75/363 (O.J. 1975, L. 167/1 and 14). Both were amended by Dir. 82/76 (O.J. 1982, L. 43/21). See Case 246/80, above n. 15. See also decision 75/364 of the Council to set up an Advisory Committee on medical training and a Committee of Senior Officials on public health (O.J. 1975, L. 167/17–19).

Nurses (responsible for general care): Dir. 77/452 (O.J. 1977, 176/1) (amended by Act of accession of Greece (O.J. 1979, L. 291/91)) and Dir. 77/453 (O.J. 1977, L. 176/8).

Dental practitioners: Dir. 78/686 (O.J. 1978, L. 233/1) amended by Act of accession of Greece (O.J. 1979, L. 291/91) and Dir. 78/687 (O.J. 1978, L. 233/10).

Veterinary surgeons: Dir. 78/1026 (O.J. 1978, L. 362/1) amended by Act of accession of Greece (O.J. 1979, L. 291/92) and Dir. 78/1027 (O.J. 1978, L. 362/7). See Cases 271/82, *Auer* v. *Ministère Public* [1983] E.C.R. 2727 and 5/83, *Rienks*, judgment of December 15, 1983 [1983] E.C.R. 4233.

For *doctors, nurses, dental practitioners* and *veterinary surgeons* see Dir. 81/1057 (O.J. 1981, L. 385/25) on the acquired rights of holders of diplomas.

Midwives: Dir. 80/154 (O.J. 1980, L. 33/1) amended by Dir. 80/1273 (O.J. 1980,

above-mentioned directives were, over the past years, the object of numerous requests for interpretation by the Court which considered that, even in the absence of the necessary implementation directives, Articles 52 and 59 have since the end of the transitional period direct effect and the prohibition of discrimination based on nationality which is provided therein can therefore be invoked by nationals of the Member States in any national court or tribunal.[19]

Other activities present similar problems to those encountered by the liberal professions. Both for "establishment" and for "services" the Treaty provides for the Council to draw up a general programme for the abolition of existing restrictions[20]; these programmes set out the general conditions under which freedom of establishment and freedom to provide services is to be attained in the case of each type of activity. These programmes were implemented and further complemented by dozens of Directives laying down detailed provisions concerning transitional measures in respect of activities of self-employed persons.[21]

All the above-mentioned directives concerning both the liberal professions and other activities provide for measures ensuring

---

L. 375/74) following Greek accession and Dir. 80/155 (O.J. 1980, L. 33/8).
Lawyers: Dir. 77/249 (O.J. 1977, L. 78/17), limited to the freedom to provide services.
Carriers of goods and passengers: Dir. 77/796 (O.J. 1977, L. 334/37) and Case 273/82 *Commission* v. *Italy* [1983] E.C.R. 3075.

[19] See *e.g.* the following Cases where the Court upheld the right to practice a liberal profession in another Member State: Case 2/74 *Reyners* v. *Belgium* [1974] E.C.R. 631: Case 71/76 *Thieffry* v. *Conseil de l'Ordre des Avocats de Paris* [1977] E.C.R. 765 and Case 107/83 *Ordre des avocats du barreau de Paris* v. *Klopp*, judgment of July 12, 1984, (not yet published). Case 33/74 *van Binsbergen* v. *Bedrijfsvereniging Metaalnijverheid* [1974] E.C.R. 1299 and Case 11/77 *Patrick* v. *Ministère des Affaires Culturelles* [1977] E.C.R. 1199, concerning the right for a British subject to practice as an architect in France. For illegal exercise of veterinary profession see Case 136/78 *Ministère* v. *Auer* [1979] E.C.R. 437. See Case 246/80 *Broekmeulen* v. *Huisarts Registratie Commissie* [1981] E.C.R. 2311 on the interpretation of Dir. 75/362 concerning Doctors.

[20] J.O. 1962, 32 and 36. These programmes provided for the liberalisation of 123 groups of activities, mostly situated in the industrial and craft sectors.

[21] A complete list of directives can be found in Sweet and Maxwell, *Encyclopedia of European Community Law*, Pt. C 13. See Case 115/78 *Knoors* v. *Secretary of State for Economic Affairs* [1979] E.C.R. 399, concerning conditions for access to and exercise of activities of self-employed persons in manufacturing and processing industries.

freedom in regard to the right of establishment and the right to provide services. These fundamental rights will be examined hereafter.

Further Reading

II. *Free Movement of Persons*

D. O'Keefe, "Practical difficulties in the application of Art. 48 of the EEC Treaty" (1982) 19 C.M.L. Rev. 35.

P. Berckx, "De nationaliteitsvoorschriften voor betrekkingen in overheidsdienst en het vrije verkeer van werkenmers binnen de EEG" (1982) jg. 37 Tijdschr. voor Bestuurswetenschappen en Publiekrecht, Brussel 246.

H. v. Impe, "De nationaliteitsvoorwaarden en het beginsel van het vrije verkeer van werknemers binnen de EEG" (1982) jg. 37 Tijdschr. voor Bestuurswetenschappen en Publiekrecht, Brussel 259.

E. Denza, "Le passeport européen" (1982) 260 Rev. du M.C. 489.

G. Druesne, "Liberté de circulation des personnes, les prolongements de la libre circulation des salaires—droit de séjour et progrès social" (1982) Rev. Trim. de dr. Eur. 556.

Ami Barar, "Court recommendation to deport and free movement of workers in EEC Law" (1981) 6 E.L. Rev. 139.

A. C. Evans, "Entry formalities in the European Community" (1981) 6 E.L. Rev. 3.

III. *Freedom of Establishment*[22]

The right of establishment was briefly examined in the previous section insofar as its exercise is required for freedom for self-employed persons to move within the Community. As was pointed out, this freedom also applies to companies and firms formed in accordance with the law of a Member State and having

---

[22] EEC, Arts. 52 to 58. It should be noted that in pursuance of Art. 66, Arts. 55 to 58 also apply to the matters covered by the Treaty provisions concerning "services," *i.e.* Arts. 59–65.

their registered office, central administration or principal place of business within the Community.[23]

Freedom of establishment includes "the right to take up and pursue activities as self-employed persons and to set up and manage undertakings, agencies, branches or subsidiaries."[24] The abolition of restrictions on freedom of establishment is limited to discrimination based on nationality. In other words, with regard to the right to establish themselves in a Member State in order to pursue economic activities, nationals of other Member States must be treated in the same way as natural or legal persons who are nationals of the host-State.[25] As pointed out above, Article 52 has direct effect[26] even if the Council fails to issue the necessary directives to implement the general programme to attain freedom of establishment or for the mutual recognition of diplomas.[27]

The Treaty provisions concerning the right of establishment and the right to provide services are very similar,[28] but there are differences resulting from the fact that although the actual economic activity carried on by a person or company under both rights might be the same, "establishment" requires a more or less permanent settlement (residence) in another Member State, *i.e.* a base from which services are provided. "Services," on the other hand, can be provided from a "homebase" and might require only occasional temporary entry into another Member State.[29]

Restrictions to the freedom of establishment often result from differences in the laws of the Member States concerning companies. Article 54(3)(g) therefore provides for the co-ordination of the safeguards which are required by Member States of companies and firms for the protection of the interest of members and others. This provision was, from the beginning, widely interpreted by the Commission which embarked back in 1968 on an

---

[23] See EEC, Art. 58(2) for a definition of "company or firm."
[24] EEC, Art. 52.
[25] Of interest in this respect is Case 115/78 *Knoors* mentioned in n. 21.
[26] See above, p. 131.
[27] EEC, Arts. 54(2) and 57(1). See case-law referred to above in n. 19.
[28] See above n. 22.
[29] See, *e.g.* Case 33/74 *van Binsbergen* v. *Bedrijfsvereniging Metaalnijverheid* [1974] E.C.R. 1299.

ambitious programme aiming at harmonising company law in general.[30]

In this context mention must also be made of possible restrictions to the freedom of establishment and to provide services resulting from national procedures regarding public works contracts.[31] Directives were therefore issued by the Council

---

[30] The *first* Dir. 68/151 (J.O. 1968, L. 65/8; O.J. 1968 (I), 41) on the co-ordination of safeguards which for the protection of the interests of members and others are required by Member States of companies within the meaning of Art. 58 concerns *inter alia* disclosure of particulars, validity of obligations entered into on behalf of the company and nullity of companies with limited liability.
The *second* Dir. 77/91 (O.J. 1977, L. 26/1) deals with the formation of public liability companies and the maintenance and alteration of their capital.
The *third* Dir. 78/885 (O.J. 1978, L. 295/36) concerns merger between companies and requires publication to the shareholders of the merger plan, accounts and reports.
The *fourth* Dir. 78/660 (O.J. 1978, L. 222/11) provides for similar legal requirements concerning the financial information that must be made public.
The *fifth* draft Dir. (Commission proposal O.J. 1983, C. 240/2) concerns the structure of public limited companies and the powers and obligations of their organs. The latest amendments of the proposals concern the board structure: Member States have a choice between requiring a two-tier structure with a supervisory and a management board, or giving the companies a choice between a two-tier structure and a one-tier structure (*i.e.* a single administrative board). As for employee participation it is to be regulated by the Member States in accordance with one of four alternative models. (Not to be confused with the so-called "Vredeling" Directive on procedures for informing and consulting employees; see below).
The *sixth* Dir. (O.J. 1982, L. 378/47) provides for required publications prior to admission on a stock exchange.
The *seventh* Dir. (O.J. 1983, L. 193/1) concerns group accounts.
The *eighth* Dir. (O.J. 1984, L. 126/20) on approval of persons responsible for carrying out statutory audits of accounting documents.
See also Dir. 77/187 (O.J. 1977, L. 61/26) on the safeguarding of employers' rights and advantages in the case of mergers, takeovers and amalgamations.
For the above-mentioned draft "Vredeling" Directive see O.J. 1980, C. 297/3. The draft provides for procedures for informing and consulting the employees of transnational companies.
Mention should also be made of the proposals for a uniform European company law, making it possible to set up a "European Company"; see J.O. 1970, C. 124/1.
See also the Convention of February 29, 1968 on the mutual recognition of companies and bodies corporate, whose object is to enable legal persons to avail themselves fully of the Community freedoms; see Bull. Suppl. 2/1969.
[31] For public supply contracts which can constitute restrictions on the free movement of goods prohibited by Arts. 30 *et seq.* see above, elimination of quantitative restrictions, p. 116.

concerning the abolition of restrictions on freedom to provide services in respect of public works contracts and on the award of public works contracts to contractors acting through agencies or branches.[32]

Exceptions to the freedom of establishment

Although it constitutes one of the fundamental principles of the Community, Member States may invoke certain exceptions in order to restrict its implementation. In the first place, the Treaty rules do not apply to activities which in a given Member State are connected, even occasionally, with the exercise of official authority.[33] This exception must however be restricted to those activities referred to in Art. 52 which in themselves involve a direct and specific connection with the exercise of official authority.[34]

Secondly, Member States may under certain conditions apply the provisions laid down by law, regulation or administrative action providing for special treatment for foreign nationals on grounds of public policy, public security or public health.[35]

As will be seen, the same exceptions apply to the freedom to provide services which is examined hereafter.[36]

IV. *Freedom to Provide Services*[37]

As was mentioned in the chapters on free movement of persons

---

[32] Dir. 71/304 (J.O. 1971, L. 185/1; O.J. 1971 (III), 678); this Directive is based upon Arts. 54 (2) and 63 (2). See also Dir. 71/305 (*ibid.* at 185/5 and 682) concerning the co-ordination of procedures for the award of public works contracts based upon Arts. 57 (2), 66 and 100. In regard to the latter see Case 76/81 *Transporoute* v. *Minister of public works* [1982] E.C.R. 417.

[33] EEC, Art. 55 (1). See Dirs. 78/1026 and 78/1027 (O.J. 1978, L. 362/1 and 7) concerning veterinary surgeons; for the first time the Member States declared not to prevail themselves of the possibility to invoke the exception. Under para. 2 the Council may declare the provisions on freedom of establishment non applicable to certain activities: no such declaration exists.

[34] Case 2/74 *Reyners* v. *Belgium* [1974] E.C.R. 631. See also Cases 152/73 *Sotgiu* v. *Deutsche Bundespost* [1974] E.C.R. 153 and 149/79 *Commission* v. *Belgium* [1980] E.C.R. 3881 concerning the interpretation of the similar provisions of Art. 48 (4).

[35] EEC, Art. 56 (1). See Dir. 64/221 (J.O. 850/64; O.J. 1963–1964, 117). Also Dirs. 72/194 (J.O. 1972, L. 121/32; O.J. 1972 (II), 474) and 75/35 (O.J. 1975, L. 14/14).

[36] EEC, Art. 66.

[37] EEC, Part II (Foundations of the Community), Title III (Free movement), Chap. 3, Arts. 59–66.

(non-wage earners) and freedom of establishment, the free movement is a prerequisite for the right to provide services, while many provisions regarding "establishment" also apply to "services."[38] This is the case with those articles providing that companies and firms formed in accordance with the law of a Member State or having their registered offices, central administration or principal place of business within the Community shall be treated as natural persons who are nationals of Member States.[39]

Freedom to provide services applies to nationals of Member States who are established in a State of the Community other than that of the person for whom the services are intended.[40]

The freedom to provide services consists in the right temporarily to pursue activities in the State where the services are provided "under the same conditions as are imposed by that State on its own nationals."[41] This freedom also implies the freedom for the beneficiary of the service to enter another Member State for that purpose without being restricted by limitations imposed on the transfer of payments.[42]

According to the Court the essential requirements of Article 59 of the Treaty became directly and unconditionally applicable at the end of the transitional period[43] and have direct effect.[44]

Freedom to provide a service does not prevent a Member State, because of the particular nature of the service to be provided, imposing also upon persons providing services while established in another Member State specific requirements where they have as their purpose the application of professional rules justified by the general good—in particular rules relating to organisations, qualification, professional ethics, supervision and

---

[38] EEC, Art. 66 provides that Arts. 55 to 58 (Chap. 2 on the Right of establishment) shall apply to the matters covered by Chapter 3 on "Services."

[39] EEC, Art. 58.

[40] EEC, Art. 59.

[41] EEC, Art. 60.

[42] Joined Cases 286/82 and 26/83 *Luisi and Carbone* v. *Ministero del Tesoro*, [1984] E.C.R. 377.

[43] See Case 33/74 *van Binsberge Bedrijfsvereniging Metaalnijverheid* [1974] E.C.R. 1299 and joined Cases 110 and 111/78 *Ministère Public and A.S.B.L.* v. *van Wesemael* [1979] E.C.R. 35 at 52 (26).

[44] *i.e.* must be upheld by national courts and tribunals; see Case 13/76 *Donà* v. *Mantero* [1976] E.C.R. 1333.

liability—which are binding upon any person providing that kind of service.[45]

It is interesting to note that the Court refers to a "single market for services" and the refusal to provide services on a non discriminatory basis to all nationals of Member States constitutes a violation of the Treaty rules.[46]

It was pointed out above, in regard to free movement of goods, that not only direct limitations in the form of customs duties or quantitative restrictions, but also measures with equivalent effect are prohibited,[47] in the same way not only overt discrimination based on the nationality of the person providing the service is contrary to Articles 59 and 60(3) of the Treaty but also "all forms of covert discrimination which, although based on criteria which appear to be neutral, in practice, lead to the same result."[48]

Another parallel can be drawn here, this time with the free movement of persons where according to the Court, the rights provided for in the Treaty apply only to nationals of other Member States[49]: the provisions of the EEC Treaty on freedom to provide services cannot apply to activities whose relevant elements are confined within a single Member State.[50]

It is not clear under the Treaty provisions what kind of activities come within the rules concerning freedom to provide services. As the Court pointed out at a very early stage, the rules of the EEC Treaty only apply to economic activities within the meaning of Article 2[51]; this however does not *per se* exclude any activity. So for instance rules or national practices, even adopted by a sporting organisation can be incompatible with Article 7 and, as the case may be, with Articles 48 to 51 (free movement of persons) or 59 to 66 (freedom to provide services).[52]

---

[45] Case 33/74, above n. 43.
[46] Case 7/82 *G.V.L.* v. *Commission* [1983] E.C.R. 483, where the Court held that such refusal affects trade between Member States (trade in services) which is prohibited by Art. 86 (1).
[47] See above, Free Movement of Goods, p. 111.
[48] Joined Cases 62 and 63/81 *Seco* v. *Evi* [1982] E.C.R. 223 at 235 (8).
[49] See above, Free Movement of Persons, p. 125.
[50] Case 52/79 *Procureur du Roi* v. *Debauve* [1980] E.C.R. 833 at 857 (15). See also Case 62/79 *Coditel* v. *Ciné Vog Films* [1980] E.C.R. 881.
[51] Case 36/74 *Walrave* v. *Union Cycliste Internationale* [1974] E.C.R. 1405 at 1417 (4).
[52] Case 13/76 *Donà* v. *Mantero* [1976] E.C.R. 1333.

It is also important to note that Articles 48, 59(1) and 60(3) have direct effect in the legal orders of the Member States and therefore confer on individuals, rights which national courts must protect.[53]

Exception to the freedom to provide services

The same exceptions apply as those provided for the freedom of establishment,[54] *i.e.* activities which in a given Member State are connected, even occasionally, with the exercise of official authority[55] and limitations resulting from provisions laid down by law, regulation or administrative action providing for special treatment for foreign nationals on grounds of public policy, public security or public health.[56]

Further Reading

III. *and* IV. *Freedom of Establishment and Freedom to Provide Services*

J. Séché, "Le rapprochement des législations destiné à faciliter le droit d'établissement et la libre prestation des services en matière d'assurances" (1981) Cah. de Dr. Eur. 190.

S. Wendling, "La liberté d'établissement et la libre prestation de service dans la CEE; 20 ans de réalisation des programmes généraux de libération de l'établissement et des services" (1982) 255 Rev. du M.C. 132.

E. Steindorf, "Berufsfreiheit für nicht-wirtschaftliche Zwecke im EG-Recht" (1982) Neue juristische Wochenschrift 1902.

Philippe P. Chappatte, "Freedom to provide insurance services in the European Community" (1984) 9 E.L. Rev. 3.

C. W. Nobes, "The harmonisation of company law relating to the published accounts of companies" (1980) 5 E.L. Rev. 38–50.

Jane Welch, "The Fifth Draft Directive—a false dawn?" (1983) 8 E.L. Rev. 83.

---

[53] *Ibid.*
[54] EEC, Art. 66.
[55] EEC, Art. 55, see above under Freedom of Establishment, p. 133.
[56] EEC, Art. 56, see *ibid.*

T. E. Cooke, "The Seventh Directive—an accountant's perspec-
tive" (1984) 9 E.L. Rev. 143.

V. *Free Movement of Capital*[57]

All restrictions on the movement of capital belonging to persons
resident in Member States and any discrimination based on the
nationality or on the place of residence of the parties or on the
place where such capital is invested shall, according to the
Treaty, be progressively abolished. However, the elimination is
only required "to the extent necessary to ensure the proper
functioning of the common market."

According to the Court the scope of that restriction, which
remained in force after the expiry of the transitional period, varies
in time and depends on an assessment of the requirements of the
common market and on an appraisal of both the advantages and
risks which liberalization might entail for the latter, having
regard to the stage it has reached and, in particular, to the level of
integration attained in matters in respect of which capital
movements are particularly significant.[58] It is quite clear therefore
that the provisions concerning free movement of capital have no
direct effect.[59]

The provisions concerning the abolition of restrictions were
implemented by a Council directive requiring Member States to
grant foreign exchange authorisation in respect of various categories of capital movement.[60]

The term "persons" in Article 70 refers both to natural and legal
persons, *i.e.* companies and firms within the meaning of Article
58.

Free movement of capital must be distinguished from the free
movement of payments, the latter being closely connected with
the other basic freedoms in such a way that these basic freedoms
would become inoperative if connected payments were not
liberalized.[61] The same cannot be said of capital movements in
the sense of Article 67.

---

[57] EEC, Arts. 67–73.
[58] Case 203/80 *Casati* [1981] E.C.R. 2595.
[59] For direct effect, see below, Chap. 7, Community Law, p. 257.
[60] See First Directive as amended by the Second Directive (J.O. 1960, 921 and 1963,
62; O.J. 1959–1962, 49 and 1963–1964, 5). These directives were enacted
pursuant to EEC, Art. 69.
[61] See below, Free Movement of Payments, p. 141.

Exceptions to the free movement of capital[62]

If movements of capital lead to disturbances in the functioning of the capital market in a Member State the Commission must authorise it to take protective measures.[63] In cases of secrecy or urgency, the Member State may take such measures on its own initiatives.[64]

It is clear from the foregoing that if the Treaty provisions concerning the free movement of goods, persons, services and the freedom of establishment have reached a fair degree of implementation, the same cannot be said of the provisions concerning free movement of capital. This lack of implementation can be explained by the absence of explicit Treaty obligations, by the monetary difficulties experienced by several Member States and by the fact that notwithstanding the EEC Treaty and the establishment of the European Monetary System,[65] the Member States for whom the control of international capital movements remains an important instrument of their monetary and economic policies, have retained large powers in these fields.[66]

VI. *Free Movement of Payments*[67]

Member States must authorise payments from a debtor in one Member State to a creditor or beneficiary residing in another but only in so far as they are connected with the free movement of goods, services and capital. The freedom to make payments must therefore be distinguished from the freedom to move capital or current payments connected with the movement of capital

---

[62] EEC, Art. 73. See in this respect Dir. 72/156 (J.O. 1972, L. 91/13; O.J. 1972 (I), 296).

[63] See *e.g.* O.J. 1976, L. 268/59 authorizing Italy to maintain certain restrictions. Regarding the U.K. see O.J. 1978, L. 45/30.

[64] From the judgment of the Court in the *Casati* case (see above n. 58) it follows that Member States are free to impose control measures and to enforce such measures by criminal penalties on capital movements and currency transfers on which no Community rules have yet been enacted requiring the Member States to liberalize such transactions (Fifteenth General Report (1981) 306).

[65] See below, p. 214.

[66] See EEC, Arts. 103 (conjunctural policy), 104, 108 and 109 (balance of payments), 105 (economic policies) and 107 (rates of exchange).

[67] EEC, Art. 106.

between Member States.[68] On the other hand, means of payment as such—silver or gold coins—even when they are legal tender in a Member State are not covered neither by the provisions regarding payments nor by those concerning free movement of goods.[69]

The connection referred to between free movement of payments and the other basic freedoms including free movement of persons and freedom of establishment not mentioned in Article 106, is obvious. Indeed, the other freedoms would be quite useless if the financial results from those transactions could not be "repatriated". It follows from this close connection that the freedom to move payments from one Member State to that of the creditor or beneficiary and in the currency of the Member State where the latter resides, also has direct effect, *i.e.* confers upon the nationals of the Member States rights which the national courts must uphold.

In regard to payments for goods, services and capital the national provisions concerning foreign currencies have been progressively abolished.[70] As for obstacles to payments in conjunction with invisible transactions, *i.e.* tourism, transport of goods and persons, publicity, subscriptions, etc. their progressive elimination is done in accordance with the provisions governing the abolition of existing restrictions on freedom to provide services.[71]

Further Reading

V. *Free Movement of Capital*

J. Louis, "Free movement of capital in the community; The Casati Judgement" (1982) 19 C.M.L. Rev. 443.

---

[68] EEC, Art. 67. See above, Free Movement of Capital, p. 140.

[69] Case 7/78 *Regina* v. *Thompson* [1978] E.C.R. 2247; *idem* Case 203/80. See above n. 58.

[70] Dir. 63/340 (J.O. 1609/63; O.J. 1963–1964, 31). The General Programme for the removal of restrictions on the freedom to supply services (J.O. 1962, 32), referred to above n. 17 contains a timetable for the removal of restrictions upon the transfer of funds and payments.

[71] EEC, Art. 106 (3). See Annex III to the EEC Treaty and Dir. 63/474, (J.O. 2240/63; O.J. 1963–1964, 45). See joined Cases 286/82 and 26/83, *Luisi and Carbone* v. *Ministero del Tesoro* [1984] E.C.R. 377.

W. Kiekens, "Het vrije kapitaalverkeer in de EEG" (1982) jg. 46 Bank en Financiewezen.

Michael Petersen, "Capital movements and payments under the E.E.C. Treaty after Casati" (1982) 7 E.L. Rev. 167.

Peter Oliver, "Movement of capital between the Member States. Article 67(1) EEC and the Implementing Directives" (1984) 9 E.L.R. 401.

PART TWO: THE COMMON POLICIES

The provisions concerning agriculture and transport are, in the EEC Treaty, classified in Part Two "Foundations of the Community," while competition, approximation of laws, economic policy, etc., are to be found in Part Three "Policy of the Community." This separation seems unsatisfactory since the proper functioning and development of the common market requires common objectives and common action in all fields of the economy. In this second part the main policies will therefore be examined whether they are provided for by the Treaty itself or were initiated by acts of the Community institutions.

I. *Agriculture*

Although the Treaty specifies[72] that the common market shall extend to agriculture and trade in agricultural products[73] and that, save as otherwise provided, the rules laid down for the establishment of the common market apply to agricultural products,[74] it also provides that the operation and development of the common market for agricultural products must be accompanied by the establishment of a common agricultural policy.[75]

---

[72] EEC. Art. 38 (1).
[73] *i.e.* "Products of the soil: of stock farming and of fisheries and products of first-stage processing directly related to these products (EEC, Art. 38 (1)). These products are listed in Annex II to the Treaty (EEC, Art. 38 (3)). In 1960, a number of products were added to the list, see Third General Report (1960), 209. See also Reg. 7 a) (J.O. 1961, 71; O.J. 1959–1962, 68).
[74] EEC, Art. 38(2).
[75] EEC, Art. 38 (4).

This apparent contradiction between the inclusion of agriculture within the Common Market on the one hand and the conditional operation and development of the Common Market for agricultural products on the other is symptomatic of the particular place agriculture occupies within the Community. It is also indicative of the problems faced by the drafters of the EEC Treaty since, in theory at least, one could have established a common market without agriculture. Some Member States produce more than they consume; others depend heavily on imports. The latter would undoubtedly have preferred to continue to import their food from third countries where these products are much cheaper[76]: there existed from the start a fundamental conflict of interests.

Furthermore, agriculture was, long before the establishment of the Communities, a particular problem in each European country and elaborate and costly national measures to aid agriculture existed everywhere.

Thirdly, agriculture presents some very particular problems which clearly differentiates it from industrial products.[77]

On the other hand however, agriculture constitutes in all the Member States a sector closely linked with the economy as a whole[78] and it is mainly for that reason that the principle of inclusion of agriculture in the Common Market was agreed upon. But, in order to take into account its particular nature, the inclusion took place under special terms: the operation and development of the Common Market for agricultural products was to be accompanied, as pointed out above, by the establishment of a common agricultural policy among the Member States[79] and the necessary adjustments were to be carried out by degrees.[80] In other words, the general rules governing the establishment of the Common Market are to be applied "save as otherwise provided in the Treaty"[81] which means *inter alia* that

---

[76] The U.K. is a case in point.
[77] EEC, Art. 39 (2) (*a*) refers to the "particular nature of agricultural activity which results from the social structure of agriculture and from structural and natural disparities between the various agricultural regions."
[78] EEC, Art. 39 (2) (*c*).
[79] EEC, Art. 38 (4).
[80] EEC, Art. 39 (2) (*b*) and 40 (1).
[81] See, *e.g.* EEC, Art. 42. See also Reg. 26 concerning the application of Arts. 85 and 86; (J.O. 1962, 993; O.J. 1959–1962, 129).

the provisions of the Treaty relating to the common agricultural policy have precedence, in case of any discrepancy, over the rules relating to the establishment of the Common Market.[82] But it also means that in the absence of specific provisions the general rules of the Treaty are fully effective for agricultural products after the end of the transitional period.[83] As for the existing national measures they were to be replaced by a "common organisation of agricultural markets"[84] which took the form of various European market organisations.

THE COMMON AGRICULTURAL POLICY (CAP)

Immediately after the entry into force of the Treaty a conference of the Member States was convened[85] by the Commission with a view to making a comparison of their agricultural policies, in particular by producing a statement of their resources and needs. On the basis of those findings the Commission submitted proposals for a Community policy in the field of agriculture.[86]

As a first step the Council adopted a number of basic principles which were to determine the future orientation of the CAP: free movement of agricultural products within the Community, establishment of a commercial policy jointly with the CAP and a common price level for all agricultural products throughout the Community. The anticipated results were an economic balance between supply and demand (read: self-sufficiency) and fair earnings for those employed in agriculture.[87] With regard to third countries, a uniform system of levies was to be established and, finally, the national measures for structural reforms were to be co-ordinated.[88] It is obvious that all these objectives are not necessarily compatible.[89] After nearly 25 years of operation with

---

[82] Case 83/78 *Pigs Marketing Board* v. *Redmond* [1978] E.C.R. 2347.
[83] Case 48/74 *Charmasson* v. *Minister for Economic Affairs and Finance* [1974] E.C.R. 1383.
[84] EEC, Art. 40 (2).
[85] EEC, Art. 43 (1). The conference was held at Stresa, Italy, in July 1958. See Resolution of the conference in J.O. 281/58 and First General Report (1958), 87 *et seq.*
[86] See Third General Report (1960), 186 *et seq.*
[87] See in this respect the objectives listed in Art. 39 (1).
[88] See Third General Report (1960), 186 *et seq.*
[89] See Case 5/73, *Balkan-Import-Export* v. *Hauptzollamt Berlin-Packhof* [1973] E.C.R. 1091 where the Court found that the various objectives of the common agricultural policy taken separately appear to conflict with one another and that the Community institutions must, where necessary, allow temporary priority to one of them.

outstandingly positive results, the problems created by appalling overproduction in some sectors with the resulting increases in Community expenditure make a revision of the CAP more urgent than ever.[90]

But, back in 1960 the task facing the Community was of a different nature and it was decided to act in two domains: a market and price policy through the establishment of common organisations for agricultural products and a structural policy. Both policies will be examined hereafter.

1. Common organisation of agricultural markets

The establishment of a common organisation of agricultural markets is provided for by the Treaty leaving, however, a choice as to the form such organisation should take.[91] From the onset it was agreed that the common organisation is based on the following principles:

(1) unity of the market: free movement of agricultural products throughout the Community;

(2) Community preference: protection of the common market against low-priced imports from third countries, thereby encouraging consumers to prefer community products;

(3) financial solidarity: the CAP must be totally financed out of Community funds; for this purpose the European Agricultural Guidance and Guarantee Fund was set up.

If a single market for agricultural products was operative at the end of the sixties, the beginning of the seventies was marked by several monetary crises which have resulted in the formation within the EEC of several markets interlinked by a system of monetary compensatory amounts[92] applied to imports and

---

[90] See the communiqué of the European Council held at Stuttgart in June 1983, Bull. 6–1983, 19.

[91] EEC, Art. 40 (2).

[92] Monetary compensatory amounts (mca's) are levies (or refunds) applied by Member States on agricultural products imported (or exported) from (to) other Member States in order to offset the reduction (increase) in the price of those products due to changes in the exchange rates; *e.g.* the re-evaluation of the DM makes German agricultural products non competitive on the French market hence refunds or export subsidies are paid to German farmers; the French products on the other hand become cheaper on the German market, hence levies imposed on those products entering Germany to protect the national production and the income of German farmers.

See Reg. 974/71 on certain measures of conjunctural policy to be taken in

exports within the Community. Several times steps were undertaken by the Commission for their gradual phasing out: until now without much success. However, the setting-up of the European Monetary System on March 13, 1979 was accompanied by an agreement on a so-called "agri-monetary package" including the policy to be followed with regard to the dismantling of existing mca's and the conditions for the creation of new ones following changes in the central rates.

The common organisation of agricultural markets must be limited to the pursuit of the objectives set out in the Treaty[93] and may include all measures necessary to attain them such as regulation of prices, aids for the production and marketing of various products, storage and carry-over arrangements and common machinery for stabilising imports or exports.[94]

The form chosen by the Commission and the Council for the common organisation was the European market organisation[95] and for practically all the agricultural products[96]—potatoes, honey and alcohol are the only exceptions[97]—such a market organisation was set up over the years. It is important to note that once the Community has legislated for the establishment of the common organisation of the market in a given sector, Member

---

agriculture following the temporary widening of the margins of fluctuation for the currencies of certain Member States (J.O. 1971, L. 106/1; O.J. 1971 (I), 257). The system, although contrary to the spirit if not letter of the Treaty, was upheld by the Court (Case 9/73 *Schlüter* v. *Hauptzollamt Lörrach* [1973] E.C.R. 1135 at 1158 (33)).

[93] See EEC, Art. 39.

[94] EEC, Art. 40 (3); an example of special measures is Dir. 75/268 on mountain and hill-farming and farming in less-favoured areas (O.J. 1975, L. 128/1).

[95] EEC, Art. 40 (2) (c). These organisations are "based on the concept of the open market to which every producer has access and which is regulated solely by the instruments provided for by these organisations", Case 83/78 *Pigs Marketing Board* v. *Redmond* [1978] E.C.R. 2347 at 2371 (57).

[96] There are to date 21 market organisations for the following products: fats (Reg. 136/66), cereals (Reg. 2727/75), pigmeat (Reg. 2759/75), eggs (Reg. 2771/75), poultry (Reg. 2777/75), rice (Reg. 1418/76), sugar (Reg. 3330/74), plants and flowers (Reg. 234/68), milk (Reg. 804/68), beef (Reg. 805/68), cider, cocoa, etc., (Reg. 827/68), processed food from vegetables (Reg. 516/77), tobacco (Reg. 727/78), wine (Reg. 317/79), flax and hemp (Reg. 1308/70), fish (Reg. 100/76), hops (Reg. 1696/71), seeds (Reg. 2358/71), fruit and vegetables (Reg. 1035/72), dehydrated fodder (Reg. 1117/78) and goat meat (Reg. 1837/80).

[97] From the end of the transitioned period, existing national market organisations become subject to the general Treaty rules, see Case 68/76 *Commission* v. *France* [1977] E.C.R. 515.

States are under an obligation to refrain from taking any measure which might undermine or create exceptions to it.[98]

The first proposals for a market organisation—for cereals—were submitted to the Council in 1961 and the first regulation setting up a common organisation for the markets in cereals was adopted in 1962.[99] It provided for a transitional period during which the existing national market organisations remained in force and were progressively replaced by the European organisation. The definitive market organisation for cereals was established in 1967. Since this organisation is most typical for the organisation of agricultural markets, it will be examined in some detail below.

Not all market organisations are identical and they can be classified into three groups according namely to the guarantee they offer the producers:

(a) for wheat, coarse grains, sugar and dairy products: a system of target and intervention prices, intervention purchases to be made under certain conditions, within the Community, and external protection in the form of variable levies;

(b) for beef and veal, pigmeat, poultry and eggs, support is offered mainly through external protection;

(c) for fruit, vegetables and wine, where the determinant factor is quality control,[1] only the standardised or graded products will be allowed on the market; in addition, measures to reduce production and a customs duty are applicable.

For a proper understanding of the functioning of the market organisations, the one applying to cereals is examined hereafter in some detail.

The common organisation of the market in cereals.[2] Broadly speaking this organisation is based on a price and a trading

---

[98] Case 83/78, see above n. 95, at 2371 (56).
In this respect it is also important to note that matters not dealt with in the regulations setting up the market organisations are subject to the general rules of the Treaty pursuant to Art. 38.

[99] Reg. 19 (J.O. 1962, 933).

[1] See Case 29/82 *van Luipen* [1983] E.C.R. 151 concerning compulsory membership of a private control-institution.

[2] Reg. 120/67 (J.O. 1967, 2269; O.J. 1967, 33); this regulation was superseded by Reg. 2727/75 (O.J. 1975, L. 281/1).

system. The price system consists mainly of a target price and a basic intervention price, while the trading system is based on a threshold price and an export refund and on import and export licences; in other words the market organisation provides guaranteed prices within the Community and protection against third countries.

As can be seen, "prices" play an essential role in a market organisation[3]; this is because one of the basic ideas is that the income of the farmer should derive from his sales on the market and not from subsidies payed to him by the public authorities (deficiency payments).

The *target price*[4] is the price at which it is expected the cereal can be sold on the Community market during the next marketing year[5] beginning sometime during the next calendar year.[6] It is not a fixed price for the product in question—it does not bind anybody; it is intended to help the farmers plan their production by giving them an indication as to their possible income from the sales of that product.

The target price is established once a year,[7] before August 1, by the Council on a proposal from the Commission and after consulting Parliament.[8]

The *intervention price* is the price at which designated national authorities must buy the cereals offered to them[9]; it constitutes

---

[3] See Case 223/78 *Grosoli* [1979] E.C.R. 2621.

[4] This target price is also a maximum price since, as will be seen, imported cereals can be bought at that price within the Community and are thus competitive at that price level.

[5] A "marketing year" begins after harvest-time; for cereals it runs from Aug. 1 to July 31 of the following year (Reg. 2727/75, Art. 3).

[6] The target price is set ahead of the marketing period and before the "sowing" takes place.

[7] For the 1983/1984 period the common wheat target price was established at 261,41 ECU/Tonne (O.J. 1983, L. 163/1). The target price applies for a standard quality determined by the Council for each cereal; it is fixed for Duisburg (Germany) at the wholesale stage, goods delivered to warehouse, not unloaded. Duisburg was chosen since it is the area with the lowest production of cereals. The target, intervention and threshold prices are subject to monthy increases due to additional storage and other financial costs accruing after the harvest (Reg. 2727/75, Art. 6).

[8] This is the procedure provided for in EEC, Art. 43 (2); it is not required in all cases: the threshold price for instance is established without consultation of Parliament. In practice, all price decisions are taken unanimously.

[9] Reg. 2727/75, Art. 4 (1).

for the farmers the guarantee that their products, in case they cannot sell them on the market at a higher price, will at least be bought at the intervention price which is, of course, lower than the target price.[10] The intervention price is fixed annually,[11] before August 1, simultaneously with the target price by the Council on a proposal from the Commission and after consultation of Parliament.[12]

The *threshold price* is the price fixed for certain cereal products imported from third countries. This is made necessary to protect the Community farmers against cheap, mostly subsidised foreign products. The level at which it is established ensures that for the products imported through Rotterdam, the selling price on the Duisburg market is equivalent to the target price. Since the products have to be transported from Rotterdam to Duisburg, the threshold price is arrived at by deducing from the target price for the Duisburg area the transport costs of cereals from Rotterdam to Duisburg. The threshold price is fixed, for the same standard quality as the target price, by the Council acting by a qualified majority[13] on a proposal from the Commission[14] before March 15, for the following marketing year.[15] Since imported products are generally speaking cheaper than the Community products, a *levy* is imposed on them equal to the difference between the threshold price and the most favourable c.i.f. price at Rotterdam. The levies are fixed daily by the Commission in the form of regulations. By

---

[10] For the 1983/1984 period the common wheat single intervention price was set at 184,58 ECU per tonne (O.J. 1983, L. 163/1) as against a target price of 261,41. Since the target price is set for Duisburg, *derived intervention prices* are fixed for a number of other places (there are about 40 main market centres). The level of these derived prices are set in such a way that the differences between them correspond to the disparities in prices to be expected in a normal harvest, under natural conditions of price formation, thereby allowing for the free movement of cereals within the Community (Reg. 2727/78, Art. 4 (1)). Duisburg being the area with the lowest production, the price there will be higher than in areas of high production; all the other market centres have a lower intervention price (*ibid*. para. 4).

[11] For a standard quality at the wholesale stage; see above n. 7.

[12] See above n. 8.

[13] In practice this decision is taken unanimously.

[14] Reg. 2727/75, Art. 5 (5); note the difference with the procedure for fixing the target and intervention prices, see above n. 8.

[15] See nn. 7 and 9.

thus making imported products at least as expensive as (if not more so than) Community products, the consumer will give preference to the latter (Community preference), although he pays a higher price than he normally would on the world market. This is a clear case where the short-term interest of the consumer runs counter to the long-term necessity for an efficient and competitive European agriculture. Since self-sufficiency is one of the objectives, farmers have to be "kept alive" during the time required for restructuring farming in Europe.

Export *refunds*[16] are provided to enable producers to export their surplus cereals on the world markets where, as was pointed out, agricultural prices are generally speaking lower than in the Community. Refunds are the same for the whole Community and may vary according to use or destination; they are equal to the difference between quotations or prices on the world market and Community prices; they are fixed at regular intervals by the Commission after consultation with a Management Committee. Such a Committee was set up within each market organisation to allow the Member States to follow at close hand the implementation of the agricultural policy without imposing the heavy procedure of formal Council decisions, but providing nonetheless the possibility of bringing a matter before the Council in case of disagreement with a Commission decision.[17]

Finally, *import and export licences*[18] are required for all imports into or all exports from the Community; they are issued by the Member States to any applicant irrespective of his establishment in the Community. They were established mainly for statistical purposes.

The implementation of a common market organisation requires an administrative machinery which the European Commission does not possess; this task was therefore entrusted to the existing bodies of the Member States.[19] Not only are import and export licences delivered by the national authorities, but they also collect the levies[20] and pay the refunds.[21] Similarly, the

---

[16] Reg. 2727/75, Art. 16.

[17] For the Management Committees, see above, p. 49, n. 7.

[18] See Case 109/82 *Interagra* v. *FORMA* [1983] E.C.R. 127.

[19] See Case 217/81 *Interagra* v. *Commission* [1982] E.C.R. 2233.

[20] See joined Cases 178, 179 and 180/73 *Belgium and Luxembourg* v. *Mertens* [1974] E.C.R. 383.

[21] See Case 167/82 *Nordgetreide* v. *Hauptzollamt Hamburg-Jonas* [1983] E.C.R. 1149. See also Case 217/81 *Interagra* v. *Commission* [1982] E.C.R. 2233.

purchase of agricultural products at the intervention prices is the responsibility of the national intervention offices. In case of conflict concerning the application of the Community measures, responsibility lies with the Member States, not with the Community institutions,[22] even now that the agricultural levies have been attributed to the Community as own resources. The responsibility of the Community for all legislative acts in the agricultural field of course remains.[23]

2. Social-structural policy in agriculture

One of the objectives assigned to the CAP is "to increase agricultural productivity by promoting technical progress and by ensuring the rational development of agricultural production and the optimum utilisation of the factors of production, in particular labour."[24] The common organisation of agricultural markets described above aims at a market equilibrium through prices and trade systems; they do not, however, constitute a solution for the fundamental problems of agriculture within the Community[25]; at the most they are a palliative, providing a temporary breathing space needed to carry out the required structural reforms, or as the Commission pointed out: the question of agricultural incomes cannot be dealt with exclusively by a price policy.[26]

Seeking a more durable solution, the Commission submitted to the Council in 1968 a "Memorandum on the Reform of Agriculture in the EEC" (Agriculture 1980).[27] Two and a half years later the Council adopted a Resolution on new guidelines for the common agricultural policy[28] closely following the measures

---

[22] See Case 46/75 *IBC* v. *Commission* [1976] E.C.R. 65 and Case 250/78 *DEKA* v. *EEC* [1983] E.C.R. 421.

[23] See *e.g.* Case 238/78 *Ireks-Arkady* v. *Council and Commission* [1979] E.C.R. 2955.

[24] EEC, Art. 39 (1) (*a*).

[25] These problems result mainly from (1) a large and ageing agricultural population (increased by the accession of Greece), (2) the limited size of the average farm which makes mechanization difficult and (3) outdated production and marketing methods. In regard to the latter, see Reg. 355/77 (O.J. 1977, L. 51/1).

[26] Seventh General Report (1973), 247.

[27] An analysis of this document also referred to as the "Mansholt Plan" is given in the Second General Report (1968), 135. It can be summarised as follows: starting from (1) the social-economic situation in the Community's agriculture, the Memorandum sets out (2) the aims of an agricultural policy, (3) the concrete measures to be taken and (4) an estimate of the costs.

[28] J.O. 1971, C. 52/1.

proposed in the Memorandum. In the same Resolution the Council stated that state aids in conflict with the common measures should be eliminated and considered that success in the agricultural field depended on progress made in other domains, such as economic and monetary union, regional policy and social policy. The Resolution was implemented by several directives establishing the basic principles for joint action by the Community and the interested Member States in the socio-structural field.

The *first directive*[29] on the modernisation of farms, provides for the introduction by Member States of a system of selective incentives to farms where the farmer practises farming as his main occupation. To qualify for the incentives, the farmer must draw up a plan for the development of the farm business which shows that upon implementation of the plan, the modernised farm will be capable of providing for one or two persons the same revenue as that which is enjoyed by persons employed in non-agricultural work in the same region.

The *second directive*[30] concerns measures to encourage the cessation of farming and the reallocation of land for structural improvement. It provides for the grant of an annuity or a lump sum payment to those farmers aged between 55 and 65, who have practised farming as their main occupation and leave the land. At least 85 per cent. of the land released in this manner must be made available either to farmers benefiting from the first directive or reallocated for afforestation, recreational activities, public health or other purposes.

The *third directive*[31] provides for vocational retraining of persons engaged in agriculture who wish to take up an occupation outside agriculture.

Member States were given a year (until April 20, 1973, extended to December 31, 1973) to implement these directives,[32] and the draft of the implementing measures had to be submitted to the Commission for its opinion.

---

[29] Dir. 72/159 (J.O. 1972, L. 96/1; O.J. 1972, 324). See Case 107/80 *Cattaneo Adorno* v. *Commission* [1981] E.C.R. 1469.

[30] Dir. 72/160 (J.O. 1972, L. 96/9; O.J. 1972, 332).

[31] Dir. 72/161 (J.O. 1972, L. 96/15; O.J. 1972, 339).

[32] See Case 113/82 *Commission* v. *Germany* [1983] E.C.R. 1173. In 1973, the Council adopted a directive for the regional differentiation of certain measures provided for in the three above-mentioned directives (Dir. 73/440, O.J. 1973, L. 356/85).

Mention should also be made of a directive on mountain and hill farming in certain less-favoured areas,[33] which together with the three other directives constitutes the basic provision for socio-structural reform in agriculture.[34]

The directives were only relatively successful, particularly in the less-developed regions which are most in need of structural reform. In order to improve the results the directives were complemented by a whole series of other structural measures[35] and amended by adapting some implementing conditions to the particularities of backward areas[36]

3. Financing the CAP

The principle of financing the expenditure resulting from the implementation of the measures referred to above, both in the market and price field and for socio-structural policy, has always been that the financial consequences should be borne by the Community.[37] For this purpose the European Agricultural Guidance and Guarantee Fund which forms part of the Community budget was established.[38] In 1985, the total appropriation for commitments in agriculture amounted to about 18 billion ECU,[39] *i.e.* 65.91 per cent. of the total budget of about 28 billion ECU.

4. Future of the CAP

Every year the CAP absorbs between 60 and 70 per cent. of the Community's budget leaving little room for other Community

---

[33] Dir. 75/268 (O.J. 1975, L. 128/1).

[34] For other structural measures see Twelfth General Report (1978), 181. See also Thirteenth General Report (1979), 162.

[35] For other structural measures see Twelfth General Report (1978), 181; see also Thirteenth (1979), 162 and Sixteenth General Report (1982), 177.

[36] Dir. 72/159 was amended by Dir. 81/528 (O.J. 1981, L. 197/41) and Dir. 72/161 by Dir. 81/529 (*ibid.* at 44).

[37] Reg. 25, Art. 2 (2) (J.O. 1962, 991; O.J. 1959–1962, 126).

[38] See above, Financing Community Activities, p. 81.

[39] Those 18 billion ECU approx. are distributed as follows among the main activities of the agricultural fund:
  1. Support for agricultural markets (Guarantee) .... 18 Billion ECU
  2. Structural measures (Guidance + specific measures) .... 655,967,700 ECU
  3. Fisheries .... 154,481,400 ECU
In 1985 the total amount is about 19 billion ECU, *i.e.* 66 per cent. of the EEC budget.

policies. Furthermore the expenditure of the CAP is unevenly distributed over the Member States and paradoxically, the richer Member States are collecting most of the resources of the agricultural fund.

From 1974 to 1979 expenditure on supporting agricultural markets grew by 23 per cent. per year. After a relative stabilisation in 1980–1982 largely because of a favourable situation on world markets, expenditure started rising again; in the first half of 1983 farm spending was up a frightening 40 per cent. over the year before! Clearly, something must be done. The Community has come to rely more and more on subsidised exports and on subsidized sales in Member States in order to dispose of its growing production. And with demand likely to increase less rapidly than in the past because of the economic crisis and a lower rise in population, the situation is likely to get worse. Furthermore, thanks to scientific research and development, there is a constant improvement in crops and breeds of animals, machinery and techniques; this has led, *e.g.* in the case of animal production to the setting up of agricultural enterprises for which land is no longer a limiting factor. This development has aggravated the danger of overproduction which has been experienced particularly in the dairy sector: between half and two-thirds of total Community output of butter and skimmed milk powder is disposed of at high rates of subsidy. The Community tried to stem the worsening of this situation by imposing a 2 per cent. levy, the so-called "co-responsibility levy."[40] But it was in vain.

In 1982 the Commission submitted to the Council a memorandum on the adaptation of the CAP: "Guidelines for European agriculture,"[41] with a view to curbing increases in the cost of the policy and at the request of the European Council held at Stuttgart in June 1983 the Commission presented a report and proposals concerning the "Adjustment of the common agricultural policy."[42] In this document the Commission states that the CAP has had considerable success but that Europe must adapt its agricultural policy and that this is not a technical affair,

---

[40] Community Report, Vol. 3, n. 7, 2–3. On the legality of the levy see Case 138/78 *Stölting* v. *Hauptzollamt Hamburg-Jonas* [1979] E.C.R. 713: is legal.

[41] Bull. Suppl. 4/81, Memorandum supplementing the Commission's report on the mandate of May 30, 1980. See also "Further guidelines for the development of the CAP," Bull. 6–1983, 60.

[42] Bull. Suppl. 4/83.

but a political challenge. It also points out that the budgetary costs of the CAP are a consequence of the measures adopted to implement its social and economic objectives. For these reasons, the adaptation of the policy cannot be made according to exclusively budgetary criteria, but rather with the aim of fulfilling the fundamental objectives in the most cost-effective way. If it cannot be the Community's aim to stop the development of its agriculture, it has no choice but to adapt its policy of guarantees for production: hitherto the price guarantees for most products have been unlimited; this situation cannot continue and therefore the market organisation will have to be adapted. In other words, Europe's agricultural producers will have to participate more fully in the cost of disposing of production beyond a certain threshold. What the Commission now proposes is to limit the guarantees offered by the CAP; this could be done in various ways: (a) lowering the yearly increase in the intervention price if production exceeds a global quantum; (b) limiting the aid paid under the market regulation to a global amount; (c) participation of producers, by means of a levy, in the cost of disposing of additional production or in the cost of net exports or, (d) production quotas at national level, or at the level of the enterprise.

Alongside the introduction of guarantee thresholds, the Commission considers it necessary to pursue a restrictive price policy.

Finally, the Community will have to revise its agricultural trade policy along the following lines: international co-operation, the development of an export policy and revision of the external protection system in those cases where the Community is taking measures to limit its own production.

As can be seen the fundamental elements of the CAP as set out in this section remain, but their implementation will be radically changed in some respects. No doubt this will hurt, but as for many other sectors, it becomes unavoidable to modify legislation that was enacted under totally different economic circumstances.

Further Reading

PART TWO. THE COMMON POLICIES

I. *Agriculture*

Annual Commission Report on the agricultural situation in the Community.

G. Berardis, "The Common organisation of agricultural markets and price regulations" (1980) 17 C.M.L. Rev. 539.

F. Kouloussi, "Vers une politique commune des structures agricoles" (1982) 254 Rev. du M.C. 89.

Dr. P. Tiedemann, "Rechtsprobleme der Agrarmarktintervention" (1980) Heft 3 Europarecht, 15. 219.

C. Megret, "Chronique agricole" (1982) 3 Rev. Trim. de Dr. Eur. 568.

M. Tracy, "L'agriculture et le développement régional" (1982) 255 Rev. du M.C. 120.

S. Neri, "la jurisprudence de la Cour de Justice relative à l'application de la législation agricole communautaire" (1982) 5–6 Cah. Dr. Eur. 507.

P. Gilsdorf, "The system of monetary compensation from a legal standpoint" (1980) 9 E.L. Rev. 341 and 433.

II. *Fisheries Policy*

Although fisheries is undoubtedly part of "Agriculture,"[43] it has acquired a momentum of its own and is therefore generally considered as an autonomous policy. Since the 1939–1945 war, fisheries products have established themselves as an important food resource. The sector provides only 250,000 jobs in the Community, compared with 8.5 million in agriculture, but the industry is of crucial economic importance in many otherwise disadvantaged coastal areas.[44]

However, it was not until 1970 that the first decisions concerning fisheries were taken:

---

[43] See Case 141/78 *France* v. *United Kingdom* [1979] E.C.R. 2923. As was pointed out in the section on the Agricultural policy, the Treaty provisions concerning agriculture (EEC, Arts. 39 to 46) apply to the products listed in Annexe II to the Treaty; this list includes "Fish, crustaceans and molluscs." Since fish is subject to the Treaty provisions on agriculture, a common policy is likewise required (See EEC, Art. 38(4)).

[44] "The Common Fisheries Policy," European File, 11/83; this publication was largely used for writing this section.

1. The principle of common access to all fishing grounds in the Community was established[45];
2. A common market organisation for fish was set up, based on the establishment of producer organisations and the operation of price support mechanisms and protection for the Community market[46];
3. Co-ordination of the structural policies of the Member States with financial help from the Community[47] with a view to modernising the Community fishing fleets.[48]

The basic principle of common access was adopted subject to a five-year derogation in a three mile zone of coast where the local population was heavily dependent on inshore fishing for its means of livelihood.[49] The Council was also empowered to adopt the necessary conservation measures in cases where there was a risk of over-fishing in a Member State's coastal waters.[50] This structure was modified following enlargement of the Community to Denmark, Ireland and the United Kingdom since the fisheries' interests of these countries were rather different from those of the original members.

For a ten-year period, until the end of 1982, Member States were authorised to restrict fishing in waters under their sovereignty or jurisdiction, situated within a limit of six nautical miles, to vessels which fish traditionally in those waters and which operate from ports in that geographical coastal area.[51] It was provided also that the Council would decide on the provisions which would become applicable after December 31, 1982 on the basis of proposals from the Commission and a report on the economic and social development of coastal areas and the state of the stocks.[52] By that time, however, the state of affairs in the fisheries sector had radically changed.

---

[45] See Reg. 2141/70 (J.O. 1970, L. 236/1; O.J. 1970 (III), 703) based upon EEC, Arts. 42 and 43 but also 7 and 235. This Reg. was superseded by Reg. 101/76 (O.J. 1976, L. 20/19), Art. 2 (1).

[46] See Reg. 2142/70 (J.O. 1970, L. 236/5; O.J. 1970 (III), 707), superseded by Reg. 100/76 (O.J. 1976, L. 20/1) and by Reg. 3796 81 (O.J. 1981, L. 379/1).

[47] Between 1971 and 1982 this help amounted to 200 million ECU.

[48] Reg. 2141/70, see above n. 45.

[49] *Ibid.* Art. 4.

[50] *Ibid.* Arts. 2(1) and 5.

[51] Act of accession, Arts. 100(1) *et seq.*

[52] *Ibid.* Art. 103.

From 1975 on, a number of countries on the Atlantic coastline extended their exclusive national fishing zones to 200 miles. This limit had been endorsed by the International Convention on the Law of the Sea. Consequently the Member States of the Community also extended their fishing limits with effect from January 1, 1977 to 200 miles off their North Sea and North Atlantic coasts.[53]

The extension of fishing limits all over the world is closely linked with the exhaustion of fish stocks which first became a problem in the early 1970's. Indeed, since the European fishing fleets were excluded from distant rich fishing grounds, they had to fall back on their national fishing zones which increased competition and the risk of overfishing. It is only by strict conservation measures that large catches at reasonable cost can be guaranteed in the future.

It is obvious that the establishment of a common fisheries policy became urgent and vital for the Community fishing industry which is also faced with strong competition from third countries. After years of discussion, such a policy was finally agreed upon[54]: it has four main spheres of operation which are briefly examined hereafter:

1. Access to fishing grounds and conservation of stocks

All waters within the community 200-mile zone are, in principle, open to all Community fishermen, but Member States may reserve fishing to their own fleets and those with traditional rights within a 12 mile limit.[55]

The conservation and management of Atlantic and North Sea fish stocks is controlled by the fixing of total allowable catches (TACs) fixed annually by the Council for all species threatened by overfishing and by technical conservation measures such as authorized mesh sizes, areas where fishing is prohibited, etc. The TACs are divided into national quotas according to an agreed upon key based upon traditional fishing activities, the specific needs of regions which are especially dependent on fishing and

---

[53] See Council Resolution of November 1976 on "Certain External Aspects of the Creation of a 200 miles Fishing Zone in the Community" (O.J. 1981, C. 105/1 and Bull. 10–1976, 23 *et seq.*).

[54] The agreement was reached on January 25, 1983; see Bull. 1–1983, 7 and the principal regulations published in O.J. L. 24 of January 27, 1983.

[55] Such rights are defined, in each case, by Article 6 of Reg. 170/83 (O.J. 1983 L. 24/1). See also Regs. 171/83–181/83 (*ibid*).

the loss of fisheries in the waters of non-member countries.[56] Member States are no longer entitled to exercise any power of their own in the matter of conservation measures in the waters under their jurisdiction.[57]

2. Community market organisation

In the section on agriculture[58] it was pointed out that the common market for agricultural products must be accompanied by the establishment of a common agricultural policy among the Member States[59] and that the CAP was to take the form of European market organisations.[60] Such an organisation was set up for fish in 1970[61] and radically revised in 1981.[62] The main features of this market organisation for fish concern marketing standards, producer organisations, a price system with guide and withdrawal prices and an external trade policy.

3. Structural policy

The first rules laying down a common structural policy for the fishing industry were enacted in 1970.[63] Following enlargement, a new regulation was adopted in 1976.[64] These provisions enabled the Community financially to support through the

---

[56] See Arts. 3 and 4 of Reg. 170/83 (see Case 63/83 *Kirk*, judgment of July 10, 1984, (not yet published)), and Reg. 172/83 (O.J. 1983 L. 24/30) concerning TACs and quotas, and Reg. 171/83 (O.J. 1983, L. 24/14) amended by Reg. 2931/83 (O.J. 1983, L. 288/1) concerning technical measures. See also Reg. 2057/82 establishing certain control measures for fishing activities by vessels of the Member States (O.J. 1982, L. 220/1) amended by Reg. 2931/83 (O.J. 1983, L. 288/1). See also Commission declaration concerning duty of Member States in absence of Council Decision (O.J. 1982, C. 199/2) and annual General Reports.

[57] Except in complementing and implementing Community measures and for local stocks, see Art. 5 Reg. 170/83, Arts. 19 and 20 Reg. 171/83 and Art. 14 Reg. 2057/82. See Case 21/81 *Openbaar Ministerie* v. *Bout* [1982] E.C.R. 381 at 388 (6): the power to adopt measures relating to conservation has belonged fully and definitively to the Community since the expiration on January 1, 1979 of the transitional period laid down by Art. 102 of the Act of Accession.

[58] See above, Agriculture, p. 143.

[59] EEC, Art 38 (4).

[60] EEC, Art 40 (2) (*c*).

[61] Reg. 2142/70 (J.O. 1970, L. 236/5; O.J. 1970 (III) 707) and Reg. 100/76 (O.J. 1976, L. 20/1). See Eighteenth General Report (1984), 189.

[62] O.J. 1981, L. 379/1; this regulation became fully applicable on January 1, 1983.

[63] Reg. 2141/70 (J.O. 1970, L. 236/1; O.J. 1970 (III), 703).

[64] Reg. 101/76 (O.J. 1976, L. 20/19).

agricultural fund fish processing and marketing development projects, building of inshore fishing vessels, refitting vessels and creation or extension of fish farming schemes.

On the other hand the European Regional Development Fund[65] and the European Investment Bank offer grants and loans respectively for infrastructure investments, such as harbours, processing factories, ships and research centres.

Much more is needed, however, and in October 1983 the Council agreed on two Regulations and one Directive for a three year programme of measures[66] (1) to adjust capacity by laying up temporarily or permanently certain fishing vessels, (2) for re-deployment of the Community fishing capacity and (3) to encourage investment, *i.e.* construction and modernization of certain fishing vessels, aquaculture facilities and installations to facilitate restocking and develop the fishing industry generally.

4. External arrangements

Since 1976 the Community has been exclusively competent to handle international fishing negotiations. Fishing agreements were signed with a number of third countries[67] in order to safeguard traditional fishing rights of Community vessels or seek new opportunities.

Multilateral agreements have also been concluded with a view to the Community's participation in the international agreements covering the North-West, North-East, East, Central and South-East Atlantic, the Antarctic salmon in the North Atlantic Ocean,[68] fishing and conservation of the living resources in the Baltic Sea and the Balts. and in the Antarctic.[69]

---

[65] The ERDF spent 9.6 million ECU on the fishing industry in 1981–1982.

[66] Regs. 2908 and 2909/83 and Dir. of Oct. 4, 1983 (O.J. 1983, L. 290/1, 9 and 15).

[67] *e.g.* Norway, Sweden, the Faeroes (O.J. 1983, L. 115/1), Spain (O.J. 1983, L. 30/1), the U.S., Canada and several developing countries (Senegal, Guinea, Guinea-Bissau, Equatorial Guinea (O.J. 1983, L. 237/13) and Sao Tome: O.J. 1985, L. 114/51). See Case 812/79 *Attorney General* v. *Burgoa* [1980] E.C.R. 2787 concerning the interpretation of Art. 234 and the compatibility of the rules concerning the conservation of fishery resources with international law, and especially the London Fisheries Convention of 1964.

[68] O.J. 1982, L. 378/24. The Convention for the conservation of salmon entered into force on October 1, 1983 (O.J. 1983, L. 282/63).

[69] O.J. 1983, L. 237/5 and Eighteenth General Report (1984), 188.

It might be interesting at this point to quote a Commission publication:

> "After seven years of tough negotiations, the common fisheries policy has taken its place as a fully-fledged Community policy. It was not an easy achievement. A great deal of effort and good will was needed on all sides. The ultimate success of the negotiations proves that it is possible to reconcile differences of view and allow the common European interest to prevail. A new European policy has been born. This is an important sign that, slowly, step by step, the construction of Europe is proceeding."[70]

Further Reading

II. *Fisheries Policy*

C. Swords, "The external competence of the EEC in relation to international fisheries agreements" (1979) 2 Leg. ISS. Eur. Integr. 31–64.

R. Churchill, "Revision of the EEC's Common Fisheries Policy" (1980) 5 E.L. Rev. 1–37, 95–112.

R. White, "Fishing rights of non-Member States in Community waters" (1981) 6 E.L. Rev. 398–402.

M. E. Martins Ribeiro, "Compétence communautaire et compétence nationale dans le secteur de la pêche" (1982) 2–3 C. de Dr. Eur. 144.

D. Booss, "La politique commune de la pêche, quelques aspects juridiques" (1983) Rev. du M.C. 269, 404.

III. *Transport Policy*

On January 22, 1983 the Parliament brought before the Court of Justice an action against the Council for failure to act in the field of transport.[71] Parliament's aim is to obtain from the Court a declaration that the Council has failed to fulfil its obligation to

---

[70] European File, 11/83, 7.
[71] Case 13/83 *Parliament* v. *Council* (O.J. 1983, C. 49/9). Bull. 1–1983, 35. This step constitutes the final stage in the procedure instituted under EEC, Art. 175 by a resolution of Parliament (O.J. 1982, C. 267/62).

take steps called for by the Treaty to establish a common transport policy. This parliamentary reaction is indicative of the state of affairs in the field of transport, which, as will be seen, is rather unsatisfactory.

Together with the basic freedoms and agriculture, transport constitutes the "Foundations of the Community."[72] However transport is basically a service, and could therefore, when carried out in another Member State, come within the ambit of the provisions concerning the freedom to provide services. It was therefore found necessary to provide that this field "shall be governed by the provisions of the Treaty relating to transport."[73]

What did the drafters of the Treaty mean when they referred to the "distinctive features of transport?"[74] Most kinds of transport require heavy investments which, due to widely varying demand, often remain idle and unproductive for long periods. There is an enormous discrepancy between the infrastructure needed for various means of transport: some, like railways and inland shipping, need a specially designed infrastructure, while others, like road transport, use the road network jointly with millions of other users; another characteristic is that some means of transportation are in the hands of the State and are forced to offer services which are not economically justifiable. But whether nationalised or not, all forms of transport are subject to severe requirements with regard to public safety. Finally, air and sea transport, extending far beyond the limits of the Community, are the object of many international agreements and regulations.

On the other hand, transport is a necessary complement to the basic freedoms: free movement of goods would remain ineffective if transport conditions were discriminatory; the same applies to the freedom to offer services and, to a certain extent, the free movement of persons. Notwithstanding its particularities, transport is therefore an inherent part of the common market.

---

[72] No particular meaning should be attached however to this classification: the competition policy and the social policy which are to be found in Part Three of the Treaty play as fundamental a role in the EEC. However, agriculture and transport are the only "economic" activities which are explicitly regulated in the Treaty.

[73] EEC, Art 61(1). See Case 167/73 *Commission* v. *French Republic* [1974] E.C.R. 359.

[74] EEC, Art. 75 (1).

Implementation.[75]

Article 84(1) provides that the Treaty provisions concerning transport only apply to "transport by rail, road and inland waterway." It is in this well-defined field that the Council is required to develop a common transport policy comprising common rules for transport between the Member States, conditions allowing non-resident carriers to operate transport services in other Member States and all other appropriate measures.

The Commission at first proposed to the Council the adoption of general principles covering all aspects of a common transport policy.[76] It soon appeared, however, that a global approach was not politically possible and that the only way to obtain at least some results, would be to proceed gradually by presenting packages of concrete proposals which would allow the Council to reach compromises gained by limited mutual concessions. During the past 10 years, the approach to working out a common transport policy has become increasingly pragmatic and it has been possible to work out at least some practical solutions to problems currently affecting transport. A first step was a procedure for prior examination and consultation in respect of certain laws, regulations and administrative provisions of the Member States.[77]

The Community rules enacted so far concern mainly access to the market and rates, and conditions of carriage.[78] In regard to the latter, the Treaty specifically prohibits discrimination which takes the form of carriers charging different rates for the carriage of the same good over the same transport links[79] and wide powers were conferred upon the Commission whose agents may require information from any carrier and who may impose fines

---

[75] EEC, Art. 75. According to the Court, the Treaty confers wide legislative powers upon the Council as regards the adoption of appropriate common rules. This includes matters which concern social policy, road safety and equality of competition between transport undertakings; Case 97/78 *Schumalla* [1978] E.C.R. 2311.

[76] Tenth EEC General Report (1967), 231.

[77] J.O. 1962, 720; O.J. 1959–1962, 96. This decision was complemented by others (J.O. 1966/583; O.J. 1965–1966, 92 and O.J. 1978, L. 54/16 and 18).

[78] EEC, Art. 84 (1). See, *e.g.* a directive on the establishment of common rules for certain types of carriage of goods by road between Member States (O.J. 78/1962) amended in January 1982 (O.J. 1982, L. 27/22); *id.* for combined road/rail carriage (O.J. 1979, L. 5/33).

[79] EEC, Art. 79 (1). See Reg. 3568/83 on the fixing of rates (O.J. 1983, L. 359/1).

in case of refusal to provide information or when false information is provided or when discrimination is established.[80]

As for *State aid*, this is declared compatible with the Treaty if it meets certain conditions[81] while the imposition by a Member State of rates and conditions involving any element of support or protection in the interest of one or more particular undertakings or industry is prohibited, unless authorised by the Commission.[82]

Mention should be made in this context of the famous tachographs[83] for road transport vehicles and minimum rest periods for truck-drivers.[84]

Of course, these measures do not constitute a harmonious globally-conceived transport policy; this will remain impossible as long as agreement cannot be reached on conditions of access to the markets and on publication of rates and conditions of carriage; the latter would provide the users with the necessary information to make their free choice, and the Commission with an instrument to exercise an effective control.

Mention should be made here of an important development resulting from a judgment of the Court of Justice: it concerned the interpretation of Article 84(2) and the question whether or not sea and air transport were covered by the EEC Treaty. The Court stated that, as long as the Council has not decided otherwise, sea and air transport were excluded from the rules of Title IV of Part

---

[80] Reg. 11/60, J.O. 1960/1121 and Dir. 83/643 on physical inspections (O.J. 1983, L. 359/8).

[81] See EEC, Art. 77; see also Art. 92, which however refers to incompatibility with the common market.

[82] EEC, Art. 80. See, *e.g.* O.J. 1982, L. 234/5. See Case 1/69 *Italy* v. *Commission* [1969] E.C.R. 277, concerning rates and conditions involving an element of support.

[83] See Case 128/78 *Commission* v. *United Kingdom* [1979] E.C.R. 419 at 429 (12): the importance of this judgment goes far beyond the tachograph question, since the Court declared that "for a State to break, according to its own conception of national interest, the equilibrium between the advantages and obligations flowing from its adherence to the Community brings into question the equality of Member States before Community law."

[84] Reg. 543/69 (J.O. 1969, L. 77/49; O.J. 1969 (I), 170); see Case 69/74 *Auditeur du travail* v. *Cagnon et Taquet* [1975] E.C.R. 171: provisions to be observed both by crew members and the employer; Case 65/76 *Derycke* [1977] E.C.R. 29: rules apply both to independent and to employed drivers, and Case 47/79 *Nehlsen* v. *Bremen* [1979] E.C.R. 3639: vehicles of public authorities.

Two of the Treaty, but that it is, on the same basis as other modes of transport, subject to the general rules of the Treaty.[85]

With regard to transport *infrastructure*, the Commission made its first proposals in 1976[86]; in 1981, the Council approved a Resolution on support for projects of Community interest[87] and in 1982 it adopted a regulation[88] on the granting of limited financial support in the field of transport infrastructure. A similar regulation was adopted in 1984.[89]

Relations with *third countries* are particularly important for the Community, especially since the enlargement to include Greece which has no common frontier with other Member States so that transport to and from that country has (except for sea transport) to come via third countries.[90] Of great importance in this respect is the judgment of the Court of Justice concerning the capacity of the Community to establish contractual links with third countries.[91] The same principle applies to participation by the Community in multilateral agreements.[92]

Notwithstanding some concrete action in the field of transport, one must unfortunately conclude with the Commission that the Council failed to come up with solutions to certain main items such as financial support for transport infrastructure projects of Community interest, road-tax structures, the weights and dimensions of commercial road vehicles and inter-regional air services.

Further Reading

III. *Transport Policy*

G. Close, "Art. 84 E.E.C.: The Development of Transport Policy in the Sea and Air Sections" (1980) 5 E.L. Rev. 188–208.

---

[85] Case 167/73 *Commission* v. *French Republic* [1974] E.C.R. 359 at 371 (31).
[86] Bull. 6–1976, 15.
[87] Bull. 12–1981, 53.
[88] O.J. 1982, L. 376/10.
[89] Reg. 1889/84, O.J. 1984, L. 177/4.
[90] See for instance negotiations with Yugoslavia on the establishment of through international railway tariffs, Bull. 6–1982, 56.
[91] Case 22/70 *Commission* v. *Council* [1971] E.C.R. 263 (the so-called AETR case).
[92] See *e.g.* the Agreement on the International Carriage of Passengers by Road by means of Occasional Coach and Bus services (ASOR) (O.J. 1982, L. 230/39 and 1983, L. 309/33).

P. D. Dagtoolou, "Air transport and the European communities" (1981) 6 E.L. Rev. 335, 356.

A. Bredimas and J.G. Tzoannos, "A common shipping policy for the E.C." (1981) J. of C.M. Stud. 95.

H. G. Lubberdink, "De positie van de commissie vervoervergunningen ter discussie" (1982) S.E.W. 745.

IV. *Competition Policy*

Competition, according to the Commission, is the best stimulant of economic activity since it guarantees the widest possible freedom of action to all. An active competition policy, pursued in accordance with the provisions of the treaties establishing the Communities, makes it easier for the supply and demand structures continually to adjust to technological development. Through the interplay of decentralised decision-making machinery, competition enables enterprises continuously to improve their efficiency, which is the *sine qua non* for a steady improvement of living standards and employment prospects within the countries of the Community. From this point of view, competition policy is an essential means for satisfying to a great extent the individual and collective needs of our society.[93]

It follows that competition policy is not an end in itself. It constitutes another instrument, at the disposal of the Community, to ensure that the objectives set out in the Treaty are attained. One of those objectives, it will be remembered, is economic integration through the operation and development of the common market which in turn is characterised by the basic freedoms. The ultimate test of any Community policy and any behaviour of Member States and persons in respect of Community rules is whether or not those freedoms are guaranteed to the full. This applies in the first place to free movement of goods, which is the most important of the freedoms. Trade between Member States therefore becomes the overriding criterion for compatibility with Community obligations. This rule applies especially in the field of competition.[94]

---

[93] First Report on Competition Policy (11).
[94] See also joined Cases 56 and 58/64 *Consten and Grundig* v. *Commission* [1966] E.C.R. 299 at 341.

The Treaty does not define the concept "competition,"[95] but refers to certain measures which interfere with competition and are therefore prohibited, subject to exemptions granted by the Commission. Generally speaking, the rules of competition aim at preventing the introduction by Member States and private parties of new obstacles to trade within the common market once the traditional protective measures such as customs duties and quotas have been abolished. The Treaty Chapter on competition contains broadly two sets of rules: those applying to enterprise, prohibiting trade restrictions through agreement and abuse of a dominant position—and rules concerning aids granted by States, the latter having effects comparable to quantitative restrictions. Other treaty provisions, concerning public enterprises[96] and state monopolies,[97] must also be considered as competition rules applying to Member States.

This does not mean, however, that Community competition policy is essentially negative. With regard to co-operation between undertakings, the Commission's declared intention is to reinforce the competitive position of enterprises, not only within the Community, but on the world market as well. This is achieved by excluding from the Treaty's prohibition agreements which have a positive effect on industrial development within the Community, such as co-operation agreements between small and medium-sized enterprises and specialisation agreements in research and manufacture. Similarly, it will be noticed that the Treaty does not prohibit all kinds of state aid, and the Commission considers that, when judiciously applied, it is an indispensable instrument for regional development. These various aspects will be examined hereafter.

1. Competition rules applying to undertakings[98]

(1) *Agreements[99] between undertakings (Article 85)*

Agreements between enterprises, which may affect trade

---

[95] The preamble of the Treaty refers to "fair" competition, but this has no practical significance; for a definition of the kind of competition that must be protected see Case 26/76 *Metro* v. *Commission* [1977] E.C.R. 1875 at 1904 (20).

[96] EEC, Art. 90.

[97] EEC, Art. 37.

[98] EEC, Arts. 85 to 89.

[99] The Treaty refers to "agreements between undertakings, decisions by associations of undertakings and concerted practices"; unless otherwise indicated they will be collectively referred to as "agreements."

between Member States and which have as their object or effect distortion of competition, are prohibited and automatically void, except where an exemption was granted by the Commission. Parties to any agreement must therefore ensure that it does not impede the free movement of goods throughout the Community nor distort competition within the common market. If it were otherwise, it can safely be assumed that the agreement is void and can only be implemented at the risk of the parties. This applies even when the agreement has been notified to the Commission as part of a request to have the prohibition declared inapplicable to the said agreement. Although this rule is simple enough in its generality, it requires some explanation as regards the precise significance of various terms.

Agreements and concerted practices. Agreements must be understood as legally enforceable contracts. This follows from the wording of the second paragraph of Article 85 according to which prohibited agreements are void, *i.e.* not binding; the term agreements therefore does not and cannot include non-binding arrangements such as "gentleman's agreements."[1] The latter may, however, constitute a concertation between parties, which, when it is followed by prohibited behaviour, constitutes together with this practice a "concerted practice." Agreements, on the other hand, are prohibited whether or not they are implemented, indeed the Treaty refers to agreements which have as their "object or effect" distortion of competition. In other words, in the case of an agreement the question whether or not competition was actually distorted is irrelevant, as long as the clauses clearly show the intention of the parties to distort competition.[2] So, normally speaking, there must exist a contract, preferably a document, permitting the scrutiny of its clauses. In the case of a

---

[1] Gentleman's agreements and other arrangements binding in honour only are not, in this writer's view, prohibited, unless they are actually followed by prohibited practices. In its decision of July 16, 1969 (J.O. 1969, L. 192/5) *ACF Chemiefarma*, the Commission considered an arrangement referred to as a gentleman's agreement to be an "agreement" because it expressly laid down written provisions binding the parties with regard to their conduct on the market. See also Opinion of Mr. Gand, Case 41/69 *ACF Chemiefarma* v. *Commission* [1970] E.C.R. 661 at 714 (3). See a recent example of concerted practice in joined Cases 100–103/80 *Musique Diffusion Française* v. *Commission* [1983] E.C.R. 1825.
[2] See Case 56/65 *Société Technique Minière* v. *Maschinenbau Ulm* [1966] E.C.R. 235 at 249.

suspected concerted practice on the other hand, the Commission's examination will concern in the first place the behaviour of the parties; the sole fact that this behaviour actually distorts competition is not sufficient for it to fall under the prohibition of the Treaty, prior concertation between the parties must be proved also. Parallel price increases for instance, are not in themselves prohibited; they could indeed be purely coincidental or the result of a particular market situation known as oligopoly with price leadership.[3] But parallel price increases are prohibited when they are the result of a concertation between the parties, *i.e.* some form of arrangement like a gentleman's agreement. The difficulty for the Commission, in such a case, lies with the proof of the existence of such a concertation which more often than not will have to be based on circumstantial evidence.[4]

Decisions by associations of undertakings must be understood to include the constitutive act of a trade association and its internal rules,[5] decisions made in accordance with those rules, which are therefore binding upon the members of the association,[6] and also recommendations such as the fixing of "target prices" by an association.[7] Any such decision which affects trade between Member States and distorts competition within the common market is automatically void.

Associations refers also to any grouping of associations of undertakings with or without legal personality including non-profit making associations; a *de facto* association of associations was considered by the Commission to be an association of undertakings.[8]

---

[3] See, *e.g. Pittsburg Corning* (J.O. 1972, L. 272/35). In Case 85/76 *Hoffmann-La Roche* v. *Commission* [1979] E.C.R. 461 at 520 (39) the Court refers to "parallel courses of conduct which are peculiar to oligopolies."

[4] See, *e.g.* Case 48/69 *I.C.I.* v. *Commission* [1972] E.C.R. 619 at 662 and joined Cases 40, etc. /73 *Suiker Unie et al* v. *Commission* [1975] E.C.R. 1663; in both cases the Court admitted the existence of concerted practices; not admitted in joined Cases 29 and 30/83 *Royale Asturienne and Rheinzink* v. *Commission*, judgment of March 28, 1984 (not yet published).

[5] *ASPA* (J.O. 1970, L. 148/11).

[6] *Bomée-Stichting* (O.J. 1975, L. 329/30).

[7] Case 8/72 *Cementhandelaren* v. *Commission* [1972] E.C.R. 977 at 991 (29). See also joined Cases 209, etc. /78 *van Landewyck* v. *Commission* [1980] E.C.R. 3125 at 3254 (102).

[8] *Cecimo* (J.O. 1969, L. 69/13). See also joined Cases 209, etc., /78, *van Landewyck* above n. 7.

Undertakings may or may not have legal personality.[9] In the latter case they must have some recognised legal status[10] otherwise they would not be able to carry out economic activities, *i.e.* conclude legally binding agreements, bring actions in the Court of Justice and be liable for the payment of fines. In other words, they must have "legal autonomy." The question whether or not an entity has the required legal status allowing it to operate on the market must be decided according to the applicable national law. The term undertaking also covers individuals, public enterprises and even Member States when they carry out commercial and economic activities.[11]

Besides having legal autonomy, an entity must also have "economic independence"[12] in order to qualify as an undertaking within the meaning of Article 85. This provision does not concern agreements between undertakings belonging to the same concern and having the status of parent company and subsidiary, if the undertakings form an economic unit within which the subsidiary has no real freedom to determine its course of action on the market, and if the agreements are concerned merely with the internal allocation of tasks as between the undertakings.[13] Once these two conditions are fulfilled, the two enterprises must, for the implementation of the competition rules, be considered as

---

[9] This follows *inter alia* from the wording of EEC, Art. 52 which in regard to the freedom of establishment refers to the right to set up and manage "undertakings, in particular companies or firms"; the latter are defined by Art. 58 as "constituted under civil or commercial law, including co-operative societies, and other legal persons governed by public or private law, save for those which are non-profit making"; it seems therefore that where the Treaty refers to entities having legal personality, the terms "company" or "firm" are used, while "undertaking" is broader and also includes economic entities without legal personality.

[10] This is the case, *e.g.* with the Dutch "Vennootshap onder Firma," the English "Partnership," and the German "Offene Gesellschaft."

[11] The economic or commercial character of these activities is what distinguishes undertakings in the sense of Art. 85 from other bodies that are engaged, *e.g.* in artistic or scientific work. For individuals, see *Reuter/BASF* (O.J. 1976, L. 254/40) and for Member States, Case 83/78 *Pigs Marketing Board* v. *Redmond* [1978] E.C.R. 2347.

[12] See Cases 22/71 *Béguelin Import* v. *G. L. Import Export* [1971] E.C.R. 949 at 959 (8) and 10/83 *Hydrotherm* v. *Compact*, judgment of July 12, 1984, (not yet published).

[13] See Case 15/74 *Centrafarm* v. *Sterling Drug* [1974] E.C.R. 1147 at 1167 (41). The Commission had reached a similar decision in *Christiani and Nielsen* (O.J. 1969, L. 165/12).

one single undertaking. The same applies when an agreement is concluded between two subsidiaries.[14]

If the relationship between a parent company and its subsidiary can thus result in the non applicability of Article 85, it can on the other hand bring the parent company within the jurisdiction of the Community competition rules, even when it is situated outside the Community. Indeed, when the subsidiary does not determine its own market behaviour, the latter becomes the responsibility of the parent company. Whether or not this parent company is situated within the Community becomes irrelevant since its decision has effects within the Community.[15]

Effect on trade between Member States constitutes a criterion which serves, in the first place, to determine the field of application of the Community competition rules: it is "to the extent that the agreement may affect trade between Member States that the interference with competition caused by that agreement is caught by the prohibition in Community law found in Article 85, while in the converse case it escapes those prohibitions."[16]

An agreement "may" affect trade when it "is capable of constituting a threat, either direct or indirect, actual or potential, to freedom of trade between Member States in a manner which might harm the attainment of the objectives of a single market between States."[17] Preventing, *e.g.* undertakings from importing certain products into a Member State from another one, or prohibiting them from re-exporting those products to other Member States, indisputably affects trade between Member States since they constituted a limitation of the freedom of

[14] See *Kodak* Dec. (O.J. 1970, L. 147/24).
[15] See, *e.g.* Case 48/69 *I.C.I.* v. *Commission* [1972] E.C.R. 619 at 662; Case 6/72 *Europemballage and Continental Can* v. *Commission* [1973] E.C.R. 215; joined Cases 6 and 7/73 *Commercial Solvents* v. *Commission* [1974] E.C.R. 223; Case 27/76 *United Brands* v. *Commission* [1978] E.C.R. 207 and Case 85/76 *Hoffman-La Roche* v. *Commission* [1979] E.C.R. 461.
[16] Case 56/65 *Société Technique Minière* v. *Maschinenbau Ulm* [1966] E.C.R. 235 at 249.
[17] Joined Cases 56 and 58/64 *Consten and Grundig* v. *Commission* [1966] E.C.R. 299 at 341. The Court added that the fact that an agreement encourages an increase, even a large one, in the volume of trade between States is not sufficient to exclude the possibility that the agreement may "affect" trade in the above mentioned manner. The Court also stated that trade may be affected even though the agreement does not concern imports or exports: Case 43/69, *Bilger* v. *Jehle* [1970] E.C.R. 127 at 135 (5).

movement of goods.[18] For instance with regard to agreements containing a clause granting an exclusive right of sale, the Court stated that they do not necessarily by their very nature contain elements incompatible with the common market and that, in this respect, special attention should be given to whether the agreement is capable of partitioning the market in certain products between Member States.[19] It must also be noted that the effect on trade does not have to be actual; indeed the word "may" refers to a "possible" effect on interstate commerce.

Competition is adversely affected when any kind of agreement, decision or action by undertakings directly affects the market and is detrimental to production or sales to purchasers or consumers because it limits freedom of choice. On the other hand, effective competition exists when a producer is forced to take into account the market behaviour of other producers within the relevant market.[20]

Interference with competition may result from all or some of the clauses of the agreement itself. If only some clauses of the agreement interfere with competition, only those will be void, not necessarily the whole agreement. When the intention to distort does not result from the agreement itself, then, as was mentioned above, the consequences of the agreement should be considered and factors must be found which show that competition has in fact been affected.[21]

The Court of Justice has further developed and specified the meaning of distortion of competition by adding that competition must be prevented, restricted or distorted to an *appreciable* extent.[22] For instance, an "exclusive dealing agreement, even with absolute territorial protection, may, having regard to the weak position of the persons concerned in the market and the

---

[18] *Ibid.*
[19] See Case 22/71 (*Béguelin*) n. 12.
[20] For the concept "relevant market" see below, Abuse of dominant position, p. 179.
[21] See Case 56/65 (*Technique Minière*, above n. 2, *ibid*).
[22] See Case 56/65 (*Technique Minière*, above n. 2 *ibid*.) For more details as to the meaning of the term "appreciable" see the Commission's Notice concerning agreements of Minor Importance of December 19, 1977; (O.J. 1977, C. 313/3). See also the following Commission decisions: SOCEMAS (J.O. 1968, L. 201/4) and *Intergroup Trading* (*Spar*) (O.J. 1975, L. 212/23) where the effects were considered to be minor; but in *Reuter/BASF* (O.J. 1976, L. 28/19) this was not the case. See also Case 319/82 *Ciments et Betons* v. *Kerpen*, judgment of December 14, 1984 (not yet published).

products in question, escape the prohibition of Article 85."[23] In other words, *de minimis not curat lex* also applies to the Community competition rules.

Another point emphasised by the Court is that the appreciation of the effects on competition may not be purely theoretical but the "competition in question must be understood within the actual context in which it would occur in the absence of the agreement in dispute." One must take into account, therefore, the nature and quantity, limited or otherwise, of the product covered by the agreement, the position and importance of the parties on the market for the products concerned, the isolated nature of the disputed agreement or, alternatively, its position in a series of agreements, the severity of the clauses limiting trade or, alternatively, the opportunities allowed for other commercial competition in the same product by way of parallel re-exportation and importation.[24]

According to the Treaty, distortion of competition must take place *within the common market*. It follows that an agreement between two undertakings situated within the Community which limits competition within a third country is not prohibited by Community law,[25] unless of course the behaviour of the parties to the agreement outside the Community indirectly affects interstate trade and competition within the Community.[26] Another consequence is that an agreement concluded between undertakings situated outside the Community, but having effect on interstate trade and competition within the Community, is prohibited by the Treaty. The same applies of course when one of the parties is situated within the Community.[27] And finally, it should be noted that the expression "within the Community" does not necessarily refer to competition in all Member States or even in some of them: adverse effect on competition in one single Member State is also to be considered as taking place within the

---

[23] Case 5/69 *Völk* v. *Vervaecke* [1969] E.C.R. 295 at 303 or Case 30/78, *Distillers Cy* v. *Commission* [1980] E.C.R. 2229 at 2265 (28).

[24] See Case 56/65 (*Technique Minière*, above n. 2, *ibid.* at 250) and Case 99/79 *Lancôme* v. *Etos* [1980] E.C.R. 2511 at 2536 (24).

[25] *e.g.* *Rieckermann* (J.O. 1968, L. 276/25).

[26] *e.g.* joined Cases 6 and 7/73 *Commercial Solvents* v. *Commission* [1974] E.C.R. 223 at 252 (33). This is sometimes referred to as the extra-territorial effects of the Community Competition law. This however is misleading: competition law does not apply outside the Community, it applies to the effects agreements have within the Community and therefore to the parties.

[27] *e.g.* *Franco-Japanese Ballbearings* (O.J. 1974, L. 343/19).

Community, and forbidden when interstate trade is also affected; this will practically always be the case when the agreement covers the whole territory of one Member State.[28]

Nullity (Article 85 (2)). Any agreements or decisions prohibited by the Treaty are automatically void.[29] This statement requires some clarification: a distinction must be made between "new" agreements and "old" ones. What distinguished the two groups is the question whether they were concluded before or after March 13, 1962. The latter date refers to the moment when Regulation 17, the first regulation implementing Articles 85 and 86, became effective.[30] Nullity applies without reservation to all *new agreements* (*i.e.* those concluded after March 13, 1962[31]) prohibited by the Treaty, whether or not they were notified[32] to the Commission in a procedure to obtain an exemption from the prohibition under Article 85 (3), or whether they were exempted from notification.[33] In other words these new agreements can only be implemented at the parties' own risk: it is up to them to determine whether or not their agreement is prohibited under the Treaty; if there is any doubt and the agreement is implemented anyway, there is always the possibility that a court finds, even years later, that it is and always was void, with all the consequences thereof, including for third parties.

The situation is different with *old agreements* (*i.e.* those which were in existence before March 13, 1962). The Court held[34] that in those cases the general principle of contractual certainty, particularly when the agreement has been notified in accordance with Regulation 17, requires that national courts may only declare the agreement to be automatically void after the Commission has taken a decision by virtue of that regulation. Since certain old agreements are exempted from notification, another distinction

---

[28] *e.g.* Case 8/72 *Cementhandelaren* v. *Commission* [1972] E.C.R. 977 at 999 (29).

[29] EEC, Art. 85 (2).

[30] J.O. 204/62; O.J. 1959–1962, 87.

[31] For the new Member States: Denmark, Ireland and U.K., this date became June 30, 1979; for Greece it is January 1, 1981 but "old" agreements had to be notified before July 1, 1981, Act, Annexe One, V, Competition.

[32] Reg. 17, Art. 4; thus notification has no suspensive effect. As to what constitutes a proper notification see Case 106/79 *Vereniging Boekhandels* v. *Eldi Records* [1980] E.C.R. 1137 and Case 30/78 *Distillers Cy* v. *Commission* [1980] E.C.R. 2229.

[33] Case 48/72 *Brasserie de Haecht* v. *Wilkin (No. 2)* [1973] E.C.R. 77 at 86 (9, 10).

[34] Case 59/77 *De Bloos* v. *Bouyer* [1977] E.C.R. 2359 at 2369 (8).

must be made between the latter—these are simply valid—and the old agreements which must be notified in order to be exempted—these are "provisionally valid" since they may still become void if the exemption is refused by the Commission.[35] But this provisional protection from which notified old agreements benefit ceases to exist from the date on which the Commission informs the parties that it has decided to close the file on the case concerning them; from then on national courts before which the direct effect of the prohibition of Article 85 (1) is relied upon may decide whether or not the agreement is in accordance with the Treaty. The possibility therefore exists that although the Commission has decided not to open procedures against an old agreement, a national court may on the basis of information available to it, find the agreement to be void.[36]

The declaration of inapplicability of the prohibition (Article 85 (3)). A declaration of inapplicability, or exemption, may be given by the Commission,[37] and by the Commission only,[38] under certain limited conditions, either for individual agreements or for categories of agreements.[39] Exemption in individual cases may only be granted once the Commission has been notified of the agreement concerned and the four conditions provided in Article 85 (3) are fulfilled:

(1) the agreement must contribute to improving the production or distribution of goods or to promoting technical and economic progress;

(2) consumers must get a fair share of the resulting benefit;

(3) the agreements may not impose restrictions which are not indispensable for the objectives under (1) and (2);

(4) the agreement may not afford the parties the possibility of eliminating competition in respect of a substantial part of the products in question.

---

[35] Case 13/61 *Bosch* v. *Van Rijn* [1962] E.C.R. 45 at 52.

[36] Case 99/79 *Lancôme* v. *Etos* [1980] E.C.R. 2511 at 2535. The same applies *a fortiori* to new agreements: Case 31/80 *L'Oréal* v. *De Nieuwe AMCK* [1980] E.C.R. 3775.

[37] Before Reg. 17 became effective only the national authorities in the Member States could grant such an exemption (EEC, Art. 88); with the entry into force of the said Reg. this exclusive right passed to the Commission (Reg. 17, Art. 9 (1)).

[38] Case 31/80 (*L'Oréal*) above n. 36 at 3790 (13).

[39] EEC, Art. 85 (3).

The exemptions may not enter into force on a date earlier than the date of notification[40]; they must be issued for a specified period and conditions and obligations may be attached thereto; they may be renewed but also revoked even with retroactive effect.[41]

Exemptions for *categories of agreements*. By regulation the Council decides on the principle of the exemption[42] and delegates to the Commission[43] the task of working out the details. This technique was used in two instances: certain categories of exclusive dealing agreements and categories of specialisation agreements.[44]

Application of competition rules to certain agreements. After this brief analysis of Article 85 it might be useful to indicate how they have been applied by the Commission and the Court of Justice to the main types of agreements.[45]

---

[40] Reg. 17, Art. 6 (1). Agreements should therefore be notified on the day they become effective, otherwise parties run the risk of having to consider this agreement void between the date of entry into force of the agreement and the date on which the exemption becomes effective, *i.e.* at the earliest the date of notification.

[41] Reg. 17, Art. 8.

[42] EEC, Art. 87 (2) (*b*).

[43] EEC, Art. 155.

[44] Council Reg. 19/65 was the first to be adopted pursuant to this provision; it empowered the Commission to exclude by regulation from the prohibition certain agreements concluded between only two undertakings in which one party agrees to purchase only from the other. (J.O. 1965, 533; O.J. 1965–1966, 35). This was done by Commission Reg. 67/67 on the application of Art. 85 (3) to certain agreements by which undertakings bind themselves not to manufacture certain products and leave it to the other parties. (J.O. 1967, 849; O.J. 1967, 10) and by Reg. 2349/84 concerning certain categories of patent licensing agreements (O.J. 1984, L. 219/15). Reg. 67/67 was replaced by Reg. 1983/83 (O.J. 1983, L. 173/1) and Reg. 1984/83 (O.J. 1983, L. 173/5). See Case 170/83 *Hydrotherm* v. *Compact*, judgment of July 12, 1984, (not yet published). See also Council Reg. 2821/71 (J.O. 1971, L. 285/46; O.J. 1971, 1032;) followed by Commission Reg. 2779/72 on the application of Art. 85 (3) to categories of specialisation agreements (J.O. 1972, L. 292/23; O.J. 1972 (28–30 Dec.) 80) amended by Reg. 2903/77 (O.J. 1977, L. 338/14). This Regulation was replaced by Reg. 82/3604 (O.J. 1982, L. 376/33): it widens the scope of the previous one to include specialization taking the form of joint production. See also draft Reg. for exemption of patent licences in accordance with Art. 5 of Reg. 19/65. (O.J. 1979, C. 58/11).

[45] This passage is based on Bellamy and Child, *Common Market Law of Competition* (Sweet and Maxwell, 1978) with the kind permission of the authors.

The following are very likely to fall under the prohibition of Article 85: (a) agreements relating to prices and conditions of sale[46]; (b) limitations on markets and productions[47]; (c) agreements whereby a vendor agrees not to compete within the market of the purchaser[48]; (d) exclusive dealing agreements such as supply agreements[49]; collective exclusive dealings[50]; and (e) joint purchasing[51] and joint selling agreements.[52]

Special mention should be made of exclusive dealing agreements, *i.e.* agreements between suppliers and intermediaries providing for limitation of the commercial activities of one or both parties. These agreements are prohibited as soon as they provide geographical restrictions since this carries the risk of reintroducing partitions within the common market.[53] Of particular interest are the *selective distribution agreements, i.e.* limitation of the sales points of a given product[54] and distribution systems in general.[55]

Reference should also be made to *industrial property rights* with respect to the Community competition rules although these rights are generally used by their owners to prevent import into a given country and therefore enter into conflict with the principle of free movement of goods under Article 30 of the Treaty; it is in regard to this principle that most cases concerning property rights brought before the Court have been decided upon.[56] The position of the Court can be summarised as follows: the Treaty

---

[46] See, *e.g. International Quinine* (J.O. 1969, L. 192/5) and Case 41/69 *ACF Chemiefarma* v. *Commission* [1970] E.C.R. 661.

[47] See, *e.g. Julien Van Katwijk* (J.O. 1970, L. 242/18).

[48] See, *e.g. Reuter BASF* (O.J. 1976, L. 254/40).

[49] See, *e.g. Bayer Gist* (O.J. 1976, L. 30/13).

[50] See "First Report on Competition Policy," 35 *et seq.* and Case 71/74 *Frubo* v. *Commission* [1975] E.C.R. 563. See also Reg. 67/67 above, n. 44.

[51] See, *e.g. Belgian Industrial Timber*, Bull. 10–1975, 23.

[52] See, *e.g. SEIFA* (J.O. 1969, L. 173/8).

[53] See, *e.g.* joined Cases 40, etc./73, *Suiker Unie* v. *Commission* [1975] E.C.R. 1663 at 2006 (535).

[54] See *Omega* (J.O. 1970, L. 242/22), *SABA* (O.J. 1976, L. 28/19), *BMW* (O.J. 1975, L. 29/1), *Junghans* (O.J. 1977, L. 30/10), Case 107/82 *AEG* v. *Commission* [1983] E.C.R. 3151 and Case 86/82 *Hasselblad* v. *Commission*, judgment of February 21, 1984, (not yet published).

[55] See, *e.g. Fedetab* (O.J. 1978, L. 224/29) and joined Cases 228 and 229/82, judgment of February 28, 1984, (not yet published).

[56] In Case 78/70 *Deutsche Grammophon* v. *Metro* [1971] E.C.R. 487 the Court found that the use of property rights was contrary to the Community's competition rules. See below, Industrial Property Rights, p. 226.

provisions do not affect the existence of exclusive rights attached to patents and licences, trademarks and copyright, but may limit their use in so far as it restricts trade between the Member States.

(2) *Abuse of dominant position (Article 86)*

Interstate trade and competition can be adversely affected not only by several undertakings acting or behaving jointly, but also by an individual enterprise or a group of undertakings enjoying a dominant position within the common market or in a substantial part of it. Article 86 therefore must be understood in conjunction with Article 85 which it complements; together they constitute the common rules of the Community competition policy based on the basic principle set out in Article 3 (*f*) which provides for the institution of a system ensuring that competition in the common market is not distorted, thereby requiring *a fortiori* that competition must not be eliminated. This requirement is so essential that without it, numerous provisions of the Treaty would be pointless. Thus the restraints on competition which the Treaty allows under certain conditions because of the need to harmonise the various objectives of the Treaty are limited by that fundamental requirement.

The methods used to eliminate competition are irrelevant: both practices which may directly affect the market and are detrimental to production or sales, to purchasers or consumers, and changes to the structure of an undertaking which lead to competition being seriously disturbed in a substantial part of the common market, are prohibited by Article 86.[57]

The concept "dominant position" relates to a position of economic strength enjoyed by an undertaking which enables it to prevent effective competition being maintained on the relevant market,[58] by giving it the power to behave to an appreciable extent independently of its competitors, customers and ulti-

---

[57] *Continental Can* (J.O. 1972, L. 7/25) and Case 6/72 *Europemballage and Continental Can* v. *Commission* [1973] E.C.R. 215. This case constitutes the first major breakthrough in the implementation and interpretation of Art. 86. The Court states that the latter must be based upon the spirit, general scheme and wording, as well as on the system and objectives of the Treaty; see *ibid.* at 243. Most of the remarks made above about Art. 86 are taken from this judgment.

[58] To determine whether an undertaking occupies a dominant position it is necessary first to determine the relevant market, Case 22/78 *Hugin* v. *Commission* [1979] E.C.R. 1869 at 1895 (5).

mately of the consumers. It follows from the case law of the Commission[59] and the Court of Justice[60] that to be considered as "dominant," the position of an undertaking must be viewed in relation to a relevant product and a geographical market. The definition of the relevant market is of essential significance because the possibilities of competition can only be judged in relation to those characteristics of the products in question by virtue of which those products are particularly apt to satisfy an inelastic need and are only to a limited extent interchangeable with other products.[61] In order to be regarded as constituting a distinct market, the products in question must be individualised not only by the mere fact that they are used for a given purpose, but by particular characteristics of production which make them specifically suitable for this purpose and within a given area.[62]

A substantial market share as evidence of a dominant position is not a constant factor and its importance varies from market to market according to the structure of these markets, especially as far as production, supply and demand are concerned[63] and in this

---

[59] The most important Commission decisions concerning Art. 86 were taken in the following Cases: *GEMA* (J.O. 1971, L. 134/15), *Continental Can* (above n. 57), *ZOJA* (J.O. 1972, L. 229/51), *General Motors* (O.J. 1975, L. 23/14), *United Brands* (O.J. 1976, L. 95/1), *Hoffmann-La Roche* (O.J. 1976, L. 223/27), *ABG/OIL companies* (O.J. 1977, L. 117/1), *Michelin* (O.J. 1981, L. 353/33), *GVL* (O.J. 1981, L. 370/49), *GEMA statutes* (Bull. 12–1981, 29) and *British Telecommunications* (O.J. 1982, L. 360/36). See also the arrangement with I.B.M. (Europe 3905, August 3, 1984, 3).

[60] The most important Court rulings were given in the following Cases: Case 6/72 (*Europemballage*, above, n. 57); Case 26/75 *General Motors* v. *Commission* [1975] E.C.R. 1367; joined Cases 6 and 7/73, *Commercial Solvents* v. *Commission* [1974] E.C.R. at 223; Case 13/77, *GB-INNO-BM* v. *ATAB* [1977] E.C.R. 2115; Case 27/76 *United Brands* v. *Commission* [1978] E.C.R. 207; Case 77/77 *BP* v. *Commission* [1978] E.C.R. 1513; Case 85/76 *Hoffmann-La Roche* v. *Commission* [1979] E.C.R. 461: the existence of a relevant market was not established; Case 22/78 *Hugin* v. *Commission* [1979] E.C.R. 1869: trade between Member States was not affected, and Case 7/82 *GVL* v. *Commission* [1983] E.C.R. 483.

[61] For an example of not-interchangeable products see Case 85/76 (*Hoffmann-La Roche*) above n. 60, at 547 (111).

[62] Case 6/72 (*Europemballage* above n. 57, at 217 (14)). The concept of the relevant market in fact implies that there can be effective competition between the products which form part of it and this presupposes that there is a sufficient degree of interchangeability between all the products forming part of the same market in so far as a specific use of such products is concerned (Case 85/76 *Hoffmann-La Roche* above n. 60, at 462 (3)).

[63] A market share of 80 per cent. clearly creates *ipso facto* a dominant position. When the market share is smaller additional criteria must be taken into consideration. In Case 85/76 (*Hoffmann-La Roche* above n. 60) the Court rejected

context substitution with regard to both demand and production constitutes an essential element of appreciation. Dominance is not only a question of sheer size, but it can also derive from a combination of several factors which taken separately, would not necessarily be determinative.

More difficult is the definition of "abuse," except that it has to be specified with regard to competition: any behaviour of an undertaking enjoying a dominant position which interferes with one of the basic freedoms or the free choice of purchasers or consumers or freedom of access to business, must be viewed as limiting competition and therefore as an "abuse." The Treaty refers to abuse "of" a dominant position, but this does not mean that a link of causality must exist between the dominant position and abuse.[64] Indeed, the strengthening of the position of an undertaking may constitute an abuse and be prohibited regardless of the means and procedure by which it is achieved. The concept of abuse is an objective concept relating to the behaviour of an undertaking in a dominant position which is such as to influence the structure of the market and which through recourse to methods different from those which condition normal competition has the effect of hindering the maintenance or growth of still existing competition.[65]

Regulation 17.[66] Regulation 17 is the first regulation "to give effect to the principles set out in Article 85 and 86"[67] and generally speaking, it sets out the procedure to be followed when the Commission decides:

as irrelevant a number of additional criteria mentioned by the Commission in its decision, but lists those which it considers important, such as the relationship between the market share of the company in question and the shares of the next largest, the technological lead, the existence of a highly developed sales network and the absence of potential competition (at 524 (48)). See also Case 22/78, *Hugin* above n. 60.

[64] See *e.g.* Case 85/76 (*Hoffmann-La Roche*, above n. 60 at 541 (91)): use of economic power is not required.

[65] In connection with the provisions of Art. 86, mention should be made of the Commission proposals for a regulation on the control of concentrations between undertakings (O.J. 1973, C. 92/1, amended O.J. 1982, C. 36/3 and C. 252/15).

[66] J.O. 1962, 204; O.J. 1959–1962, 87.

[67] EEC Treaty, Art. 87.

(1) to give a *negative clearance*[68] (Article 2): this is issued at the request[69] of undertakings which want to make certain that their agreement is not prohibited by Article 85 or 86. Before granting a negative clearance, the Commission must publish the essential content of the application and invite interested parties to submit observations[70];

(2) to oblige undertakings to put an *end to infringements*, when it finds that they exist, either upon application of Member States or natural or legal persons[71] or upon its own initiative (Article 3).[72] In this connection attention should be drawn to the limitation period in proceedings under competition[73];

(3) to issue a declaration *granting an exemption* from the prohibition of Article 81 (1) (Article 6)[74];

(4) to *investigate* into undertakings (Article 14): Commission officials are empowered to examine the books, take copies, ask for oral explanations and enter any premises.[75] Written

---

[68] Complete lists of decisions taken by the Commission are to be found in the annual Reports on Competition Policy published in conjunction with the General Reports. The first decision taken under Reg. 17 concerned a request for negative clearance: *Grosfillex-Fillistorf*, March 11, 1964 (J.O. 915/64); the last decision to date was issued on July 14, 1975, *Intergroup Trading Spar* (O.J. 1975, L. 212/3). About 14 decisions were taken in all and the disuse of this procedure can be explained by the greater security which has existed since the Commission and the Court defined the various concepts of the Treaty provisions.

[69] See Reg. 27 fixing form, content and other details concerning application and notifications (J.O. 1962, 1118; O.J. 1959–1962, 132); it was amended by Reg. 1133/68 (J.O. 1968, L. 189/1; O.J. 1968, 400) and Reg. 1699/75 (O.J. 1975, L. 172/11).

[70] Reg. 17, Art. 19 (3).

[71] For the right to file a complaint with the Commission under Art. 3 (2) (*b*) see Case 125/78 *GEMA* v. *Commission* [1979] E.C.R. 3173.

[72] In Case 792/79 R *Camera Care* v. *Commission* [1980] E.C.R. 119, the powers which the Commission holds under Article 3 include the power to take interim measures which are indispensable for the effective exercise of its functions (at 131 (18)). See also joined Cases 228 229/82 R *Ford-Werke* v. *Commission* [1982] E.C.R. 3091 where interim measures were suspended by the President of the Court.

[73] Enforcement procedures are subject to a limitation period of five years (Reg. 2988/74, Arts. 4–6, O.J. 1974, L. 319/1).

[74] See above: declaration of inapplicability of the prohibition of Art. 85 (1).

[75] See Case 136/79 *National Panasonic* v. *Commission* [1980] E.C.R. 2033 where the Court held that this right does not infringe the fundamental rights of undertakings and that the latter do not have the right to be heard in case of an investigation procedure.

communications between lawyer and client, in so far as they have a bearing on market activities, fall within the category of documents of which the Commission may require production. But Regulation 17 protects the confidentiality of written communications between lawyer and client when 1) such communications are made for the purpose and in the interests of the client's rights of defense and 2) they emanate from independent lawyers, that is to say lawyers who are not bound to the client by a relationship of employment (legal privilege)[76];

(5) to impose *fines* or *penalties* (Articles 15 and 16).[77]

In cases (1), (3) and (5), the Commission, before deciding, must make known to the undertakings concerned the points to which it objects and which it has taken into consideration, and give the undertakings an opportunity to express their views thereon (Article 19),[78] and invite interested third parties to submit their observations. In those cases, the Commission must also consult the Consultative Committee on Cartels and Monopolies.

---

[76] Case 155/79 *AM & S* v. *Commission* [1982] E.C.R. 1575 at 1611 (22).

[77] In several cases fines have been imposed by the Commission for infringement of Art. 85 (1): *e.g. Hoffmann-La Roche* (O.J. 1976, L. 223/27), *National Panasonic* (O.J. 1982, L. 354/28) and *Toltecs-Dorcet* (O.J. 1982, L. 379/19), in one case for submitting incomplete information: see Bull. 11–1971, 55 (5) and in other cases the Commission imposed a periodic payment for each day the undertaking failed to fulfil an obligation imposed by the Commission: *MA-Statuut* (O.J. 1980, L. 318/1). On the determination of the amount of the fine see joined Cases 100–103/80, *Musique Diffusion Française* v. *Commission* [1983] E.C.R. 1825 at 1904 and joined Cases 96, etc., /82 *I.A.Z.* v. *Commission* [1983] E.C.R. 3369 at 3417 (52), and decision of August 6, 1984 concerning the zinc producer group (O.J. 1984, L. 220/27). The Court has approved the Commission's new practice of suspending the collection of fines (when the decisions imposing fines are subject to appeal) only on condition that (1) interest is paid in respect of the period of suspension and (2) a bank guarantee is lodged covering the amount of the fine and the interest. See Case 107/82R *AEG* v. *Commission* [1982] E.C.R. 1549; Case 86/82 R *Hasselblad* v. *Commission* [1982] E.C.R. 1555 and Case 263/82 R *Klökner-Werke* v. *Commission* [1982] E.C.R. 3995.

[78] See Reg. 99/63 (J.O. 1963, 2268; O.J. 1963–1964, 47) laying down implementing provisions for those hearings. See Case 85/76 (*Hoffmann-La Roche*, above n. 60) where the Court laid down the general rule that the right to be heard is a basic principle of Community law in all procedures that may lead to the imposition of fines.

See also the creation of the post of Hearing Officer and the Notice on procedures for applying the competition rules of the EEC and ECSC Treaties: O.J. 1982, C. 251/2.

See Twelfth Report on Competition Policy, 38.

Commission announcements. To clarify its competition policy the Commission has issued announcements, notices or communications concerning the following subjects:

(a) *Exclusive agency contracts made with commercial agents*[79]: the Commission declared that contracts concluded with commercial agents in which such agents, with respect to a particular part of the common market, undertake to negotiate business transactions for the account of an undertaking, or to do so in the name and for the account of the latter, or to do so in their own name and for the account of the latter, are not prohibited by Article 85 (1).

(b) *Patent licences agreements*[80]: some clauses specifically mentioned in this communication are not covered by the prohibition of Article 85 (1);

(c) *Co-operation agreements*[81]: in this notice the Commission first indicates that it encourages co-operation between small and medium-sized enterprises, where such co-operation enables them to work more rationally and increases their productivity and competitiveness on a larger market; the Commission then lists a number of agreements which do not restrict competition;

(d) *Agreements of minor importance*[82]: this announcement also follows from the desire of the Commission to promote cooperation between small and medium-sized enterprises. The notice lists a number of criteria which allow undertakings to acquire the certainty that their agreement does not fall under the prohibition of Article 85 (1).

(e) *Subcontracting agreements*[83]: the notice offers a general guide as to clauses often contained in subcontracting agreements and which are not caught by Article 85 (1).

---

[79] J.O. 1962, 2921.
[80] J.O. 1962, 2922, See also Case 24/67 *Parke, Davis* v. *Centrafarm* [1968] E.C.R. 55 and several other judgments *inter alia*, Case 16/74 *Centrafarm* v. *Winthrop* [1974] E.C.R. 1183 and Case 258/78 *Nungesser* v. *Commission* [1982] E.C.R. 2015.
[81] J.O. 1968, C. 75/3. See also Reg. 82/3604 on the application of Article 85(3) to categories of specialisation agreements (O.J. 1982, L. 376/33).
[82] J.O. 1977, C. 313/3. This Notice replaces the Notice published in J.O. 1970, C. 64/1.
[83] O.J. 1979, C. 1/2.

(f) *Imports of Japanese products*[84]: the Commission reminds undertakings concluding agreements with Japanese firms and which are intended to restrict imports of Japanese products into the Community that such agreements do not fall outside Community competition rules because one of the parties is situated outside the Community. It urges those undertakings concerned to notify those agreements.

Relationship between Community and national competition rules. In one of its judgments,[85] the Court of Justice had to answer the question whether or not Community and national competition law could be applied simultaneously to the same agreement. The Court ascertained that Community and national law consider cartels from different points of view; the former regards them in the light of the obstacles which may result for interstate trade, while the latter proceeds on the basis of considerations which are particular to it. This implies that one and the same agreement in principle, may be the object of two sets of parallel proceedings. However, if the ultimate general aim of the Treaty is to be respected, the parallel application of the national system can only be allowed in so far as it does not prejudice the uniform application throughout the common market of the Community rules on cartels and the full effect of the measures adopted in implementation of those rules.

The Court based this rule on the fact that:

"the EEC Treaty has established its own system of law, integrated into the legal systems of the Member States, and which must be applied by their courts. It would be contrary to the nature of such a system to allow Member States to introduce or to retain measures capable of prejudicing the practical effectiveness of the Treaty. The binding force of the Treaty and of measures taken in application of it must not differ from one state to another as a result of internal measures, lest the functioning of the Community system should be impeded and the achievement of the aims of the Treaty placed in peril. Consequently, conflicts between the rules of the Community and national rules in the matter of

---

[84] J.O. 1972, C. 111/13.
[85] Case 14/68 *Wilhelm* v. *Bundeskartellamt* [1969] E.C.R. 1.

the law on cartels, must be resolved by applying the principle that Community law takes precedence."[86]

As long as this rule is applied, national authorities may take action against an agreement in accordance with their national law, even when an examination of the same agreement, from the point of view of its compatability with Community law, is pending before the Commission.[87]

However, to avoid conflict, the best solution is that as soon as the Commission starts proceedings, the national authorities, and this includes tribunals, should suspend their procedure.[88] But it is for the national judge to decide whether there is cause to suspend proceedings in order to allow the parties to obtain the Commission's standpoint, unless of course it is established that the agreement does not have any perceptible effect on competition or trade between Member States or that there is no doubt that the agreement is incompatible with Article 85.[89]

---

[86] *Ibid*. at 14 (6).

[87] This means that when, *e.g.* the Commission has made it known that it intends to grant an exemption from the prohibition of Art. 85 or has granted such an exemption, national authorities may no longer prohibit or declare void the agreement concerned on the basis of their national law, otherwise the agreement would be void in one Member State and valid in all the others. Similarly, national authorities may not consider an agreement which was found by the Commission to be prohibited under Art. 85 to be valid. However, when applying national law, national authorities are under no obligation to take into account possible infringements of Community law, as long as the Commission has not opened proceedings, and nothing prevents those authorities from prohibiting agreements under national law which are void under Community law or from imposing fines upon the undertakings concerned, even if fines were already imposed by the Commission, just as, *vice versa*, the Commission is not prevented from imposing fines after an undertaking has been fined under national law. See Case 7/72 *Boehringer* v. *Commission* [1972] E.C.R. 1281 at 1289: when the two cases are identical, the fines should be offset against one another.

[88] In Case 48/72 *Brasserie de Haecht* v. *Wilkin-Janssen*, the Court considered that "whilst the principle of legal certainty requires that in applying the prohibition of Article 85, the sometimes considerable delays by the Commission in exercising its powers should be taken into account, this cannot however absolve the (national) court from the obligation of deciding on the claims of interested parties who invoke the automatic nullity" [1973] E.C.R. 77 at 87 (11).

[89] *Ibid*. The national judge is in the same position here as when parties ask for a preliminary ruling (EEC, Art. 177, see above).

2. Competition rules applying to Member States

As was mentioned at the beginning of the section on competition, obstacles to the free movement of goods can result not only from illegal behaviour of undertakings but also from interference by national authorities: both are prohibited by the Treaty. Member States can affect trade and competition by establishing or maintaining state monopolies, by acting through public enterprises or by granting subsidies to undertakings. The Treaty provides rules for the abolition of such interference and for the prevention of their recurrence.

(1) *State Monopolies of a commercial character*[90]

Member States were required by the Treaty to adjust their monopolies of a commercial character[91] so as to ensure that, by the end of the transitional period,[92] no discrimination regarding the conditions under which goods are procured and marketed exists between nationals of the Member States.

At the time of the entry into force of the Treaty about a dozen such monopolies existed in the six original Member States[93]; the timetable of the Treaty was not respected by the Member States and in 1978 the Commission reported that it hoped "that by the end of the year its work on state monopolies of a commercial character will have reached a point where none of the remaining monopolies are at variance with Article 37 of the EEC Treaty."[94]

However in 1980 the Commission had to report once more that the adjustments to the remaining monopolies could not be completed,[95] in fact it concerned the French and Italian manufactured tobacco monopolies. With regard to the former the

---

[90] EEC, Art. 37. A state monopoly is a body through which a State, in law or in fact, directly or indirectly supervises, determines or appreciably influences imports or exports between Member States.

[91] Commercial means that production monopolies are not affected by the Treaty because in a real common market these monopolies do not constitute an obstacle to free trade. Neither are the common agricultural organisations affected (see above, Agriculture, p. 143) since, on the basis of Art. 38 (2) they have precedence over other Treaty provisions; Case 83/78 *Pigs Marketing Board* v. *Redmond* [1978] E.C.R. 2347. The same applies to service monopolies: Art. 37 does not apply: Case 271/81 *Commission* v. *France* [1983] E.C.R. 2079.

[92] December 31, 1969.

[93] See First Competition Report, 160.

[94] Eighth Competition Report, 181.

[95] Tenth Competition Report, 159.

Commission considered in 1983 that the measures taken by the French Government were such as to bring the monopoly into line with the Treaty provisions.[96] This leaves one particular problem with Italy[97] and the necessary measures still to be taken in Greece.[98]

(2) *Public enterprises*[99]

A public enterprise, in the sense of Article 90, is any undertaking[1] whatever its public or private status, on whose economic behaviour the state can exert influence, *e.g.* by virtue of its direct or indirect financial participation or by legal provisions governing its establishment. It follows that the essential element is the "control" a national authority can exercise over an enterprise.[2] The logical consequence of this subordinate position of the enterprise in respect to a public authority, is that it places upon the latter the responsibility for the behaviour of the enterprise. Therefore, whether the undertaking referred to in Article 90 (which is by definition under state control) acts illegally on instructions of the national authority[3] or whether the latter has not taken the necessary measures to prevent such enterprise from acting in that way, it is the Member State—to be understood here as any public authority—which is considered as having acted.

This explains why Article 90 imposes obligations exclusively upon the Member State—not on the enterprises—and why Article 90 (3) provides that the Commission shall, in order to

---

[96] Twelfth Competition Report, 149. See however Bull. 3–1983, 35: opening of procedures against France concerning the alcohol monopoly.

[97] *Ibid.* at 150; see Case 78/82 *Commission* v. *Italy*, [1983] E.C.R. 1955.

[98] Art. 40 of the Act of Accession, O.J. 1979, L. 291/1.

[99] EEC. Art. 90.

[1] Undertaking to be understood as defined for Art. 85 (1); see above, p. 171.

[2] A parallel can be drawn here with the above-mentioned relationship between a parent company and its subsidiary; see Art. 85(1) above p. 171.

[3] Member States might indeed be tempted to implement through the undertakings they control certain measures which are prohibited when taken directly by the State. Art. 30 constitutes a good example: it prohibits any restriction on imports or exports; if a Member State in a notice of public contracts indicates that it will only consider tenders proposing national products, it would violate Art. 30. If an undertaking were to do the same, no action could be taken. The Member State might, therefore, order an undertaking under its control to issue the notice in its stead.

ensure the application of the provisions of Article 90, address directives and decisions only to the Member States.[4]

An interesting provision of Article 90 is that concerning undertakings "entrusted with the operation of services of general economic interest,"[5] since they shall be subject to the Treaty rules, in particular those on competition, only "in so far as the application of such rules does not obstruct the performance in law or in fact, of the particular task assigned to it."

Owing to the very important role played by "public enterprises" as producers and traders within the common market, it is to be expected that the provisions of Article 90 will be applied much more vigorously in the future.

(3) Aid granted by States

The common market, as described in the preceding sections, implies that all those who operate therein do so only with their own resources and at their own risk. These resources can be artificially increased and the risks reduced by agreements between enterprises, as well as by State aid. Aid, whatever its form or size, invariably modifies market conditions and, therefore, affects competition and inter-state trade.

Article 92 states that aids are incompatible with the common market when they distort competition and affect trade between Member States; it seems difficult to imagine state aid favouring certain[6] enterprises and not distorting competition nor affecting trade between the Member States.[7]

---

[4] See Dir. 80/723 on the transparency of financial relations between Member States and public undertakings (O.J. 1980, L. 195/35), see Tenth Competition Report, 163. The validity of this Dir. was challenged without success in the Court of Justice: joined Cases 188 to 190/80 *France, Italy and U.K. v. Commission* [1982] E.C.R. 2545.

[5] See Case 10/71 *Ministère Public Luxembourg v. Muller* [1971] E.C.R. 723. The provisions of Art. 90 are relevant only for these undertakings which are in competition with other enterprises which are not controlled by the State. See also Cases 155/73 *Sacchi* [1974] E.C.R. 409 and 127/73 *BRT v. Sabam and NV FONIOR* [1974] E.C.R. 313.

[6] The reference to "certain" enterprises establishes a distinction between what is commonly considered as "aids," *i.e.* measures favouring a limited number of undertakings, and general economic measures which favour all the undertakings operating within a given country; the latter measures are not caught by Art. 92. Distortions resulting from those general measures must be eliminated through approximation of legislation; see below, p. 229.

[7] See Case 330/79 *Philipp Morris v. Commission* [1980] E.C.R. 2671: the Court rejected by implication the applicant's argument that in order to show that an

However, state aid can also constitute an instrument of structural development policy when certain legitimate objectives of economic growth cannot be attained solely by the interplay of market forces, or not within an acceptable time-limit, or not without unacceptable social frictions. The Treaty therefore, having stated the principle of incompatibility of state aid with the common market, provides for certain categories of aid which either are or may be considered by the Commission to be compatible with the common market.[8]

To allow the Commission to declare certain aids compatible with the common market, Member States must notify the Commission of any plans to grant or alter aids. Until the Commission has decided on the compatibility of the plans,[9] the Member State concerned may not put its proposed measures into effect. If the Commission comes to the conclusion that the aid cannot be considered compatible with the common market, it opens a procedure which allows all interested parties to express their opinion; once this is done, the Commission takes a final decision. During the procedure, the measures may not be applied, unless the Council decides that they are compatible.

---

aid falls within the terms of Art. 92 (1), the Commission must apply the tests which determine the existence of restrictions on competition under Arts. 85 and 86 (relevant market, market structure, etc.). The Court held that simpler grounds (a more favourable treatment of some firms affects inter-State trade) are adequate. See however judgment of November 14, 1984, Case 323/82 *Intermills* v. *Commission* (not yet published). With regard to Art. 92 (3) the Court confirmed that the Commission enjoys a measure of discretionary power.

[8] Any aid therefore which does not fall within one of those categories is automatically prohibited (see, *e.g.* J.O. 1972, L. 10/22: Belgian aid to under-takings in difficulty which the Commission ordered to be abolished). The possibility exists of extending the categories of aid which can be declared admissible by the Commission: Art. 92 (*d*), *e.g.* Dir. 81/363 on aid to shipbuilding (O.J. 1981, L. 137/39) which creates the category of production aids to shipbuilders. See Case 74/76 *Iannelli* v. *Meroni* [1977] E.C.R. 557 at 574 (11): the incompatibility is "neither absolute nor unconditional."

For a Commission's refusal see, *e.g.* O.J. 1979, L. 217/17. See also Case 730/79 *Philipp Morris* v. *Commission* [1980] E.C.R. 2671: it was the first time a potential beneficiary of an aid contested the Commission's decision prohibiting a Member State from granting said aid.

[9] According to Art. 93 (3), the Commission must be notified "in sufficient time to enable it to submit its comments"; as for the Commission, once it has been informed, it has, according to the Court, two months to make up its mind; see Case 122/73 *Nordsee* v. *Germany* [1973] E.C.R. 1511 at 1522 (4) and Case 71/83R *Commission* v. *France* [1983] E.C.R. 2621.

If a Member State were to apply an aid either without waiting for the procedure to be closed or without informing the Commission, the following could happen: any interested party can ask the national judge to declare the aid illegal,[10] the Commission can ask the Court to adopt interim measures requiring the Member State to cease the infringement,[11] and finally having declared the aid to be incompatible, the Commission can "require from the recipients of the aid the repayment, within certain time limits, of the grants awarded."[12]

Apart from a category of aid, which is compatible *de jure*,[13] the Treaty provides for aid which can be declared compatible by the Commission; these are regional development aid and aid to certain industries.

(a) *Regional development aid*[14]: The implementation of the Treaty provisions in regard to regional aid has presented the Commission with considerable problems: the granting of aid has remained a national responsibility and the fact that the Community's regional policy is in its initial stage has made the co-ordination of national policies in this field very difficult. It constitutes furthermore a very sensitive matter, since in certain Member States the choice of the development areas is often influenced by internal political considerations; the powers of the Community in this field are therefore sometimes resented as an interference with national "policies."

The absence of co-ordination did result in the implementation by Member States of policies seeking to attract new industries to their depressed areas by offering more and better incentives than

---

[10] Indeed, the last sentence of Art. 93 (3) has direct effect: Case 120/73 *Lorenz* v. *Germany* [1973] E.C.R. 1471 at 1483 (8).

[11] Cases 31/77 R and 53/77 R *Commission* v. *U.K.* and *U.K.* v. *Commission* [1977] E.C.R. 921.

[12] Case 70/72 *Commission* v. *Germany* [1973] E.C.R. 813 at 828 (10).

[13] *e.g.* aids having a social character, aids which make good the damage caused by natural disasters and aids granted in Germany to areas affected by the division of the country. Although these aids are compatible, they must be notified to the Commission which must make sure that they fall within these categories.

[14] The Treaty distinguishes between under-developed regions and other regions where aids for development are needed; where the latter are concerned the aids may not "adversely affect trading conditions, to an extent contrary to the common interest," while no such condition is provided for the depressed areas.

their neighbours, thereby initiating stiff competition between the Member States or even their own regions. The Commission, therefore, in close liaison with the Member States, developed "principles of co-ordination of national regional aid schemes"[15] which have since 1971 constituted the main feature of the Community's policy in this field. Plans to alter existing aids or to introduce new ones are examined as to their compatibility with the common market by the Commission, on the basis of these principles.[16]

(b) *Aid to certain industries*: The application of the Community rules to industrial aid, as opposed to regional aid, is easier generally speaking since their scope is much more limited and the measures more clearly defined. In this field also, the Commission undertook to clarify and publicise its policy by a communication to the Council describing the general principles in industry aid and outlining the specific criteria used in the scrutiny of national schemes.[17] Guidelines have also been developed in particular where an industry is in a crisis; this is the case for shipbuilding,[18] textiles,[19] man-made fibres[20] and steel.[21]

(c) *General aid schemes*: General aid is any measure granting assistance to undertakings but which is not justified by the need

---

[15] The first principles which applied only to the "central regions" of the six original Member States are embodied in a Commission communication to the Council (J.O. 1971, C. 111/7) and adopted in the form of a resolution by the representatives of the governments of the Member States in Council (J.O. 1971, C. 111/1; O.J. 1974 (2nd) IX, 57). See also Act of Accession, Art. 154; in pursuance of this provision, the Commission sent to the Council an adapted version of the Principles of co-ordination in 1973 (Bull. 6–1973, 23). The latest version of the Principles was sent to the Council in December 21, 1978 (O.J. 1979, L. 31/9).

[16] See, *e.g.* O.J. 1982, L. 312/18: Belgium and L. 290/39 Denmark.

[17] Eighth Competition Report 132 and Bull. 5–1978, 28.

[18] Five successive Directives were issued by the Council, see Eleventh Competition Report, 129 and O.J. 1985 L. 2/13..

[19] General principles for the textile industry were elaborated in 1971 and refined and extended to 1976; see the various reports on Competition policy. See Case 84/82 *Federal Republic* v. *Commission*, where the Court annulled a decision authorising an aid; judgment of March 20, 1984 (not yet published).

[20] Request to the Member States for appropriate measures (Seventh Competition Report, 164).

[21] See ECSC Treaty and Dec. 81/2320, O.J. 1981, L. 228/14; see above, p. 102.

to develop the region where the undertaking invests or to restructure the industry to which the undertaking belongs. These schemes do not fall within one of the categories provided for by the Treaty as being suitable to be considered compatible with the common market. The Commission, therefore, is unable to take a definitive position on such aid schemes and requires the Member States, when applying these schemes, to notify in advance either the regional or sectoral programmes adopted to implement them, or failing this, the significant cases of aid grants.[22]

It is clear that in the field of state aids the Commission has been given wide powers to ensure that the measures, which the Member States intend to implement to achieve national regional and industrial objectives do not jeopardise the Community's endeavours to attain the aims set out in the Treaty.

Conclusion with regard to competition policy. Community competition policy must be seen, not as an end in itself, but as an effective instrument in the hands of the Commission to ensure that the objectives set out in the Treaty are attained. The prohibitions provided by Articles 85 and 86 are of great importance, and logical interpretation as much as systematic application is an essential requirement for the indispensable legal certainty. Furthermore, without the knowledge that the rules are strictly and objectively implemented, it will not be possible to convince the undertakings operating within the common market that fulfilling the Treaty obligations is in their own interest as much as in the interest of the purchasers and consumers.

The same considerations apply of course to the incompatibility of state aid with the common market, the adjustment of state monopolies and the abolition of illegal measures in the case of public enterprises. The Member States have a right to know how the Commission intends to interpret and apply the relevant provisions and must have the assurance that the Commission will prosecute any failure of other Member States to comply with the Treaty obligations in this particularly sensitive field.

More important, however, are the discretionary powers vested in the Commission, especially by Articles 85 (3) and 92 (3). It is with its power to declare the prohibition of Article 85 (1) inapplicable in certain cases, that the Commission is in a position

---

[22] See Competition Reports.

to pursue a real policy. Agreements, mergers, dominant positions, etc., tend to reinforce the competitive position of Community undertakings on the common market and on the world markets. Economic strength and technological progress require co-operation between undertakings and between the latter and the public authorities. Similarly, by considering aid compatible with the common market under certain conditions, the Commission is able to develop, in close co-operation with the Member States, a Community structural policy which will contribute to the development of economic activities throughout the Community.

The policies developed through the implementation of the competition rules are further strengthened by the contributions from the financial instruments which the Community administers; mention should be made here of the orientation section of the agricultural fund, the regional fund, the social fund, the ECSC funds, the Euratom funds, the Community borrowing and loan facilities and the European Investment Bank. The ultimate goal of all these policies and instruments is the same, *i.e.* to strengthen the structure of the regions and Community industry. It is essential to keep all this in mind in order to see the competition rules in their true relation to Community objectives.

Further Reading

IV. *Competition Policy*

Annual Commission Report on Competition Policy.

Dr. J.W. Aarts, "Mededingingspolitiek en economische crisis" (1980) S.E.W. 16.

J.T. Lang, "Community Antitrust Law—compliance and enforcement" (1981) 18 C.M.L. Rev. 335–363.

L. Focsaneanu, "La jurisprudence de la Cour de Justice des communautés Européennes en matière de concurrence (1978–1981)" (1981) Rev. du M.C. 514, (1982) Rev. du M.C. 30, 194, 272, 555.

J. D. C. Turner, "Competition and the Common Market after maize seeds" (1983) 8 E.L. Rev. 103.

James Flynn, "State aid and self-help" (1983) 8 E.L. Rev. 297.

Malcolm G. Ross, "Article 37—Redundancy or Reinstatement" (1982) 7 E.L. Rev. 281.

Alan C. Page, "Member States, public undertakings and Article 90" (1982) 7 E.L. Rev. 19.

D. Thompson, "Commission hearings in competition cases" (1982) J. of W.T.L. 448.

J. Joshua, "The element of surprise; competition investigations under Art. 14 (3) of Regulation 17" (1983) 8 E.L. Rev. 3.

M. Brothwood, "The Commission Directive on transparency of financial relations between Member States and public undertakings" (1981) 18 C.M.L.R. 207–217.

J. S. Chard, "The economics of the application of Article 85 to selective distribution" (1982) 7 E.L. Rev. 83.

Valentine Korah, "Comfort letters—reflexions on the perfume cases" (1981) 6 E.L. Rev. 14.

John Usher, "Exercise by the European Court of its jurisdiction to annul competition decisions" (1980) 5 E.L. Rev. 287.

V. *Regional Policy*

Regional policy as such is not explicitly provided for under the Treaty, although some provisions[23] exist concerning the

---

[23] There are, indeed, some indications in the Treaty referring to the problems of certain regions: the fifth para. of the Recitals states that the parties are "anxious to strengthen the unity of their economies and to ensure their harmonious development by reducing the differences existing between the various regions and the backwardness of the less favoured regions"; Art. 2 refers to the promotion of a harmonious development of economic activities "throughout the Community"; Art. 39 instructs the Community to take account, in working out the CAP, of "structural and natural disparities between the various agricultural regions"; Art. 80 provides that the Commission in examining rates and conditions of transport shall take account of "the requirements of an appropriate regional economic policy, the needs of under-developed areas and the problems of areas seriously affected by political circumstances" and Art. 92 (3) provides that aids granted by States may, as an exception to the general rule, be considered compatible with the common market when they are intended "to promote the economic development of areas where the standard of living is abnormally low or where there is serious underemployment."

development of the backward areas.[24] The European Investment Bank, for instance, was set up *inter alia* to provide the necessary resources for "developing less developed regions,"[25] while the Treaty provides for the possibility to grant State aid to the problem regions in Germany and elsewhere.[26] Moreover, the drafters of the Treaty were convinced that the functioning of the common market, with the resulting development of economic activities, continuous and balanced expansion and accelerated raising of the standard of living would more or less automatically reduce, if not eliminate, regional disparities.

After all, although they were less developed, less favoured or even backward, these areas had two great advantages: large reserves of manpower much in demand for an expanding economy and vast expanses of land at a time when the central, industrialised areas were already suffering from excessive concentration.

The establishment, functioning and development of the common market did indeed achieve spectacular results in most of these areas as evidenced by a doubling and even trebling of their per capita income. This, however, was not sufficient within a Community where similar developments were taking place in the well developed areas. The result was that although the gap may not have widened between richer and poorer regions, it was kept relatively stable, depending on the method of calibration, *e.g.* GNP per inhabitant[27] or purchasing power parity. It goes without saying that such discrepancies are no longer politically or socially acceptable and create a major problem for the Community as a whole. On the one hand, it becomes increasingly difficult to achieve the required convergence of Member States' economic

---

[24] At the time the Treaty was signed, there were mainly two areas which presented serious development or other economic problems: the Mezzogiorno in Italy and the Zonenrandgebiet in Germany.

[25] EEC, Art. 130 (*a*).

[26] Art. 92 (2) provides for aids "granted to the economy of certain areas of the Federal Republic of Germany affected by the division of Germany, in so far as such aid is required in order to compensate for the economic disadvantages caused by that division."

[27] It is generally admitted that the ratio in 1960 between the average income in Hamburg and Sicily was in the order of 3 to 1, the difference being 2; after the figure doubled for Hamburg to 6 and trebled in Sicily to 3, the difference still increased by 50 per cent.

policies[28] as long as some of them—and their number has increased with enlargement—have to devote a large fraction of their resources to the development of their less favoured regions, with all the economic consequences such as inflation, balance of payment problems and exchange rate fluctuations.

Furthermore, regional imbalances within the common market may have a disruptive effect: Member States have shown dangerous tendencies to have recourse to currency devaluation and protective measures where, for instance, low productivity and inflation have resulted in increased prices and diminished competitiveness for their industries.

It was at the conference of Heads of State or of Government held in Paris in October 1972, that it was agreed that a high priority should be given to the aim of correcting the structural and regional imbalances which might affect the realisation of economic and monetary union.[29] They invited the Commission to present a report analysing the regional problems which arise in the enlarged Community and to put forward appropriate proposals. They undertook to co-ordinate their regional policies and invited the Community institutions to create a Regional Development Fund.[30]

A "Report on Regional Problems in the enlarged Community"[31] was presented to the Council in 1973, containing an analysis of the regional problems and policy instruments; the same year the Commission sent a proposal for a regulation establishing a European Regional Development Fund[32] together with other proposals[33] and a draft decision establishing a

---

[28] See EEC, Art. 2: refers to progressive approximation of the economic policies of the Member States; Art. 6: instructs Member States to "co-ordinate their respective economic policies" and according to Art. 145: the Council shall "ensure co-ordination of the general economic policies of the Member States."

[29] Bull. 10–1972, 9. This was the first "summit" at which Denmark, Ireland and the U.K. participated.

[30] It was further stated that this fund would be set up before December 31, 1973, and would be financed from the Community's own resources from the beginning of the second phase of Economic and Monetary Union; it was also provided that interventions by the Fund should take place in conjunction with national aids.

[31] Bull. Supp. 8/73. The report concluded that the main imbalances are to be found in (a) predominantly agricultural areas; (b) regions affected by industrial change, *i.e.* marked by dependency on old industries; and (c) regions of structural unemployment.

[32] O.J. 1973, C. 86/7.

[33] For more details see Bull. 10–1973, 13.

Committee for Regional Policy which would facilitate the co-ordination of the regional policies of the Member States.

It was not until March 1975 that the regulation establishing the Regional Fund was formally adopted by the Council[34] together with a decision setting up a Regional Policy Committee.[35]

It is interesting to note that, although a Regional Fund was finally set up, no provisions were made to develop a Community Regional Policy. It appears, therefore, that the Regional Fund was seen in the first place as an instrument to transfer supplementary resources to the poorest regions of the Community, although the system of partial reimbursement by the Fund of the Member States own regional aids partially defeated this purpose. Indeed nothing proves that the recipients of the Fund resources used those grants to increase the financial aid allotted to the deprived areas, although it is explicitly stated in the preamble to the Fund Regulation, that the Fund's assistance should not lead Member States to reduce their own regional development efforts, but should complement these efforts. In the absence of a real Community policy, the Fund became, in most cases, a means to transfer resources from the richer to the poorer Member States.[36]

However, since the regulation was to be re-examined after three years, the Commission was asked to make at that time the "appropriate proposals for the Community's regional policy."[37] The importance of this provision should be emphasised, because it implies that the Community itself has a responsibility for the elimination of unacceptable regional differences and, consequently that the Member States not only have lost their exclusive sovereign rights in this field, but must co-ordinate their national policies.[38]

---

[34] Reg. 724/75 (O.J. 1975, L. 73/1). This Reg. is based upon EEC, Art. 235. The creation of the Regional Fund required a modification of the Financial Regulation concerning the Community budget (O.J. 1975, L. 73/45) and the financing of the first endowment of the Fund necessitated a regulation on the transfer of funds out of the appropriations held in reserve by the Agricultural Fund (O.J. 1975, L. 73/8). It was replaced by Reg. 1787/84, see n. 51 below.

[35] O.J. 1975, L. 73/47.

[36] Fund grants for infrastructure which, as in the U.K., go directly to the local authorities which finance them are an exception, although these amounts are deducted from the borrowing ceiling of those authorities.

[37] Reg. 724/75, Art. 2(2) see above n. 35).

[38] The loss of exclusive rights follows in the first place from Arts. 92–94 (see above, Competition Policy, p. 167). Since regional policy is but one aspect of general economic policy, the obliglation to co-ordinate the national regional policies

Proposals for a Community regional policy,[39] together with amendments to the existing Fund regulation, were forwarded by the Commission to the Council in July 1977.[40] Due to difficulties encountered with the introduction in the Fund of the proposed "quota free" section, and because of a conflict which arose between the European Parliament and the Council with regard to the Fund's endowment for the period 1978–1980[41] it was not until February 1979 that the amendments were formally accepted by the Council, together with a resolution concerning the guidelines for a Community regional policy.[42] The latest regulation covers both the instruments for a regional policy and provisions regarding the fund.[43]

1. Community Regional Policy

The Commission felt that a few simple, positive actions were required as a first step towards a Community Regional Policy, rather than lengthy and general statements of intention. Consequently, measures were initiated along the following lines:

(1) *A comprehensive analysis* of the evolution of the socio-economic situation in all the regions: this will make it possible to establish a

---

with one another follows from EEC Arts. 2, 6 and 145 (see above note 28) and Council Dec. 74/120 on the attainment of a high degree of convergence of the economic policies of the Member States (O.J. 1974, L. 63/16).

[39] Bull. Supp. 2/77: "Community Regional Policy: New Guidelines."

[40] O.J. 1977, C. 161/11.

[41] At its meeting of December 1977, the European Council agreed on the endowment of the Regional Fund for the period 1978–1980 for a total of 1.850 million EUA, notwithstanding the fact that the Council had previously agreed with Parliament that the Fund resources would be considered as non-obligatory Community expenditure and, consequently, fall within the exclusive competence of Parliament. At the end of 1977, when the Community budget comprising the Fund expenditure of the first of the three years period had to be approved, Parliament increased slightly the amount fixed by the European Council, but a year later a real conflict emerged when Parliament decided on a Fund endowment of a billion EUA as against the 620 decided upon by the European Council; the final endowment was 945. The amount of resources in the following years was: 1980: 1,165; 1981: 1,540; 1982: 1,669; 1983: 2,010 and 1984: 2,140.

[42] O.J. 1979, L. 35/1 and C. 36/10.

[43] O.J. 1984, L. 169/1.

common basis of assessment of the regional problems at Community level.[44]

(2) *The regional impact assessment* (R.I.A.) of all Community policies: since all Community policies have regional implications, particularly as regards employment, account should be taken of these implications when formulating and implementing policies. On the other hand the Fund resources can be used to help implement some of those policies and should these policies have negative effects in some regions, the Community should endeavour to counteract these by positive intervention: through Community programmes (quota-free section). This would ensure that all Community policies and measures do contribute actively to the solution of regional problems and thereby to the reduction of the regional imbalances within the Community.

(3) *Co-ordination of national regional policies*: this is considered essential to achieve a balanced distribution of economic activities throughout the Community. For the practical implementation of this co-ordination the Regional Policy Committee was set up and Member States are required to establish regional development programmes according to a joint plan.[45] It should be noted that an investment may only benefit from Fund assistance if it falls within the framework of a regional development programme. There exists, therefore, a formal link between these programmes and the working of the Regional Development Fund which will be examined briefly.

---

[44] The findings of this analysis are the object of a so-called "Periodic Report" to be sent to the Council every two and a half years, so as to coincide every five years with the presentation of the Community's medium-term economic policy programme. The first report was presented in 1980 (COM(80)816 final); on the basis of this report, the Commission sent to the Council the New Regional Policy Guidelines and Priorities (COM(81)152 final). The second report was sent in March 1984 (COM (84) 40 final).

[45] O.J. 1976, C. 69/2. In accordance with Reg. 1787/84, Art. 1(3)(a), programmes are transmitted to the Commission for all regions eligible for assistance from the Fund. After examination they are submitted for opinion to the Regional Policy Committee (see, *e.g.* Seventeenth General Report (1983), 150). The Commission has made recommendations to the Member States, both as to the contents of the programmes and future actions in the field of regional policy (O.J. 1979, L. 143/7 and 9). (See also Studies-Series, Regional Policy, no. 15). See Commission Opinion on the Regional Development Programmes (O.J. 1984, L. 211/18).

2. European Regional Development Fund (ERDF)

To execute its regional policy, the Community has two instruments at its disposal: The Regional Fund and the Regional Policy Committee. Although the European Parliament and the Commission consider the Fund's endowment to be insufficient, it plays a major role in carrying out the regional policy both of the Community and the Member States.

The purpose of the Fund is to help correct the principal regional imbalances within the Community by participating in the development and structural adjustment of regions whose development is lagging behind and in the conversion of declining industrial regions.

The first Fund regulation was adopted by the Council in 1975[46] and remained in force until the end of 1984. It called for a re-examination by the Council on a proposal from the Commission every three years. After a major revision in 1979,[47] draft amendments were put forward by the Commission in October 1981 with a view to introducing some drastic changes.[48] Very slow progress was made over a period of 18 months and the discussions were interrupted by the mandate given to the Commission by the European Council of June 1983 at Stuttgart to present a report with proposals to improve the effectiveness of the Community's Structural Funds.[49] The report and proposals were transmitted to the Council in July 1983 and later amended.[50]

A new regulation was finally adopted in June 1984[51] after a "concertation" took place with the European Parliament resulting in a common declaration of the Parliament, the Council and the Commission concerning Community regional policy.[52] It entered into force on January 1, 1985.

The new regulation provides for some interesting novelties such as programme financing, continual dialogue with the Member States, economic evaluation of programmes and pro-

---

[46] Reg. 724/75 establishing a European Regional Development Fund (O.J. 1975, L. 73/1).

[47] Reg. 214/79 (O.J. 1979, L. 35/1).

[48] See Seventh ERDF Report (1981), 11.

[49] The Structural Funds are: the Agricultural Fund—Guidance Section, the Social Fund and the ERDF.

[50] Bull. Supp. 3/83 and Bull. 11–1983, 7.

[51] Reg. 1787/84 on the Regional Development Fund (O.J. 1984, L. 169/1).

[52] Bull. 6–1984, 18.

jects, technical assistance, a higher rate of financial participation and the abolition of the "quota-free" section.

The resources are distributed among the Member States according to ranges fixed in the regulation.[53] Every country is assigned a minimum contribution from the Fund corresponding to the threshold of the range and which is guaranteed in so far as the criteria of the regulation are met. As for the amount up to the ceiling of the range it will be allocated to those programmes or projects which present the greatest Community interest.

The Fund resources are used in conjunction with national regional policy measures, thereby ensuring the agreement and co-operation of the interested Member State. The ERDF participates in the financing of Community programmes, national programmes of Community interest, projects and studies.

"Programmes" means a series of coherent measures intended to solve a specific set of problems within a well-defined geographical area over a period of several years. "Community programmes," directly serve Community objectives and the implementation of Community policies and are initiated by the Commission; "national programmes of Community interest" correspond to national objectives while also serving Community objectives and policies. This insistence upon Community interest follows from the decision taken at the Stuttgart European Council concerning the increase of the efficiency of the structural Funds.

The Regional Fund also contributes to the financing of investment projects in industry, the crafts, services (including tourism) and infrastructure.[54]

As a general rule, financial contributions are limited to those areas which are designated by the Member States in agreement with the Commission[55] for the application of their own systems of regional aid.

Requests for assistance are provided by the Member States and submitted for opinion to the Fund Committee. In the case of projects the Fund contribution may either supplement national

---

[53] Reg. 1787/84, Art. 4(3): the main beneficiaries are Italy (31.94 to 42.59 per cent.), U.K. (21.42 to 28.56), Greece (12.35 to 15.74), France (11.05 to 14.74) and Ireland (5.64 to 6.83), followed by Belgium (0.90 to 1.2), Denmark (0.51 to 0.67), Germany (3.76 to 4.81), Luxembourg (0.06 to 0.08) and the Netherlands (1.00 to 1.34).

[54] *Ibid.* Art. 17.

[55] See above, Aid granted by States, p. 189.

aid or be credited to the national authorities as a partial repayment of such aid.

Of great importance was the introduction in 1979 of the "quota-free" section[56]: the resources thus available were used to finance specific Community regional development measures linked with Community policies and with measures adopted by the Community, in order to take better account of their regional dimension or to reduce their regional consequences.[57] The so-called "quota-free" section of the Fund was abolished by the new regulation but similar actions are now provided for in the form of Community programmes.

3. The Regional Policy Committee

It is composed of 22 members "selected from among senior officials responsible for regional policy" and appointed by the Member States and the Commission. Unfortunately the terms "senior" and "responsible for" have been rather widely interpreted by the Member States.

As mentioned above, this Committee was set up with a view to contributing to the co-ordination of the regional policies of the Member States; its mandate, however, is much larger since its task is to examine problems relating to the regional development, the progress that has been made or will be made towards solving the problems and the regional policy measures needed to further the achievement of the Community's regional objectives.[58] The Committee also assists the Commission in establishing the Periodical Report on the evolution of the socio-economic situation of the regions which constitutes the basis for fixing the priorities and orientations of the Community regional policy.

4. Conclusion

Community regional policy is still in the developing stage: the very first steps have just been taken to arrive at a comprehensive approach to the problems created by the regional discrepancies

---

[56] Reg. 724/75, Art. 13 (O.J. 1975, L. 73/1 amended by Reg. 214/79, O.J. 1979, L. 35/1).

[57] A first series of specific Community actions was adopted by the Council on October 7, 1980; see Fifth ERDF Report (1979) and O.J. 1980, L. 271/1. A second series was proposed in 1982 (Eighth ERDF Report (1982)) and adopted by the Council in January 1984 (O.J. 1984, L. 27/1).

[58] Dec. 75/185, Art. 2 (O.J. 1975, L. 73/47).

within the Community. The means to implement such a policy are still extremely modest but the foundations have been laid which will allow the Community to remedy one of its most dramatic shortcomings.

Further Reading

V. *Regional policy*

Annual Commission Report on the European Regional Development Fund.

Th. A.M. Wöltgens, "Europees en nationaal structuurbeleid, taakverdeling of tegenstelling?" (1979) S.E.W. 570.

P.S.R.F. Mathijsen, "Structuurbeleid van de gemeenschap versus structuurbeleid van de lidstaten" (1979) S.E.W. 547.

M. Rui Martins and J. Mawson, "The programming of regional development in the E.C.: supranational or international decision-making?" (1982) 20 J. of C.M. St. 229.

Y. Mény, "Should the community regional policy be scrapped?" (1982) 19 3 C.M.L. Rev. 373.

P.S.R.F. Mathijsen, "Regionaal beleid in crisistijd" (1982) S.E.W. 614.

N. Moussis, "Le cadre juridique de la politique régionale communautaire" (1983) 263 Rev. du M.C. 4.

VI. *Industry Policy*

If undertakings are the object of explicit Treaty provisions such as those concerning the right of establishment, the freedom to provide services and the free movement of capital on the one hand, and those concerning competition on the other, there is no reference to industry and its role in the Community.[59] It is true, of course, that two of the objectives of the Treaty are the development of economic activities and balanced expansion, both of

---

[59] The only exception being a reference to "economic activities" in Art. 92 (3) which provides that aid to facilitate the development of certain economic activities may be considered by the Commission as compatible with the common market, notwithstanding the general principle of incompatibility of State aids with the common market.

which are normally the result of industrial growth, but the drafters of the Treaty obviously did not see the need for Community intervention in the growth and adaptation process of industry at large. However, there are two exceptions: (i) the coal and the steel industries which fall within the ambit of the European Coal and Steel Community which has its own objectives and policies for achieving them[60]; and (ii) atomic energy and its uses in industry, the development of which is promoted by the Euratom Treaty.[61]

This corresponded to the more or less liberal conceptions prevailing with regard to economic policies in the fifties and which find their expression in the fundamental freedoms, which constitute the characteristics of the common market reinforced by the rules of competition. This was feasible as long as the economies of the Member States continued to develop, but as soon as the recession of the seventies set in, certain industries supported by a number of Member States requested Community intervention. Although the Heads of State or Government in 1972 considered it necessary to seek to establish a single industrial base for the community as a whole,[62] and agreed that objectives would need to be defined and the development of a common policy in the field of science and technology ensured and that "appropriate means should be drawn up by the Community's institutions before January 1, 1974,"[63] no comprehensive industry policy was decided upon.

Instead various limited measures were adopted which were applicable either to industry as a whole, *e.g.* public contracts,[64] or more specifically to certain sectors. The latter approach became the only possible one. Over the years the Community adopted measures to regulate and sometimes to help the reconversion of specific industries in crisis, such as steel, shipbuilding, textiles, and footwear[65] or to encourage the development of new technology.

---

[60] See above, The European Coal and Steel Community, p. 98.
[61] See above, The European Atomic Energy Community (Euratom), p. 104.
[62] Communiqué issued at the Paris Summit of 1972 (Bull. 10–1972, 19).
[63] Thirteenth General Report (1979), 85–90.
[64] See Dir. 70/32 (J.O. 1970, L. 13/1), Dir. 71/304 (J.O. 1971, L. 185/1; O.J. 1971 (II) 678), Dir. 71/305 (J.O. 1971, L. 185/5; O.J. 1971 (II) 682) and Dir. 77/62 (O.J. 1977, L. 13/1).
[65] Eleventh General Report (1977), 89 and 98, which also mentions the building industry, wood, paper and petrochemicals.

Steel was dealt with under the ECSC treaty; with regard to *shipbuilding*, mention was made in the section on competition of the various directives regulating the grant of aid[66]; as for *textiles*, the Community provided financial aid for industrial restructuring and conversion operations connected with the reduction of capacity in the man-made fibres industry, it initiated a second research and development programme and decided to remain a member of the Multifibre Arrangement.[67]

The Commission embarked upon a co-ordinated scheme to help the European *automobile* industry[68] and in the field of *new technologies*, it continued the execution of a multiannual programme in the field of data processing. Mention must also be made of the co-operation in automation of data and documentation for imports/exports and agriculture[69] (Caddia), microelectronic technology[70] where the Community offers financial support for research and development projects in the field of computer-assisted design for manufacturing and test equipment for very large scale integration circuits and the European telecommunications industry.[71]

In view of the importance of *information technology* for the competitiveness of the Community's entire industrial and economic fabric, the Commission undertook the formulation of a European Strategic Programme for Research and Development in Information Technology (Esprit).[72]

---

[66] With regard to regions and areas affected by the decline of the steel and shipbuilding industries see the specific actions undertaking under the quota free section of the ERDF (O.J. 1980, L. 271/9 and 16 and O.J. 1984, L. 27/9 and 15). The fifth Dir. on aid to shipbuilding was adopted in 1981 (O.J. 1981, L. 137/39); the duration of this Dir. was extended to Dec. 31, 1986 (O.J. 1985, L. 2/13).

[67] O.J. 1979, L. 326/36; the aid amounted to 14 million ECU; see also the second research and development programme on textiles and clothing (O.J. 1981, L. 367/29). An important element of any policy regarding textiles is the relationship with third countries: see, *e.g.* Reg. 636/82 (O.J. 1982, L. 76/1) and Commission Dir. (O.J. 1981, L. 347/32). Of major importance in this field is of course the Multifibre Arrangement (MFA), see Sixteenth General Report (1982), 241. See also specific ERDF action for textile regions: Reg. 219/84 (O.J. 1984, L. 27/22).

[68] Sixteenth General Report (1982), 90 and Bull. suppl. 2/81.

[69] O.J. 1982, L. 247/25.

[70] Reg. 3744/81 (O.J. 1981, L. 376/38) providing direct financial support of 40 million ECU over two years.

[71] Eighteenth General Report (1984), 104 and Bull. 3–1984, 26.

[72] Dec. 82/878/EEC (O.J. 1982, L. 369/37) and Council Dec. 84/15 (O.J. 1984, L. 81/1). See Eighteenth General Report (1984), 104.

So although there is no grand design with regard to a Community industrial policy, the EEC is finally starting to act, albeit too slowly and too modestly, in various priority industrial fields.

With regard to industrial *research and development* the Commission set up an advisory Committee in 1978 which in 1984 became the IRDAC.[73]

Further Reading

VI. *Industry Policy*

J. Faure et J.F. Marchipont, "L'industrie automobile européenne face à la concurrence internationale: vers une stratégie automobile communautaire?" (1981) 252 Rev. du M.C. 543.

C. Cova, "Le textile entre une politique communautaire et un protectionnisme qui se survit" (1982) 255 Rev. du M.C. 213.

J. van der Heyden, "De uistralingseffecten van het Europees industriebeleid op de regionale werkloosheid" (1982) Nieuw Europa 39.

H. de Jong, "Industriële ontwikkeling en industriebeleid in de E.G." (1982) S.E.W. 302.

B. Harris, "Community law and intellectual property; recent cases in the Court of Justice" (1982) 19 C.M.L. Rev. 61.

H. Roos, "De E.G. en het Midden- en kleinbedrijf" (1983) 1 Nieuw Europa 38.

J. de Puifferat, "Pour une stratégie industrielle européenne" (1983) 264 Rev. du M.C. 62.

VII. *Tax Provisions and VAT*

1. Indirect taxes

The objective of the Treaty provisions concerning taxation[74] is to ensure free movement of goods by prohibiting any discrimination in taxation between imported products and products

---

[73] O.J. 1984, L. 66/30.
[74] EEC, Arts. 95–99.

originating within a Member State.[75] As was explained, the basic freedom of movement of goods throughout the Community, obtained by the elimination of customs duties and quotas, would be meaningless without the other freedoms and furthermore, could be jeopardised by government intervention in other fields such as state monopolies, public enterprises and state aids and by actions of undertakings were it not that the Treaty contains rules to prevent such interference. The same applies to internal taxation[76]: it can be used as a powerful weapon to protect domestic products from competition by imported goods.

The Treaty therefore prohibits the imposition upon "products of other Member States" of internal taxation of any kind higher than that which is imposed directly or indirectly[77] upon similar[78] domestic products[79]; it also prohibits the imposition upon such products of internal taxes such as to afford protection to other domestic products, *i.e.* non-similar products.[80] However, the Treaty does not prohibit charges imposed upon imported products when there is no identical or similar domestic product,[81] but it would not be permissible for Member States to impose on such products charges of such an amount that the free movement of those goods within the common market would be impeded.[82]

---

[75] Case 168/78 *Commission* v. *France* [1980] E.C.R. 347.

[76] The Court found that Art. 95 constitutes, in the field of taxation, the indispensable foundation of the common market; after January 1, 1962 (beginning of the second stage) citizens within the Community can ask the national courts to enforce Art. 95 (1); in other words Art. 95 (1) has direct effect (Case 57/65 *Lütticke* v. *Hauptzollamt Saarlouis* [1966] E.C.R. 205).

[77] These terms must be widely interpreted: Case 28/67 *Molkerei-Zentrale* [1968] E.C.R. 143.

[78] Similarity exists when the products in question are normally to be considered as coming within the same fiscal, customs or statistical classification: Case 27/67 *Fink-Frucht* v. *Hauptzollamt München* [1968] E.C.R. 223 or when products have similar characteristics and meet the same needs from the point of view of the consumers: Case 168/78 *Commission* v. *France* [1980] E.C.R. 347 and Case 170/78 *Commission* v. *U.K.* [1983] E.C.R. 2265 where the Court considered discriminatory the imposition of higher taxes on wine than on beer.

[79] EEC, Art. 95 (1).

[80] EEC, Art. 95 (2); this provision has also direct effect: see Case 27/67 *Fink-Frucht*, n. 78; the function of Art. 95 (2) is to cover all forms of indirect tax protection in the case of products which, without being similar, are nevertheless in competition even partial, indirect or potential, with certain products of the importing country: Case 168/78 *France*, see n. 78.

[81] Case 90/79 *Commission* v. *France* [1981] E.C.R. 283.

[82] Case 31/67 *Stier* v. *Hauptzollamt Hamburg* [1968] E.C.R. 235.

The tax provisions do not, however, restrict the freedom of each Member State to establish the system of taxation which it considers the most suitable[83] including tax arrangements which differentiate between certain products on the basis of objective criteria such as the nature of raw material used,[84] although Article 95, for instance, prohibits a system of taxation affecting differently whisky and other spirits.[85] Since the Treaty refers to products of other Member States, products from third countries are not included.[86]

Where *export* of products is concerned, the Treaty prohibits repayment of internal taxation beyond the actually imposed charges[87]; where a cumulative multi-stage tax system applies, Member States may establish average rates.[88]

2. Harmonisation of indirect taxes[89]

If to date the common market is not yet a single market within which all products circulate freely as in a national market, this is mainly due to the existence of differences in taxation from one Member State to the other; if taxes were harmonised, there would

---

[83] Case 127/75 *Bobie* v. *Hauptzollamt Aachen-Nord* [1976] E.C.R. 1079.

[84] Case 140/79 *Chemial Farmaceutici* v. *DAF* [1981] E.C.R. 1.

[85] Case 216/81 *Cogis* v. *Ammin. delle finanze* [1982] E.C.R. 2701. The Commission points out that this judgment is in keeping with established case-law on the prohibition of tax discrimination, and confirms the exceptional nature of the judgment mentioned in the preceeding note (see Sixteenth General Report (1982), 315).

[86] Case 148/77 *Hansen* v. *Hauptzollamt Flensburg* [1978] E.C.R. 1787, not to be confused with Case 153/80 *Rumhaus Hansen* v. *Hauptzollamt Flensburg* [1981] E.C.R. 1165 where the Court held that Art. 95 also applies to tax advantages granted under the legislation of a Member State; those must be extended to products originating in other Member States. When such an advantage is made conditional upon the possibility of inspecting production on national territory it is discriminatory by nature and prohibited by Art. 95: joined Cases 142 and 143/80 *Amministrazione delle Finanze dello Stato* v. *Essevi and Salenzo* [1981] E.C.R. 1413. See also Case 38/82 *Hauptzollamt Flensburg* v. *Hansen* [1983] E.C.R. 1271.

[87] Cases 45/64 *Commission* v. *Italy* [1965] E.C.R. 857 and [1969] E.C.R. 433.

[88] EEC, Art. 97; see Dir. 68/221 (J.O. 1968, L. 115/14; O.J. 1968 (I) 114); what constitutes an average rate and how it is established is for the national courts to determine, Case 28/67 *Mölkerei-Zentrale* v. *Hauptzollamt Paderbom* [1968] E.C.R. 143.

[89] Harmonisation of direct taxes can be achieved in pursuance of Arts. 100 and 101.

no longer be any need for customs controls at the internal borders of the community.[90]

In respect of turnover taxes, excise duties and other forms of indirect taxation, the Commission must consider how the legislation of the various Member States can be harmonised.[91] On the basis of this mandate, the Commission submitted directives concerning the introduction of a common value added tax system in all the Member States. Two directives were adopted in 1967.[92] The principle of VAT as defined in the first Directive, involves the application to goods and services up to and including the retail stage of a general tax on consumption which is exactly proportional to the "production" price of the goods and services, regardless of the number of transactions which take place during the production and distribution process before the stage at which tax is charged. This implies that on each transaction VAT will be calculated on the price of the goods or services chargeable at that stage, but that the VAT already paid on the various costs components must be deducted.[93]

The second directive specifies the method of implementing the principle which is now uniformly applied in all Member States (except Greece); unfortunately, the Member States were allowed to determine for their own country the rate of the tax. The system was introduced on July 1, 1972.[94] A small part of the VAT revenues does now accrue to the Community as own resources.[95]

Several other so-called "VAT Directives" were adopted by the Council.[96]

---

[90] This is, of course, a slightly exaggerated statement since the elimination of all border controls on goods implies harmonisation of all other legislative and administrative provisions which impose various requirements in the field of packaging, quality control, technical control, etc.

[91] EEC, Art. 99.

[92] J.O. 1967, 1301 and 1303; O.J. 1967, 14 and 16. The latest modification of the First and Second Dirs. was introduced by the Act of Greek accession (O.J. 1979, L. 291/101 and 169); concerning the Second Dir. see Case 89/81 *Staatssecretaris van Financiën* v. *Hong Kong Trade* [1982] E.C.R. 1277 and Case 222/81 *Bausystem* v. *Finanzamt München* [1982] E.C.R. 2527.

[93] Case 15/81 *Schul* v. *Inspecteur der invoerrechten en accijnzen* [1982] E.C.R. 1409 at 1426 (10).

[94] See however the Fourth Dir. on the introduction of VAT in Italy (J.O. 1971, L. 283/41). VAT was introduced in the U.K. on April 1, 1973.

[95] See above, Financing Community Activities, p. 81.

[96] Third Dir. concerning the introduction of VAT in Member States (J.O. 1969, L. 320/34; O.J. 1969 (II) 55); Fourth: introduction of VAT in Italy (J.O. 1971, L. 203/41); Fifth: *id.* (J.O. 1972, L. 162/18); Sixth: concerning a uniform basis of

Mention should also be made of harmonisation directives in the field of excise duties,[97] duty free allowances in International Travel,[98] transport,[99] formation of capital[1] and mutual assistance of Tax Authorities.[2]

3. Direct taxes

The Treaty does not contain specific provisions regarding harmonisation of direct taxes, but Article 100 provides the necessary powers.[3] Several proposals for directives were submitted to the Council; very few were adopted,[4] notwithstanding the fact the Council and the representatives of the Member States recognised that harmonisation was necessary to achieve the effective liberalisation of movement of persons, goods, services and capital and to accelerate economic integration.[5]

Further Reading

VII. *Tax provisions and VAT*

R. Burke, "Tax harmonisation in the E.C." (1981) 1 Intertax 7.

assessment (O.J. 1977, L. 145/1); Eight: refund to non-community persons (O.J. 1979, L. 331/11); Ninth: postponing the Sixth (O.J. 1978, L. 194/16); Eleventh: excluding the French overseas departments (O.J. 1980, L. 90/41). Concerning sixth and ninth see Case 70/83 *Kloppenburg* v. *Finanzamt Leer*, judgment of February 22, 1984 (not yet published).

[97] See, *e.g.* Dir. 72/464 concerning taxes, other than turnover taxes, on consumption of manufactured tobacco modified in 1980 (O.J. 1980, L. 375/76). In regard to excise duties on certain alcoholic beverages, see, *e.g.* Case 170/78 *Commission* v. *U.K.* [1980] E.C.R. 417.

[98] Dir. 69/169 (J.O. 1969, L. 133/6; O.J. 1969 (I) 232) and Dir. 78/1032 (O.J. 1978, L. 366/28). The directives provide for duty-free (no turnover tax, no excise duty) allowances for goods in the personal luggage of travellers or sent non-commercially in small consignments. See Case 158/80 *Rewe* v. *Kiel* [1981] E.C.R. 1805. See also three directives in the field of tax-free allowances on imports (*e.g.* personal property when transferring normal residency property acquired by inheritance) O.J. 1983, L. 105/38.

[99] Dir. 68/297 (J.O. 1968, L. 175/15; O.J. 1968 (II) 313) exempting fuel held in tanks of commercial motor vehicles.

[1] Dir. 73/80 (O.J. 1973, L. 103/15) fixing common rates of capital duty.

[2] Dir. 77/799 (O.J. 1977, L. 336/15).

[3] See Programme for the harmonisation of direct taxes, Bull. Supp. 8/1967.

[4] See, *e.g.* Twelfth General Report (1978) 121; Fifteenth (1981) 115 and Sixteenth (1982) 118.

[5] Resolution of March 22, 1971 (J.O. 1971 C. 28/1; O.J. sp. Ed., Sec. Ser. IX, 40).

A. Easson, "Fiscal discrimination: new perspectives on Art. 95 of the EEC treaty" (1981) 18 C.M.L. Rev. 521.

G. Montagnier, "1957–1982: les fiscalités nationales, 25 ans après" (1982) 4 Rev. Tr. Dr. Eur. 625.

D. Berlin, "Jurisprudence fiscale européenne" (1982) 1 Rev. Tr. Dr. Eur. 100.

N. Moussis, "Le cadre juridique de la politique fiscale communautaire" (1983) 265 Rev. du M.C. 168.

VIII. *Economic and Monetary Policy*

The economy is one of the main responsibilities of the European Economic Community; the Treaty itself calls for "the application of procedures by which the economic policies of Member States can be co-ordinated and disequilibria in their balances of payments remedied"[6] and provides for measures to be taken by the institutions and the Member States with regard to conjunctural policy,[7] balance of payments[8] and commercial policy.[9] Mention should be made here of the programmes of the Council and the governments of the Member States on medium-term economic policy,[10] of the Monetary Committee which was set up to keep the monetary and financial situation of the Member States and the Community under review[11] and of the Annual Report on the Economic Situation in the Community adopted by the Council in pursuance of the decision of 1974 on the attainment of a high

---

[6] EEC, Art. 3 (*g*).
[7] EEC, Art. 103. Several Regs. Dirs. and Decs. were issued in pursuance of this provision; see, *e.g.* Dec. 74/120 (O.J. 1974, L. 63/16).
[8] EEC, Arts. 104–109. The most used provisions are those of Art. 105 (co-ordination of economic policy), see *e.g.* Dec. 64/300 on co-operation between the Central Banks (J.O. 1964, 1206; O.J. 1963–1964, 141) and the programmes for medium term economic policy (O.J. 1982, L. 236/1) and Art. 108 (Community action in case a Member State is in difficulties as regard its balance of payments), see, *e.g.* Dec. 71/143 setting up a machinery for medium-term financial assistance (J.O. 1971, L. 73/15; O.J. 1971 (I) 177) and Dec. 78/154 authorising the U.K. to take certain protective measures (O.J. 1978, L. 45/30).
[9] Commercial policy will be examined below, p. 236.
[10] So far five programmes covering a five year period have been adopted (see J.O. 1967, 1513; 1969, L. 129/1; 1971, L. 49/1; O.J. 1977, L. 101/1 and 1982, L. 236/10).
[11] EEC, Art. 105 (2) and the rules governing the Monetary Committee (J.O. 1958, 390; O.J. 1952–1958, 60).

degree of convergence of the economic policies of the Member States.[12]

The Annual Report 1984–1985 makes the following main points: economic activity should continue to expand, average inflation decelerated, monetary stability increased, but unemployment continued to rise: guidelines were set out to correct the structural weaknesses of the Community.[13]

The measures provided in the Treaty do not of course constitute an overall Community policy in the economic and monetary field, nor is it certain that the Member States at this point are prepared to accept a Community policy replacing their own. However, the deterioration of the general economic situation has persuaded the Member States that a greater convergence of the national economic and monetary policies was essential for their own survival and that of the Community.

1. Co-ordination of economic policies

Short-term economic and monetary policies have been co-ordinated over the years by the Commission and the Council working together, but here again a more comprehensive approach was required. At the European Council meeting in Copenhagen in April 1978, the Community agreed on a common economic policy strategy[14] in order to contribute to overall international action, to promote world economic recovery and facilitate progress towards economic and monetary union. In the light of this agreement, it was felt by the Community institutions that "concerted action" would boost the multiplier effect of national measures and alleviate the balance-of-payments and public finance constraints which limit the scope of economic policy measures. This concerted action was in turn defined by the European Council in Bremen[15] and implemented by the institutions.[16]

Economic problems are the subject of extensive scrutiny and discussion within the Community bodies, including the

[12] See Annual Economic Report, issued yearly by the Commission.
[13] European Economy, n. 22, November 1984 and Eighteenth General Report (1984), 73 and Bull. 10–1984, 14.
[14] Bull. 4–1978, 11.
[15] Bull. 6–1978, 17; the President of the European Council referred to "common approach" and "co-ordinated approach."
[16] Dec. 78/658 (O.J. 1978, L. 220/27), Bull. 7/8–1978, 22 and Twelfth General Report (1978), 70.

European Councils, particularly in the three fundamental areas of convergence, the medium-term programme and promoting investment.[17]

2. European Monetary System[18]

At its Bremen meeting in July 1978, the European Council outlined a scheme for establishing closer monetary co-operation. This was the creation of a European Monetary System (EMS) leading to a zone of monetary stability in Europe. The Council asked that the detailed rules necessary for the functioning of such a system be worked out.[19] The discussion leading to the final adoption of the EMS centres on two key questions: the system itself and the actions needed to strengthen, under the system, the economies of the less prosperous Member States.

The final system had four main characteristics: a European monetary unit,[20] an exchange rate and intervention mechanism,[21] a credit mechanism,[22] and a transfer mechanism.[23] The EMS came into operation on March 13, 1979.[24]

---

[17] Sixteenth General Report (1982), 67.

[18] The analysis of the EMS and the Resolution of the European Council of December 5, 1978 concerning the establishment of a European Monetary System is extracted from the Twelfth General Report (1978), 76.

[19] Bull. 6–1978, 17.

[20] The European monetary or currency unit, called ECU, is at the centre of the system; at its start its value and composition were identical with those of the EUA (European Unit of Account). The ECU serves as a *numéraire* (each currency has a central rate expressed in this unit), as the basis for a "divergence indicator," as denominator for claims and liabilities, arising under the intervention mechanism and credit mechanism; finally it serves also as a means of settlement between the monetary authorities of the Community.

[21] The exchange rate and intervention mechanism borrows some of its features from the "snake" which it has replaced, but it involves major innovations. The central rates of the national currencies expressed in ECU are used to establish a grid of bilateral exchange rates around which 2.25 per cent. fluctuation margins are established, except for Italy and Ireland which were given a 6 per cent. margin during the initial phase. The intervention mechanism is supported by unlimited very short-term credit facilities. Settlements are made through the European Monetary Co-operation Fund (EMCF).

[22] The existing credit mechanisms: short-term monetary support and short-term and medium-term credit are maintained and strengthened.

[23] Under the transfer mechanism the new borrowing and lending instrument and the European Investment Bank made up to 1 million EUA per year available to Italy and Ireland on special conditions for the financing of selected infrastructure projects and programmes.

[24] See regs. 3180/78 and 3181/78 (O.J. 1978, L. 379/1 and 2).

It has functioned satisfactorily since and has been an essential factor in achieving a more stable and orderly development of exchange rates in the Community and in shaping economic and monetary policies with a greater emphasis on stability and economic growth. During 1982, for instance, the monetary authorities twice realigned parities between the currencies participating in the EMS and once in 1983.[25] The conditions surrounding the realignments—both the decision-making process and the economic programmes adopted at national level—make it quite clear that the participating countries wish the EMS to function smoothly and that there is a common commitment to achieving a higher degree of convergence towards stability. In each case the countries most affected agreed to implement accompanying policies which would enhance the beneficial effects and neutralize the unwelcome results of the changes in parity.[26]

In this context mention must be made of the New Community borrowing and lending Instrument (NCI) created by the Council in 1978.[27] In empowers the Commission to contract loans and lend the money thus collected in order to promote investments which are in line with priority Community objectives in the energy, industry and infrastructure sectors, taking into account their regional impact and the need to combat unemployment.

3. Economic and Monetary Union

On the basis of a report drawn up by a committee under the chairmanship of Prime Minister and Minister of Finances of Luxembourg, Mr. Pierre Werner, the Council and the representatives of the governments of the Member States expressed their political will to establish an Economic and Monetary Union according to a plan starting in phases on January 1, 1971.[28] The final objective was the establishment of an area within which persons, goods, services and capital would move freely forming an individualised entity within the international system and having in the economic and monetary fields powers and respon-

[25] Bull. 2–1982, 18, 6–1982, 21 and 3–1983, 12.
[26] Sixteenth General Report (1982), 72.
[27] O.J. 1978, L. 298/9; 1982, L. 78/19 and 1983, L. 112/26.
  They also decided on the measures which were to be taken during the first stage ending on December 31, 1973.[29]
[28] See Council Dec. on the procedure for economic and monetary co-operation (J.O. 1970, L. 59/44; O.J. Sp. Ed. (2nd) 11) and Resolution of March 22, 1971 (J.O. 1971, C. 28/1; O.J. Sp. Ed. (2nd) IX, 40).

sibilities allowing its institutions to administer the union. Community instruments would be created whenever necessary.

If the first stage of the economic and monetary union was successfully implemented, the deteriorating general economic situation prevailing at the end of 1973 made the transition to the second stage impossible.[30]

In preparing and implementing the measures of economic policy, the Council and Commission are assisted by an Economic Policy Committee[31] and the European Institute for Economic and Social Policy Research.[32]

Further Reading

VIII. *Economic and Monetary Policy*

R. Gerster, "The I.M.F. and basic needs conditionality" (1982) 16 J. of W.T.L. 497.

J. A. Sargent, "Pressure group development in the E.C.: the role of the British Bankers Association" (1982) 20 J. of C.M.St. 269.

C. Rijnvos, "Dualisme binnen het E.M.S." (1982) 4 Nieuw Europa 163.

W. H. Hauschild, "Creditor protection in the E.C." (1982) 31 Int. and Comp. L.Q. 17.

P. Guimbretiere, "Les conditions d'un marché de l'écu" (1982) 261 Rev. du M.C. 529.

N. Moussis, "Le cadre juridique de la politique monétaire" (1982) 259 Rev. du M.C. 385.

N. Moussis, "Le cadre juridique de la politique économique" (1982) 260 Rev. du M.C. 482.

---

[29] These measures included: co-ordination of short-term economic policies, measures in the regional and structural field, co-ordination of monetary and credit policies, narrowing the fluctuations of exchange rates, etc.

[30] See however Bull. 10–1977, 15: "The Prospect of Economic and Monetary Union" and Bull. 2–1978, 16 for the action programme presented by the Commission.

[31] Dec. 74/122 (O.J. 1974, L. 63/21).

[32] See Twelfth General Report (1978), 78.

IX. *Social Policy*[33]

Apart from the extremely important measures provided by the Treaty concerning free movement of workers and related social security advantages, the Commission's task in the social field is wide and varied since it must promote "close co-operation between the Member States" in matters relating to employment, labour law and working conditions, basic and advanced vocational training, social security, prevention of occupational accidents and diseases, occupational hygiene and the right of association, and collective bargaining between employers and workers.[34]

The Treaty preamble indicates that the essential objective of the efforts of the Member States is the constant improvement of the living and working conditions of their peoples and in the enumeration of the activities of the Community, reference is made to the "creation of a European Social Fund in order to improve employment opportunities for workers and to contribute to the raising of their standard of living."[35]

The draftsmen of the Treaty expressed the conviction that this would be achieved, *inter alia*, through the functioning of the common market which would result in the harmonisation of social systems and approximation of other relevant legal and administrative provisions.[36] Their expectations were only partly fulfilled: standards of living did rise considerably but relatively speaking the poor remained poor and the rich became richer.

1. Employment

Of the various fields in which the Commission has the task to promote close co-operation between Member States, employment inevitably constitutes the most urgent one. The guiding principle for Community action in this domain is that social measures, *e.g.* national aids, intervention by the various Community funds, vocational readaptation, etc., should form an integral part of the industrial restructuring policy.[37] One may

---

[33] EEC, Arts. 117–128.
[34] EEC, Art. 118.
[35] EEC, Art. 3 (*i*).
[36] EEC, Art. 117, para. 2.
[37] Twelfth General Report (1978), 123.

repeat here what was said about other policies[38]: they cannot be seen in isolation, but constitute one aspect of the overall economic policy of the Community. Employment problems cannot be solved as such; job-creation is the result of investments which in turn are dictated by economic growth unless they are artificially induced through incentives. In times of economic recession most Member States rely very heavily on this method of direct intervention.

The Commission put forward various programmes[39] to combat unemployment and the Council adopted a resolution on the same subject[40] emphasising the link between economic policy and the job creation potential of small and medium-sized firms, local initiatives and co-operatives, the difficult situation of the young people and the reorganisation of working time. The Council also adopted a recommendation on retirement age.[41]

Nevertheless, direct measures to support the categories worst hit by the recession were required and the Commission's action gave priority in particular to young people, women, migrants and workers affected by restructuring operations in industry.[42]

With regard to *employment of women*, special reference should be made to several decisions of the Court interpreting the principle of equal treatment for men and women as regards pay, access to employment, vocational training and promotion, and working conditions.[43] In this field the other institutions of the

---

[38] The same is true, *e.g.* for competition and regional policy; see *Part Two* sections IV and V above, p. 167 and p. 195.

[39] See Community action programme to combat unemployment (Bull. 4–1982, 18).

[40] O.J. 1982, C. 186/3.

[41] O.J. 1982, L. 357/27.

[42] For more details see the annual Reports on Social Developments published by the Commission together with the General Report, in pursuance of Art. 122.

[43] Case 80/70 *Defrenne* v. *Belgium* [1971] E.C.R. 445 and Case 43/75 *Defrenne* v. *Sabena* [1976] E.C.R. 455 and more recently Case 129/79 *Macarthys* v. *Smith* [1980] E.C.R. 1275, Case 69/80 *Worringham and Humphreys* v. *Lloyd's Bank* [1981] E.C.R. 767, Case 96/80 *Jenkins* v. *Kingsgate* [1981] E.C.R. 911, Case 12/81 *Garland* v. *British Rail Engineering* [1982] E.C.R. 359, Case 19/81 *Burton* v. *British Railways Board* [1982] E.C.R. 555, Cases 61/81 *Commission* v. *U.K.* [1982] E.C.R. 2601 and 165/82 *Commission* v. *U.K.* [1983] E.C.R. 3431.

Community also took several measures[44] including directives on equal treatment.[45]

Mention should also be made here of the impressive efforts of the Community in the field of *vocational training* together with the European Centre for the Development of Vocational Training.[46]

2. European Social Fund

The Treaty provides for the establishment of a European Social Fund in order to improve employment opportunities[47] for workers and thereby contribute to raising the standard of living. The objectives are the same as those mentioned earlier and the Fund constitutes the Community's financial instrument to achieve them. The Fund is administered by the Commission which is assisted by a Social Fund Committee composed of representatives of governments, trade unions and employers organisations.[48] The Fund's resources are provided by the Community budget from the Community's own resources. The main function of the Fund is to reimburse Member States or public bodies for expenditure incurred for (a) vocational retraining and resettlement allowances and (b) unemployment benefits.

In 1983 the Council adopted a decision on the new tasks of the Social Fund and an implementing regulation[49]; accordingly the Social Fund shall participate in the financing of operations concerning (a) vocational training and guidance, (b) recruitment and wage subsidies, (c) resettlement and socio-vocational inte-

---

[44] See Commission publication: "Women and the European Community"; see also Eleventh General Report (1977), 127 and the Council Resolution on the promotion of equal opportunities for women (O.J. 1982, C. 1986/3).

[45] Dir. 75/117 (O.J. 1975, L. 45/19); Dir. 76/207 (O.J. 1976, L. 39/40); Dir. 79/7 (O.J. 1979, L. 6/24).

[46] See the Commission's communication on vocational training policies in the 1980s (O.J. 1982, C. 306/6) and one on vocational training and new information technologies (O.J. 1982, C. 162/7); see also Sixteenth General Report (1981), 128.

[47] In 1984, the first year of implementation of the new regulation adopted by the Council on October 17, 1983 (O.J. 1983, L. 289/1 and Seventeenth General Report, 1983, 134), the total amount available for assistance was 1,902.68 million ECU of which 1,859 were committed, *i.e.* 1,415.93 for actions in favour of young people of less than 25 years, 400 for those older than 25 years and 42 for innovation actions. The U.K. collected 32 per cent., Italy 22 and Greece 5, which seems rather disproportionate.

[48] See Council Decision 83/517 on the rules of the Committee (O.J. 1983, L. 289/42). See Case 44/81 *Germany* v. *Commission* [1982] E.C.R. 1855.

[49] O.J. 1983, L. 289/38 and 1. See also Commission Dec. of December 22, 1983, on the management of the European Social Fund (O.J. 1983, L. 377/1).

gration in connection with geographical mobility and (d) services and technical advice concerning job creation.[50]

Finally, *social protection* measures issued by the Community and measures regarding *living and working conditions* and health and safety[51] should be mentioned.

Further Reading

IX. *Social Policy*

Annual Commission Report on Social Developments.

H. Knorpel, "Social security cases in the Court of Justice of the E.C. 1978–1980 and 1981" (1981) 18 C.M.L.Rev. 579; (1982) 19 C.M.L.Rev. 105; (1982) 20 C.M.L.Rev. 97.

Laffan, "Policy implementation in the E.C.: the European Social Fund as a case study" (1983) XXI, 4 J. of C.M. Stud. 389.

Forman, "The equal pay principle under community law; a commentary on Art. 119 EEC" (1982) 1 Leg. Iss. of Eur. Int. 17.

A. Laurent, "E.C. law and equal treatment for men and women in social security" (1982) 121, 4 Intern. Labour Rev. 373.

B. Schulte, "Auf dem Weg zu einem Europäischen Sozialrecht?" (1982) 4 Eur. Recht 357.

N. Moussis, "Le cadre juridique de la politique sociale" (1982) 261 Rev. du M.C. 526.

A. Gruber, "Le fonds social européen à la veille d'un bilan" (1982) 2 Rev. Trim. de Dr. Eur. 251.

X. *Energy Policy*

A Community energy policy as such is not provided for under any of the European Treaties although coal, a main source of energy has been the object of Community measures since 1952 under the ECSC Treaty and the development of nuclear energy has been the objective of the Atomic Energy Community (Euratom) since 1958.

---

[50] Art. 1 (2) of the Decision, see *ibid.* at 39.
[51] For all those measures see details in the annual Reports on social developments.

The ECSC Treaty does not call for an overall energy policy and it was not until 1964 that the necessity for one was acknowledged by the Member States. In that year the governments of the Member States in Council approved a protocol concerning energy policy.[52] The objectives of such a policy were cheap supply, security of supply, harmonious substitution, stability of supply both as regards prices and quantities, free choice of the consumer and fair competition between the various sources of energy. In this framework the Council issued a directive on the maintenance of a minimum level of crude oil and for petroleum products stocks.[53]

In 1968, the Commission forwarded to the Council a document entitled "First Guidelines for a Community Energy Policy"[54] which laid emphasis on the need to adapt the structure of the Community's industry so as to enable it to meet expanding demand in the required conditions as regards costs and security of supply; it should also ensure the maintenance of a healthy competition on the market.[55] The fundamental principles of the memorandum were approved by the Council[56] which issued two regulations concerning notification of imports and investment projects in the energy field.[57]

After nine years of procrastination the Member States and the Community were caught totally unprepared for the first oil shock of 1973; yet even this major event, which was to change fundamentally the world's economic conditions to the grave detriment of the industrialised countries, could not incite the governments of the Nine to formulate, let alone implement, a common energy policy. The only action that could be obtained was a directive on measures to mitigate the effects of difficulties on the supply of crude oil and petroleum products[58] but it is left to the individual Member States to take the necessary measures.

[52] J.O. 1964, 69.
[53] J.O. 1968, L. 308/14, amended in 1972, J.O. 1972, L. 291/154; O.J. 1972 (28–30 Dec.) 69. See Case 72/83 *Campus Oil Ltd.* v. *Minister for Industry and Energy*, judgment of July 10, 1984 (not yet published).
[54] See Second General Report (1968), 251.
[55] Third General Report (1969), 251.
[56] Fourth General Report (1970), 207.
[57] J.O. 1972, L. 120/3 and 7; O.J. 1972 (II) 462 and 466. See also Reg. 1025/70 (J.O. 1970, L. 124/6; O.J. 1970 (II) 309 and O.J. 1974, L. 32/1) and two Regs. introducing registration of imports (O.J. 1979, L. 220/1 and L. 297/1); registration was suspended in 1981 (O.J. 1981, L. 52/1).
[58] O.J. 1973, L. 228/1.

The only concrete action of the Council during 1974 was the setting up of an Energy Committee[59] and the adoption of Resolutions on the objectives of a Community energy policy, objectives for 1985 and on a Community Action Programme on the rational utilisation of energy.[60] And the Commission once again submitted a memorandum this time entitled: "Towards a new energy policy strategy for the Community."[61]

In 1977, the Council adopted what the Commission calls the "politically and economically very important" Decision[62] on the exporting of crude oil and petroleum products from one Member State to another to ensure an equitable distribution in the event of supply difficulties.[63]

In order to increase the independence of the Community in matters of energy the Council adopted a framework Regulation on the granting of financial support for projects to exploit alternative energy sources.[64] Those projects may relate, for instance, to geothermal[65] sites, liquefaction and gasification of solid fuels, solar energy, wave energy or tidal energy. Another regulation was adopted on the granting of support for demonstration projects which offer substantial improvement in the efficiency with which energy is used.[66]

On June 9, 1980, the Council adopted a Resolution on the Community energy policy objectives for the 1980's and a convergence of the policies of the Member States,[67] and common approaches and initiatives in external energy relations.[68] Measures concerning coal and nuclear energy are also examined in the sections on the European Coal and Steel Community and the European Atomic Energy Community.

The conclusion to be drawn from the proceeding remarks is that no overall Community energy policy exists although some important measures were adopted in specific fields.

---

[59] *Ibid.*
[60] Bull. 12–1974, 14 and 17.
[61] Eighth General Report (1974), 191.
[62] O.J. 1977, L. 61/23 and L. 292/9.
[63] Eleventh General Report (1977), 192. For a summary description see Bull. 12–1976, 63. See also O.J. 1977, L. 292/9.
[64] O.J. 1978, L. 158/3; see Bull. 6–1982, 57.
[65] See Bull. 7/8–1982, 51.
[66] O.J. 1978, L. 158/3.
[67] O.J. 1979, C. 149/2; Bull. 5–1980, 23; see also O.J. 1979, L. 145/1.

X. *Energy Policy*

F. Müller, "Gesamteeuropäische Zusammenarbeit im Energie-bereich; ein neuer Ansatzpunkt für die Ost-West-Kooperation" (1979) Europa-Archiv 313.

G. Appollis, "La délibération de la C.J.C.E. sur la participation d'Euratom à la Convention sur la protection physique des matières et installations nucléaires" (1979) Rev. du M.C. 185.

Goybet, "La baisse du prix du pétrole chance ou ménace pour l'Europe" (1983) 266 Rev. du M.C. 187.

A.C. Evans, "E.C. Law and the problem of oil shortages" (1982) 31, 1 Int. and Comp. Law Quarterly 1.

A. Cruickshank and W. Walter, "Energy Research, development and demonstration in the E.C." (1981–82) 20 J. of C.M.S. 61–91.

XI. *Environment and Consumers*

1. Environment

At the Summit Conference at Paris in 1972, the Heads of State or Government of the enlarged Community emphasised the importance of a Community environment policy and they invited the Community institutions to establish, before July 31, 1973, a programme of action accompanied by a precise timetable.[69] A first programme proposed by the Commission was adopted by the Council and the Representatives of the Governments of the

---

[68] The importance of the relations and co-operation with third countries, and particularly with oil-producing countries does not have to be demonstrated; notwithstanding many official statements (Western Economic Summits at Versailles in 1982 and Williamsburg in 1983 and the United Nations Conferences) no concrete steps have as yet been formalised.

[69] Sixth General Report (1972), 12. See also Bull. 10–1972, 20.

Member States on November 22, 1973.[70] It set the objectives, stated the principles, selected the priorities and described the measures to be taken in the next two years. The Council adopted eleven principles of which three deserve particular mention: the necessity of preventive action; the responsibility of the polluter[71] and the need for action to be taken at the most appropriate level. From the end of 1973 the Commission submitted to the Council several drafts for regulations, directives, recommendations and resolutions under the programme of action.[72]

On March 5, 1973, the representatives of the governments of the Member States meeting in Council concluded an agreement concerning the information[73] of the Commission and the Member States with a view to harmonisation throughout the Community of priority measures to protect the environment.[74] At the international level, the Community participates actively in the work of organisations concerned with topics closely linked to the projects being carried out in the Community.[75]

---

[70] Seventh General Report (1973), 235 and O.J. 1973, C. 112/1. A resolution on the continuation and implementation of a European Community policy and action programme on the environment was adopted on May 17, 1977 (O.J. 1977, C. 139/1; see also 1982, C. 294/2); a second followed in 1977 (O.J. 1981, C. 133/1) and a third programme was adopted in 1982 (O.J. 1983, C. 46/1). For a review of the work undertaken under the second programme see Communication of the Commission (Bull. 5–1980, 44).

[71] The "polluter-pays" principle means that the expenses of preventing and eliminating pollution should, in principle, be paid by the polluter. It requires, however, careful assessment. The indiscriminate application of this principle to certain sensitive sectors of the economy, suddenly subjecting them to stricter rules, could have undesirable social and regional consequences. Special arrangements and transitional periods can avoid these consequences: implementing procedures and exceptions must be defined. This was done in a resolution of the Council (Bull. 11–1974, 11) and in a notice sent to the Member States by the Commission concerning the application of the Treaty provisions on state aids to anti-pollution investments (Bull. 11–1974, 39). Also: O.J. 1975, L. 194/1.

[72] For details see "State of the Environment," Fifth Report by the Commission (1982).

[73] O.J. 1973, C. 9/1.

[74] See General Reports: 1980, 158; 1981, 149; 1982, 152.

[75] United Nations Environment Programme, Paris Convention for the Prevention of Marine Pollution, Strasbourg Convention on the protection of International Waters (Eighth General Report (1974), 136 and Thirteenth (1979), 139), Barcelona Convention on the protection of the Mediterraneran sea against pollution from land-based sources (Fourteenth General Report (1980), 157 and Bull. 3–1983, January 2, 1976), OECD, Economic Commission for Europe, Geneva Convention on Long-range Transboundary Air Pollution, Berne

The Council set up a European Foundation for the Improvement of Living and Working Conditions.[76]

After the pollution caused by the *Amoco Cadiz* disaster, the Commission put forward a number of proposals for measures regarding the protection of the marine environment; the Council approved some measures on the control and reduction of pollution caused by hydrocarbons discharged at sea.[77]

Although the Treaty does not provide for any measures in the field of environment protection, the Community was able to develop a comprehensive policy to cope with one of the major problems of modern times; measures enacted by the institutions in respect of the environment are mainly based on EEC, Article 235.[78]

2. Consumers[79]

Guidelines for Community action in this field were laid down in a Preliminary Programme contained in a Council Resolution of 1975.[80] The programme refers *inter alia* to protection of consumer's health and safety, protection of the economic interests of the consumer (misleading advertising, unfair commercial practices, etc.), advice, help and redress, consumer information and

---

Convention on the Conservation of European Wild Life and Natural Habitats, Bonn Convention on Migratory Species of Wild Animals, U.N. Environment Programme, Committee of International Development Institutions for the Environment (Sixteenth General Report (1982), 151), Paris Convention for the prevention of Marine pollution from Land-based Sources (Bull. 3–1983, January 2, 1974), Oslo Convention for the prevention of marine pollution by dumping from ships and aircraft (*ibid.* at 75), Convention for the protection and development of marine environment of the wider Carribian region (*ibid.* at 78) and Convention on international trade in endangered species of wild fauna and flora (O.J. 1983, L. 344/1).

[76] O.J. 1978, L. 139/1.
[77] O.J. 1977, L. 240/1 and O.J. 1981, L. 355/52: Decision establishing a Community information system for preventing and combatting oil pollution of the sea (see also Fifteenth General Report (1981), 143).
[78] Policy areas for future action laid down by the Council include: the prevention of the reduction of pollution and nuisances in the atmosphere, water and soil, the battle against noise nuisances, the control of dangerous chemical substances and wastes, the promotion of "clean" technologies and co-operation with developing countries.
[79] Full details can be found in the annual Reports published by the Commission since 1977 on Consumer Protection and Information Policy.
[80] O.J. 1975, C. 92/1.

consumer consultation and representation. Unfortunately in these fields no measures were taken by the Community until now, although other measures concerning, *e.g.* the abolition of technical barriers to trade are beneficial also for the consumer.[81]

A second programme for a consumer protection and information policy was adopted in 1981.[82]

Further Reading

XI. *Environment and Consumers*

G. L. Close, "The legal basis for the Consumer Protection Programme of the EEC and priorities for action" (1983) 8 E.L. Rev. 221.

XII. *Industrial and Intellectual Property Rights*

Reference to industrial rights is to be found in Article 36,[83] which provides that notwithstanding the prohibition of restrictions on trade between Member States,[84] limitations can be justified to protect "industrial and commercial property." This expression includes the protection conferred by copyright, especially when exploited commercially in the form of licences capable of affecting distribution in the various Member States of goods incorporating the protected literary or artistic work.[85] It can be held that the expression covers all the rights mentioned in the Paris Convention on the Protection of Industrial Property.[86]

The owners of such rights enjoy a legal and absolute monopoly[87] since they can, as any property owner, claim exclusive use. By doing so they can prevent trade between Member States since the protection is afforded by each State separately. As the Court

---

[81] See Thirteenth General Report (1979), 140 and Sixteenth General Report (1982), 153.

[82] O.J. 1981, C. 133/1.

[83] Above, p. 120.

[84] EEC, Arts. 30–34.

[85] Joined Cases 55 and 57/80 *Musik-Vertrieb Membran* v. *GEMA* [1981] E.C.R. 147 at 161 (9).

[86] Reference to this Convention is made in Art. 18 (4) of the Euratom Treaty. For the revision of this convention protecting the national systems of property ownership see Bull. 11–1982, 17. See also EEC, Art. 222.

[87] However it does not constitute automatically a dominant position in the sense of Art. 86.

put it, in the absence of unification of national rules relating to such protection, industrial property rights and the differences between the national rules[88] are capable of creating obstacles to the free movement of products covered by such rights.[89] The exercise of a property right granted and guaranteed by national law therefore constitutes a derogation to certain fundamental rules of the Treaty; the question therefore arose of how to reconcile the individual property rights with the fundamental principle of free trade. The answer was given by the court[90]: the *existence* of the rights granted by a Member State is not affected by the Community provisions, but the exercise of such rights can, under certain conditions, fall under a prohibition of the Treaty.[91] Although the first Court decision dealt with industrial property rights in relation to the competition rules, the Court applied the same approach later in regard to free movement of goods.

It follows therefore that, through its exclusivity and territorial limitation (the latter following from the fact that the rights in question are granted and guaranteed by national law), the exercise of a property right constitutes a derogation to certain fundamental rules of the Treaty. Consequently such exercise must be strictly limited to what is necessary to safeguard those rights that "constitute the specific subject matter[92] of industrial and commercial property but taking into account what is actually left of this specific matter after the use the owner has made of it

---

[88] See, however, the European patent Convention, O.J. 1976, L. 17/1.

[89] Case 24/67 *Parke, Davis* v. *Centrafarm* [1968] E.C.R. 55 at 71.

[90] Community law in this field was entirely developed by the case-law of the Court of Justice.

[91] Case 24/67 (*Parke, Davis*), above, n. 89 at 73. In joined Cases 56 and 58/64 *Consten and Grundig* v. *Commission* [1966] E.C.R. 299, the trade-mark was the object of a prohibited agreement and had as its sole purpose to prevent the import of identical products from other Member States. See also Case 40/70 *Serena* v. *Eda* [1971] E.C.R. 69 and Case 78/70, below, n. 94.

[92] Case 192/73 *Van Zuylen* v. *Hag* [1974] E.C.R. 731. See also Cases 15/74 *Centrafarm* v. *Sterling Drug* and 16/74 *Centrafarm* v. *Winthrop*, both [1974] E.C.R. 1147 and 1183, where the Court defined what the subject matter is of a patent (Case 15/74 at 1162) and that of a trade-mark (Case 16/74 at 1194). See alo Case 24/67 (*Parke, Davis*) above n. 89: it follows from the reasoning of the Court that Parke, Davis was justified in opposing the import and distribution of the unpatented Italian product since otherwise its own patent would have become meaningless and Case 119/75 *Terrapin* v. *Terranova* [1976] E.C.R. 1039 from which it follows that the avoidance of confusion between two products bearing similar names constitutes also the subject-matter of the protection provided by a trade-mark.

within the Common market."[93] The Court held, for instance, that it would be in conflict with the provisions prescribing the free movement of products within the common market for a manufacturer of a protected article to exercise the exclusive right to distribute it, conferred upon him by the legislation of a Member State in such a way as to prohibit the sale in that State of products placed on the market by him or with his consent in another Member State solely because such distribution did not occur within the territory of the first Member State.[94] In other words, once the owner of a right has exercised it in such a way that its use by others in another Member State becomes legal, he can no longer claim territorial exclusivity within the common market. The situation therefore can be different in regard to products coming from a third country.[95]

The various rules elaborated with regard to property rights and free movement of goods over the years were restated by the Court as follows: (1) the Treaty does not affect the existence of property rights recognised by the law of a Member State; (2) the exercise of those rights may nevertheless, depending on the circumstances, be restricted by the prohibitions of the Treaty; (3) in as much as an exception to the fundamental principles of the Treaty is provided,[96] it applies only to the extent necessary to safeguard rights which constitute the specific subject-matter of that property; (4) the owner of a right cannot rely on national law to prevent the importation of a product which has been marketed in another Member State by the owner or with his consent; (5) it is the same when the right relied on is the result of a subdivision, either voluntary or publicly imposed, of a trade-mark which originally belonged to a single owner; (6) even when the rights belong to different proprietors, national law may not be relied on when the exercise of these rights is the purpose, means or result

---

[93] The words "for the first time" used in the *Centafarm* cases (n.92) are important because once the right has been used the subject-matter might have been "used up" and therefore no longer exists within the common market. The Court refers to "exhaustion of rights." The same principle was applied in several other cases; see joined Cases 55 and 57/80 (*Membran*) above n.85; Case 58/80 *Dansk Supermarked* v. *Imerko* [1981] E.C.R. 181; Case 187/80 *Merck* v. *Stephar and Exler* [1981] E.C.R. 2063 (patent) and Case 1/81 *Pfizer* v. *Eurim-Pharm* [1981] E.C.R. 2913 (trade-mark).

[94] Case 78/70 *Deutsche Grammophon* v. *Metro* [1971] E.C.R. 487 at 500 (13).

[95] See the *EMI* Cases 51/75, 86/75 and 96/75, all [1976] E.C.R. 811, 871 and 913.

[96] EEC, Art. 36.

of a prohibited agreement; (7) it is compatible with the Treaty provisions concerning free trade for the owner of a trade-mark to prevent the importation of products from another Member State and legally bearing a name giving rise to confusion with the trade-mark, provided there is no agreement or link between the owner and the producer in the other Member State and that their respective rights have arisen independently.[97] A specific case is that of the owner of two different trade-marks one in each of two Member States, for the same product: he may oppose the importation of those products in the other Member State by a third party.[98] It follows from the decisions of the Court that the general principles set out above, will in the present state of Community law[99] answer most if not all cases regarding the extent to which industrial and commercial property rights may be exercised with regard to the Treaty rules concerning free movement of goods and competition.[1]

In August 1984 the Commission issued a regulation on the application of a group exemption to certain categories of patent licensing agreements.[2]

Further Reading

XII. *Industrial and intellectual property rights*

C. W. F. Baden Fuller, "Economic issues relating to property rights in trademarks" (1981) 6 E.L. Rev. 162.

XIII. *Approximation of Laws*

The proper functioning of the Common Market and the implementation of common policies require approximation (or harmonisation) of the laws of the Member States[3]; consequently

---

[97] Case 119/75 (*Terrapin*) above n. 92. It is for the national courts to determine whether a risk of confusion does in fact exist bearing in mind the second sentence of Art. 36: "the exercise of a property right may not constitute a means of arbitrary discrimination."

[98] Case 3/78 *Centrafarm* v. *American Home Products Corporation* [1978] E.C.R. 1823.

[99] Case 119/75 (*Terrapin*) above n. 92, at 1061.

[1] In regard to the competition rules see Case 258/78 *Nungesser* v. *Commission* [1982] E.C.R. 2015 (exclusive license and Art. 85 (1)), Case 144/81 *Keurkoop* v. *Nancy Kean Gifts* [1982] E.C.R. 2853 (designs and models) and Case 262/81 *Coditel* v. *Cine-Vog Films* [1982] E.C.R. 3381 (copyright).

[2] O.J. 1984, L. 219/15.

[3] EEC, Art. 3 (*h*).

the Treaty provides that the Council shall issue directives for the approximation of such provisions laid down by law, regulation or administrative action in Member States as directly affect the establishment and functioning of the common market.[4]

Approximation of laws must be seen as a necessary complement to the basic freedoms and, in certain cases, as a necessary condition for an effective exercise of those freedoms. As was pointed out, the freedoms are based on the principle of free movement across national borders and non-discrimination within the Member States: individuals, goods and services must be treated in a given Member State in exactly the same way as the national individuals, goods and services.

The elimination of discriminations does not, however, suffice to make free movement effective, neither does it ensure uniform national treatment throughout the whole Community of all those who operate in the common market.

Free movement of persons, goods and services can be hampered by lack of harmonised rules, and the provisions concerning the basic freedoms consequently provide for some approximation of national rules.[5]

The same applies to turnover taxes, excise duties and other forms of indirect taxation including countervailing measures applicable to trade between Member States.[6] Over the years the Council has issued several dozens of directives.[7] These directives require unanimity in the Council and consultation of the

---

[4] EEC, Art. 100.

[5] See, *e.g.* customs matters (Art. 27), mutual recognition of diplomas (Art. 57 (1)), taxation (Art. 99), export aids (Art. 112).

[6] EEC, Art. 99. All the VAT Directives referred to above in Tax Provisions and VAT, p. 207, are based upon Arts. 99 and 100.

[7] Most directives issued by the Council on the basis of Arts. 99, 100 and 101 can be classified in the following categories: (1) Customs legislation and Commercial policy, *e.g.* Reg. on generalised tariff preferences for 1983 (O.J. 1982, L. 263/1); (2) competition and free movement of goods: more than 60 directives were issued concerning vehicles, others concern textiles, measuring instruments, insurance, chemical products, metals, etc.; (3) footstuffs: *e.g.* Dir. 80/777 (O.J. 1980, L. 229/1) concerning commercialisation of mineral waters; (4) forestry; (5) veterinary questions; (6) agriculture.

Many court cases were initiated by the Commission against Member States for failing to implement such directives: *e.g.* Case 91/79 *Commission* v. *Italy* [1980] E.C.R. 1099 and joined Cases 2 and 4/82 *Delhaize Frères* v. *Belgian State* [1983] E.C.R. 2973, the latter dealing with Dir. 71/118 concerning veterinary questions.

Detailed information can be found in the Bull. and annual General Report of the Commission.

European Parliament and the Economic and Social Committee, when the implementation of the directive involves amendment of legislation in one or more Member States.

Besides impeding the proper functioning of the Common Market, differences between the provisions laid down by law, regulation or administrative action in Member States can distort the conditions of competition between persons and undertakings situated in one state as compared to similar legal or natural persons in another.[8] If the Commission is of the opinion that such a distortion must be eliminated, it must consult the Member State concerned; if such consultation does not result in the elimination of that distortion, the Council, acting by a qualified majority, must issue the necessary directives.[9]

The Treaty thus makes a distinction between approximation of national rules which affect the common market and approximation required to eliminate distortion of competition; it is not always easy, however, to distinguish between the two.

By creating identical conditions under which persons and companies can operate throughout the Community, the approximation of laws constitutes an essential element of economic and social integration, in the same way as the basic freedoms do.

PART THREE: EXTERNAL RELATIONS

I. *Community's Jurisdiction*

Under this heading will be examined the Community's commercial policy, development policy, its relations with international organisations and the bilateral and regional relations. However, before going into details some general remarks seem necessary. Indeed, while the ECSC Treaty explicitly provides that in international relations the Coal and Steel Community enjoys "the legal capacity it requires to perform its functions and attain its objectives,"[10] and the Euratom Treaty confers upon the Atomic Energy Community the authority to enter, within the limits of its powers and jurisdiction, "into obligations by

---

[8] EEC, Art. 101.
[9] Very few directives were issued in pursuance of these provisions.
[10] ECSC Treaty, Art. 6. This international legal personality is not therefore a full one, comparable to that of an independent State.

concluding agreements or contracts with a third State, an international organisation or a national of a third State,"[11] the EEC Treaty only refers to the "establishment of a commercial policy towards third countries" and the "association of the overseas countries and territories"[12] and contains a few specific provisions.[13] The absence of a general provision has not prevented the Community from developing a particularly active external policy, with the help, *inter alia*, of the Court of Justice. In other words, the Community participates in activities which come within the ambit of international law. As a body created by an international treaty concluded between sovereign States in order to exercise activities in the international field, the Treaty confers upon the Community, as far as those States are concerned, international legal personality. But it is to the extent that other subjects of international law recognise the EEC as a member of the international community that the Community can take initiatives and play an active role in the international sphere; this recognition is no longer a problem. It is among the Member States that some disagreement still exists on the extent of the Community's jurisdiction in foreign affairs, especially with regard to the treaty-making power, *i.e.* how much of their treaty-making power was transferred to the EEC? And with regard to those powers which were transferred there remains the question whether they are to be exercised exclusively by the Community institutions or in conjunction with the Member States.

As far as the first question is concerned the views of the Court of Justice were clearly formulated in 1971[14] and repeated in later

---

[11] Euratom, Art. 101.

[12] However, EEC, Art. 210 provides that "the Community shall have legal personality" and nothing in this text limits it to activities within the Community.

[13] See EEC, Arts. 111 (trade relations with third countries), 113 (tariff and trade agreements), 131–135 (agreements with overseas countries and territories) and 238 (association).

[14] Case 22/70 *Commission* v. *Council* (better known as the AETR (European Transport Agreement) case) [1971] E.C.R. 263 at 274 (14). See also the opinions of the Court given under EEC, Art. 228: Opinion 1/75 [1975] E.C.R. 1355: compatibility with the EEC Treaty of a draft "Understanding on a Local Cost Standard" drawn up under the auspices of the OECD; Opinion 1/76 [1977] E.C.R. 741: compatibility of a draft agreement establishing a European laying-up fund for inland waterway vessels; Opinion 1/78 [1979] E.C.R. 2871:

judgments.[15] They were based on Article 210 of the Treaty which provides that "the Community shall have legal personality." According to the Court, this provision placed at the head of Part Six of the Treaty devoted to "General and Final Provisions," means that in its external relations the Community enjoys the capacity to enter into international commitments over the whole field of objectives defined in Part One of the Treaty, which Part Six supplements. Just as important is the statement that follows:

> "to establish in a particular case whether the Community has authority to enter into international commitments, regard must be had to the whole scheme of Community law no less than to its substantive provisions. Such authority arises not only from an express conferment by the Treaty but may equally flow implicitly from other provisions of the Treaty, from the Act of accession and from measures adopted, within the framework of those provisions, by the Community institutions."[16]

In other words whenever Community law has created for the institutions powers within its internal system for the purpose of attaining a specific objective, the Community has authority to enter into the international commitments necessary for the attaining of that objective even in the absence of an express provision in that connection.[17] This is particularly so in all cases in which internal power has already been used in order to adopt measures which come within the attainment of common policies.[18]

With regard to the second question—exclusive or shared jurisdiction—the Court admits a "mixed procedure," *i.e.* both Community and Member States are contracting parties when an agreement covers matters for which the Community is competent and others coming within the ambit of Member States.[19] But

---

compatibility with the Treaty of the draft International Agreement on Natural Rubber negotiated in the UNCTAD.

The Euratom treaty knows a similar procedure under Art. 103: see Ruling 1/78 [1978] E.C.R. 2151: compatibility of draft Convention of the IAEA on the Physical Protection of Nuclear Materials, Facilities and Transport.

[15] See, *e.g.* joined Cases 3, 4 and 6/76 *Kramer* [1976] E.C.R. 1279.
[16] *Ibid.* at 1308 (17/18).
[17] Opinion 1/76 (*laying-up fund*) (above n. 14) at 755.
[18] *Ibid.*
[19] Case 22/70 (*AETR*) (above n. 14) at 274 (18).

when Community powers exist, only the Community may conclude agreements with third countries.[20] This is *inter alia* the case in regard to commercial policy.[21] However this emergence of Community competence should not be seen as a sudden break; Community law being evolutive, the transfer of powers from the Member States to the Community is necessarily gradual.[22] But each time the Community, with a view to implementing a common policy envisaged by the Treaty, adopts provisions laying down common rules whatever form these may take, Member States, acting individually or even collectively, no longer have the right to undertake obligations with third countries affecting those rules.[23] As long as the Community has not exercised its right to conclude agreements, the Member States retain the power to do so[24]; but this authority is only of a transitional nature and Member States are bound by Community obligations in their negotiations with third countries: they may not enter into or renew any commitment which could hinder the Community in the carrying out of the tasks entrusted to it by the Treaty.[25] This raises the question of the consequences for the Community and community law of collective commitments undertaken by Member States. Here also the Court of Justice has, through various judgments, formulated the basic principles. For instance with regard to tariffs and trade policy the Member States have progressively transferred to the Community their jurisdiction; by doing so they have also conferred upon the Community the international rights and obligations connected with the exercise of this jurisdiction, particularly with regard to the General Agreement for Tariffs and Trade (GATT). It follows that the Community

---

[20] See, *e.g.* Case 22/70 (*AETR*) above n. 14 at 276 (31).

[21] Opinion 1/75 (*OECD*) (above see n. 14) at 1362).

[22] See Case 22/70 (*AETR*) (above n. 14) at 281 (81–92). In this respect the Court referred in particular to EEC, Art. 5.

[23] Case 22/70 (*AETR*) (above n. 14) at 274 (17). See also Opinion 1/76 (*ibid.*).

[24] See answer to Parliamentary question n. 173/77 (O.J. 1978, C. 72/1).

[25] Joined Cases 3, 4 and 6/76 (*Kramer*) (above n. 15) at 1310 (40). See EEC, Art. 111 (4) obliging Member States to bring about adjustments to tariff agreements in force with third countries. See also EEC, Art. 234 which provides that the entry into force of the Treaty does not affect existing agreements concluded between one or more Member States and one or more third countries.

itself is bound by that agreement.[26] A clear case of substitution of the Community for the Member States in the implementation of multilateral treaties bearing on the subject matter of the EEC Treaty. As for the rights which might derive for the Community from this agreement, their exercise depends on recognition by the other contracting parties.

The inner problems of the Community in this field may not of course obliterate the interests of third countries: in the various statements of the Court mentioned above, this principle was underlined several times,[27] without allowing any intervention by third States in internal matters of the Community and, more particularly, in the determination of the very complex and delicate relationship between the Community and its own Member States.[28]

A last question to be examined here is the effect of international commitments undertaken by the Community. In the first place it should be noted that such commitments constitute "acts of the institutions of the Community" and as such can be challenged in Court as to their compatibility with the Treaty.[29] In the second place provisions of international agreements concluded by the Community in conformity with the procedures provided for in the Treaty "shall be binding on the institutions of the Community and on Member States."[30] Such provisions have direct application in the Community: they can have direct effect and therefore override conflicting provisions of the national law of the Member States.[31]

---

[26] Joined Cases 21 to 24/72 *International Fruit Company* v. *Produktschap voor groenten en fruit* [1972] E.C.R. 1219 at 1227 (18). The Community has assumed these powers in pursuance of EEC, Arts. 111 and 113. See also Case 38/75 *Nederlandse Spoorwegen* v. *Inspecteur der invotoerrechten en accijnzen* [1975] E.C.R. 1439 at 1450 (21); joined Cases 267–269/81 *Amministrazione delle Finanze dello Stato* v. *SPI and SAMI* [1983] E.C.R. 801, and 290–291/81 *Singer and Geigy* v. *Amministrazione delle Finanze dello Stato* [1983] E.C.R. 847.

[27] See *e.g.* Opinions 1/75 (*OECD*) and 1/76 (*laying-up fund*) (above n. 14).

[28] See *e.g.* Ruling 1/78 (*IAEA*) (above n. 14) at 2180 (35).

[29] EEC, Arts. 173 and 177.

[30] EEC Treaty, Art. 228 (2). See also Opinion 1/76 (*laying-up fund*) (above n. 14) at 6 and 7.

[31] Case 87/75 *Bresciani* v. *Amministratione Italiana delle finanze* [1976] E.C.R. 129, at 141 (23). See also Case 65/77 *Razanatsimba* [1977] E.C.R. 2229.

II. *Commercial Policy*

The Treaty provides for the "establishment of a common customs tariff and a common commercial policy towards third countries.[32] It was pointed out above that the two are complementary, the customs tariffs being the main instrument of any commercial policy. It was also shown that the elimination of all trade barriers between the Member States required a "common" customs tariff toward third countries and it follows from what was just said that this common customs tariff could only function within the framework of a "common" commercial policy. Commercial policy is thereby transferred from the national ambit into the Community's jurisdiction.[33] This is particularly true for the customs tariffs: they can be lowered or raised according to the needs of commercial policy and the Community has exclusive power to do so. Consequently measures of commercial policy of a national character are only permissible by virtue of specific authorisation by the Community.[34] There exist two procedures for changes: the autonomous modification[35] and modifications through agreements with third countries.[36] For such agreements the Commission makes recommendations to the Council, which authorises the Commission to open the necessary negotiations.[37]

In case the implementation of the common commercial policy were to lead to economic difficulties in a Member State, the Commission may authorise that state to take the necessary protective measures,[38] which can deviate from the provisions regarding free movement of goods.[39] However the provisions concerning such measures must be interpreted restrictively since they derogate from provisions which are fundamental to the

---

[32] EEC, Art. 3 (*b*) and 9 (1). See above, p. 112.

[33] See Opinion 1/75 (*OECD*) (above n. 14) at 1364.

[34] Case 41/76 *Donckerwolke* v. *Procureur de la République* [1976] E.C.R. 1921 at 1937 (32). See, *e.g.* Commission Dec. 80/605 authorising surveillance of imports (O.J. 1980, L. 164/20).

[35] EEC, Art. 28. See also Art. 25.

[36] EEC, Arts. 111 and 113 (1).

[37] EEC, Art. 113 (3); these negotiations are conducted in close consultation with a special Committee composed of national officials appointed by the Council.

[38] EEC, Art. 115.

[39] Case 62/70 *Bock* v. *Commission* [1971] E.C.R. 897 at 909 (14).

operations of the common market and maintain an obstacle to the full implementation of the common commercial policy.[40]

Mention must be made here of a Council decision of 1961 on the progressive standardisation of agreements concerning commercial relations between Member States and third countries in order to eliminate disparities existing between the arrangements of the various Member States with third countries.[41] On the basis of this decision the Commission examines the Member States' trade arrangements with non-Member countries to check them for compatibility with the Community's developing commercial policy.[42] The Council, acting on a proposal from the Commission, authorises Member States to renew or extend existing agreements.[43] Another Council decision[44] established a consultation procedure for co-operation agreements to be concluded between Member States and third countries. Member States must inform the Commission and the other Member States of any agreement relating to economic and industrial co-operation which they propose to negotiate or renew with third countries and of any commitments and measures proposed by the authorities of the Member States concerned as part of the co-operation agreements. The Commission and a Member State may request prior consultation to ensure that the agreements are consistent with common policies, to encourage co-ordination and to examine the advisability of unilateral action which should be taken by the Commission.

The most impressive Community achievement in the field of commercial policy is constituted by the GATT multilateral trade negotiations. After the so-called Kennedy Round of 1967, in which the EEC played a major role,[45] the Community participated actively in the "Tokyo Round" of multilateral trade negotiations which started in 1973. After approval by the Council, the agreements were signed by the Commission in

---

[40] *Ibid.* See particularly Case 29/75 *Kaufhof* v. *Commission* [1976] E.C.R. 431 at 443 (6) where the Court annulled a Commission's decision granting an authorisation under Art. 115 because the Commission failed to examine the justification put forward by the Member State and whether the measures were necessary.

[41] J.O. 1961, 1274; O.J. 1959–1962, 84.

[42] See, *e.g.* O.J. 1978, L. 44, L. 123 and L. 225.

[43] See Council Dec. of November 4, 1983 authorising extension tacit renewal of certain trade agreements concluded between Member States and third countries (O.J. 1983, L. 309/30 and L. 340/13).

[44] Dec. 74/393 O.J. 1974, L. 208/23.

[45] See Tenth General Report (1966), 310 and First General Report (1967), 381.

1979[46]; they provide for cuts in industrial[47] and agricultural tariffs,[48] the strengthening of the GATT rule by drawing up a series of "codes" in non-tariff fields and the international dairy and bovine meat arrangements. Implementation of such agreements comes within the sphere of the common commercial policy.

With regard to *imports* in general, various rules exist within the Community applicable to trade with State-trading countries[49] and to other non-Member countries.[50] All the measures taken by the Community institutions in this field concern further liberalisation, thereby confirming the basically liberal common commercial policy of the Community. The various regulations and decisions concerning imports establish freedom of import for a wide range of products.[51] They also allow, however, for supervision,[52] in order to guarantee that the imports of particular products will not prejudice the interests of the Community producers, and for the introduction of safeguard measures in the event of serious danger. The most important of these measures are those which can be imposed by the Commission when applying the Community *anti-dumping* rules.[53] Several such procedures are initiated each year,[54] either at the request of Member States, any natural or legal person, or any association, not having legal personality, acting on behalf of a Community industry, which considers itself injured or threatened by

---

[46] O.J. 1980, L. 71/1.

[47] *Ibid.* at 5.

[48] *Ibid.* at 7, 11.

[49] See below and Reg. 1765/82 (O.J. 1982, L. 195/1).

[50] For more details see the annual General Reports and the Bulletin. See also Reg. 288/82 (O.J. 1982, L. 35/1) and Sixteenth General Report (1982), 234.

[51] See Twelfth General Report (1978), 250 and Thirteenth (1979), 224.

[52] See, *e.g.* system of surveillance introduced on imports of footwear (O.J. 1978, L. 188/28). See *ibid.* for voluntary restraint agreements concluded between the Community and third countries for iron and steel products, textile products and footwear.

[53] See Reg. 459/68 on protection against dumping or the granting of bounties or subsidies, by non-Member countries (J.O. 1968, L. 93/1; O.J. 1968 I, 80) based upon EEC, Arts. 111, 113 and 227. This Reg. was recently modified by Reg. 3017/79 (O.J. 1979, L. 339/1). See Case 113/77 R *NTN TOYO* v. *Council* [1977] E.C.R. 1721; Case 119/77 R *Nippon Seiko* v. *Council and Commission* [1977] E.C.R. 1867 and Case 121/77 R *Nachi Fuyikoshi* v. *Council* [1977] E.C.R. 2107; Case 191/82 *Fediol* v. *Commission* [1983] E.C.R. 2913, establishing the rights of private companies which request the Commission to take anti-dumping measures.

[54] See, Eighteenth General Report (1984), 244; see also *ibid.* at 243 on new commercial policy instrument (O.J. 1984, L. 252/1).

dumping. The Commission may then apply an anti-dumping duty on the dumped products. Other specific measures of commercial policy have been taken by the Community institutions for various products, namely to ensure that the external arrangements operate properly[55] or to counteract protectionist measures adopted by certain industrialised countries.[56]

Where *exports* are concerned, the principle of freedom of export for almost all the headings of the common external tariff was established by the Council in 1969.[57] Community quantitative export quotas for certain products are fixed by the Council, sometimes on a yearly basis.[58] Another important item of commercial policy is to be found in the export credit system, with or without insurances or guarantees, applied by various Member States.[59] In October 1970, the Council adopted two directives concerning the introduction by Member States of common insurance policies for medium and long-term transactions based on suppliers credit and intended for public and private buyers.[60] Various other directives and decisions were adopted by the Council in an effort to harmonise the policies of the Member States in this field.[61]

The Community participates in *Commodity* and *World agreements* such as the UNCTAD's integrated programme for commodities[62] and in the international Agreements for Cocoa,[63]

---

[55] See, *e.g.* for iron and steel products, Thirteenth General Report (1979), 26.

[56] See, *e.g.* for footwear, Twelfth General Report (1978), 255.

[57] Reg. 2603/69 establishing common rules for exports (J.O. 1969, L. 324/25; O.J. 1969, 590), amended by Reg. 1934/82 (J.O. 1982, L. 211/1): it updates the list of the few export restrictions still existing in certain Member States.

[58] See Reg. 915/78 (O.J. 1978, L. 119/9).

[59] For the OECD Understanding on Export Credits for Ships and the Arrangement on Guidelines for Officially Supported Export Credits ("consensus") see Sixteenth General Report (1982), 238.

[60] Dirs. 70/509 and 70/510 (O.J. 1970 L. 254/1 and 26; O.J. 1970, 762 and 782).

[61] See, *e.g.* Dir. 71/86 on harmonisation of basic provisions in respect of guarantees for short-term transactions (political risk) (J.O. 1971, L. 36/14; O.J. 1971, 71) and Dec. 73/391 on consultation and information procedure in matters of credit, insurance, credit guarantees and financial credits (O.J. 1973, L. 346/1).

[62] Sixteenth General Report (1982), 269.

[63] Bull. 11–1980, 60.

Coffee,[64] Sugar,[64a] Rubber,[65] Tin,[66] and Jute.[67] Of great importance, both for the Community and for developing countries is the
Multifibre Arrangement (MFA) which was extended until 1986[68];
under this extended arrangement new bilateral agreements were
concluded with 27 supplier countries.[69]

III. *Relations with International Organisations*[70]

In respect of all matters of particular interest to the common
market, Member States may, within the framework of international organisations of an economic character, proceed only by
common action.[71] In such a situation the only appropriate means
is concerted joint action by the Member States as members of the
said organisations.[72] This distinguishes this obligation from the
general provisions concerning commercial policy[73] which is
determined by the Community independently.

Decisions arrived at within an international organisation
in which the Community participates can constitute an international undertaking and therefore the Treaty provisions
concerning competence and procedure[74] are also applicable.

The Community also has the power to participate in international arrangements with a view to setting up new structures of
organisation endowed with the appropriate powers for taking
internationally binding decisions. The Community may, in this
connection, co-operate with a third country for the purpose of

---

[64] Bull. 9–1982, 44 and O.J. 1983, L. 308/1: provisional application by the EEC.
[64a] See Council Dec. of December 18, 1984, concerning the conclusion of the
International Sugar Agreement 1984 (O.J. 1985, L. 22/1).
[65] O.J. 1982, L. 111/22; Bull. 4–1982, 37; see above n. 14 (UNCTAD).
[66] O.J. 1982, L. 342/1; Bull. 6–1982, 66.
[67] Bull. 9–1982, 44.
[68] O.J. 1982, L. 83/8; Bull. 3–1982, 57.
[69] Sixteenth General Report (1982), 241. They provide for differential treatment of
these countries in terms of quota levels, growth rates and flexibility, depending
on their level of development and competitiveness.
[70] See European Community, international organisations and multilateral
agreements, 1983, Office for Official Publications EC.
[71] EEC, Art. 116. This article must be considered a transitional one which applies
in all fields where the Community is not yet in a position to avail itself to the full
extent of its autonomy (joined Cases 3, 4 and 6/76 (*Kramer*) (above n. 15), at 1311
(42, 43).
[72] Opinion 1/78 (*UNCTAD*) (above n. 14) at 2915 (49).
[73] EEC, Art. 113.
[74] EEC Arts. 114 and 228.

giving the organs of such an international institution appropriate powers of decision and for the purpose of defining, in a manner appropriate to the objectives pursued, the nature, elaboration, implementation and effects of the provisions to be adopted within such a framework.[75]

As regards relations with international organisations, it is up to the Commission to "maintain" them.[76] The Treaty specifically refers to the "organs of the General Agreement for Tariffs and Trade,"[77] the "organs of the United Nations and its specialised agencies,"[78] the Council of Europe[79] and the Organisation for Economic Co-operation and Development.[80]

1. United Nations (UN)

The Community, represented by the Commission, participates as observer in the meetings of the General Assembly, while the position of the Member States on the main issues debated at the United Nations is generally set out by the President of the Council of the European Communities. The Community also participates actively in the work of all the specialised agencies of the United Nations.[81] The Community as such is a contracting party to a number of United Nations conventions or international agreements[82] and participated in the third United Nations Conference on the Law of the Sea.[83]

2. Organisation for Economic Co-operation and Development (OECD)

As the Commission points out "the OECD continued to be the forum *par excellence* where the industrialised Western countries could exchange views on the major economic problems of the

---

[75] Opinion 1/76 (*laying-up fund*) (above n. 14) at 755 (5).
[76] EEC, Art. 229 (2).
[77] EEC, Art. 229 (1); see above, p. 237.
[78] *Ibid.*; see below n.81.
[79] EEC, Art. 230.
[80] EEC, Art. 231.
[81] For details see the annual General Report and the Bulletin, *e.g.* Sixteenth General Report (1982), 285 *et seq.*
[82] Sixteenth General Report (1982), 285. The Community also participated in the United Nations Conference on Trade and Development, the Industrial Development Organisation, the Environment Programme, etc.
[83] *Ibid.* at 287.

world and together work out solutions to some of them."[84] The annual ministerial meetings are attended by the Commission, which furthermore participates regularly in the work of the various OECD committees. Mention has been made already of the Arrangement on Guidelines for Officially Supported Export Credits ("Consensus") in which the Community participates.[85] The Community has also signed a co-operation agreement with the International Energy Agency (IEA) which operates within the framework of the OEDC.

3. Other international Organisations

Agreements of co-operation were also concluded by the Commission with the Committee of Ministers of the Council of Europe,[86] the Central Commission for the Navigation on the Rhine,[87] the International Bureau of Weights and Measures[88] and others.[89]

IV. *Bilateral and Regional Relations*

For practical purposes these relations can best be examined on a geographical basis.[90]

1. Europe

(1) *EFTA countries*

On January 1, 1973, the date of the first enlargement of the Community, preferential trade agreements establishing a free

---

[84] Twelfth General Report (1978), 272.
[85] See Sixteenth General Report (1982), 238 and above, Commercial Policy, p. 236.
[86] Not published.
[87] J.O. 1961, 1027.
[88] J.O. 1966, 614.
[89] See Commission Dec. laying down the methods of co-operation between the EEC and the International Commission on Civil Status (O.J. 1983, L. 260/19).
    See also the General Reports, Bull. and "the European Community, International Organisations and multilateral Agreements, 1983".
[90] The Treaties Office of the Directorate-General for External Relations of the European Commission produces a complete and up-to-date list every six months and is ready to provide documentation in response to specific requests. (Doc. I/29/84-EN of July 1984). Details about the implementation of all the agreements can be found in the yearly General Report published by the Commission at the beginning of each year.

trade area for industrial products[91] came into force with Austria,[92] Switzerland,[93] Sweden[94] and Portugal.[95] Similar agreements with Iceland,[96] Norway[97] and Finland[98] became effective in 1973 thereby completing the series of agreements between the EEC and the remaining EFTA countries after the United Kingdom joined the Community.

Mention should also be made of a fisheries agreement between the Community and the Government of Denmark and the Home Government of the Faroe Islands and more recently with Greenland.[99]

(2) *European countries of the Mediterranean*

Under the Treaty the Community may conclude with a third State an agreement "establishing an association involving reciprocal rights and obligations, common action and special procedures.[1] Such agreements were concluded with Greece[2] and Turkey[3] with a view to future accession of the countries to the European Communities. Association agreements were also concluded with Malta[4] and Cyprus[5]; they provide for the establishment of an association in stages. A preferential trade agreement establishing a free trade area was entered into with

---

[91] The preferential trade agreements are concluded pursuant to EEC, Art. 113.

[92] O.J. 1972, L. 300/93. See also O.J. 1983, L. 339/1.

[93] *Ibid.* at 189. See also O.J. 1983, L. 339/10.

[94] *Ibid.* at 96.

[95] O.J. 1972, L. 301/164.

[96] *Ibid.* at 1.

[97] O.J. 1973, L. 171/2.

[98] O.J. 1973, L. 328/1.

[99] O.J. 1980, L. 226/11. See Protocol n. 2 on the Faroe Islands annexed to the Act of Accession of the U.K., Denmark and Ireland and for Greenland, O.J. 1985, L. 29/1.

[1] EEC, Art. 238 (1).

[2] J.O. 1963, 294/63; O.J. 1974 Sp. ed. (2nd) I, Ext. rel. (1), 3, this association came to an end on accession: January 1, 1981.

[3] The association agreement with Turkey was signed in 1963 (J.O. 1964, 3687). However, because of the political situation in Turkey characterised with the absence of a pluralist parliamentary democracy and lack of respect for human rights, the association during the last couple of years "did no more than tick over" (Sixteenth General Report (1982), 253). See Eighteenth General Report (1984), 263.

[4] J.O. 1971, L. 61/1; first stage was extended several times.

[5] J.O. 1973, L. 133/1; second stage decided in 1980.

Spain[6] and a co-operation agreement was concluded with Yugoslavia.[7]

(3) *State-trading countries*

In 1974 all the existing bilateral trade agreements entered into by the individual Member States with State-trading countries expired. Thereupon the Council laid down the principles for autonomous trade arrangements for 1975 and sent the interested third countries a model for a possible agreement which the Community might conclude with each one of them. This model envisaged a long-term non-preferential agreement, based on reciprocity ensuring that both sides have equal rights and obligations. No reactions were received at first owing to the refusal of those countries to recognise the European Communities.

The first agreement with a State-trading country was signed with China in 1978[8]; followed in 1980 by agreements with Romania,[9] Hungary[10] and Czechoslovakia[11] on industrial products and in 1981 by agreements on trade in textile products; in 1981 also agreements on textile products were implemented with Poland[12] and Bulgaria.[13] Most were amended, extended or replaced by new agreements, protocols or exchanges of letters.[14]

2. Maghreb, Mashreq and Israel

Because of their geographical proximity to the Community, the countries of the Mediterranean basin are of extreme importance to the development of trade. From the outset, systems were set up to deal pragmatically with trade, to help remove the

[6] O.J. 1970, L. 182/1.
[7] O.J. 1983, L. 41/1. It is understood that this agreement also is based upon EEC, Art. 238.
[8] O.J. 1978, L. 123/1; non preferential agreement with tacit renewal on an annual basis. A second agreement on trade in textile products was initialled in 1979; see implementing regulation O.J. 1979, L. 345/1 and O.J. 1983, L. 346/91.
[9] O.J. 1980, L. 352/21. See also O.J. 1983, L. 346/1.
[10] O.J. 1981, L. 332/39.
[11] Not yet signed; see however O.J. 1981, L. 300/8.
[12] O.J. 1982, L. 107/82.
[13] O.J. 1982, L. 330/1.
[14] See publications of the Commission's Treaties Office and, *e.g.* Council Regs. 3286/80 on import arrangements (O.J. 1980, L. 353/1) and 1278/80 on import quotas (O.J. 1981, L. 376/1) and O.J. 1984, L. 381/1.

organisation of markets and production, and improve the commercial and tariff machinery. However, the disparity of these systems created difficulties. At the Paris Summit of October 19 and 20, 1972, it was stated therefore by the Heads of State or Government that the Community attaches essential importance to honouring its commitments towards the Mediterranean countries with whom agreements have been or are to be made, but that all those agreements require an overall and balanced handling.[15] The Council decided to examine a "global approach" to the problems arising in the region and, on the basis of a Commission proposal, worked out the substance of a general Community policy towards the Mediterranean countries, covering trade, economic, technical and financial co-operation and also co-operation on labour. The global approach did not meet with great enthusiasm from the three Maghreb countries (Algeria, Morocco and Tunisia) and Israel which were the first to be approached by the Commission on this subject. However, the Community pursued its efforts and over the years concluded agreements with all the countries of that region.

The first agreement was signed with Israel in 1975; it concerns free trade and co-operation.[16] With the other Mediterranean countries overall co-operation agreements were negotiated and signed during 1976 and 1977; most of them entered into force in 1978 with effect from January 1, 1979; they are all based upon Article 238. Additional protocols based upon Article 113 were concluded in the following years.

The countries concerned are: Algeria,[17] Morocco,[18] Tunisia,[19] Egypt,[20] Lebanon,[21] Jordan[22] and Syria.[23] A co-operation agreement was also concluded between the Council of Arab Economic Unity and the three European Communities: it concerns co-operation in areas of common interest involving economic development.[24]

---

[15] Bull. EC 10–1972, 9. See Sixteenth General Report (1982), 252.
[16] O.J. 1975, L. 136/1. See also further agreements and additional protocols (Commission's Treaties Office).
[17] O.J. 1978, L. 263/1.
[18] O.J. 1978, L. 264/1.
[19] O.J. 1978, L. 265/1; came into force in 1978.
[20] O.J. 1978, L. 266/1.
[21] O.J. 1978, L. 267/1; came into force in 1978.
[22] O.J. 1978, L. 268/1.
[23] O.J. 1978, L. 269/1; came into force from November 1, 1978.
[24] O.J. 1982, L. 300/23.

3. North America

The relations with the *United States* in the field of trade and commerce present particular problems if only because of the size of American industry and its export position throughout the world. The continuing recession and consequent uncertainty have given rise to protectionist pressures from American industrial and agricultural lobbies and to a more aggressive attitude towards anything that is perceived as unfair competition in international economic relations. Hence numerous difficulties.[25]

In past years the difficulties experienced have centred around steel[26] and agricultural products, not to mention the embargo on exports of oil and gas equipment. An agreement for co-operation was signed between the United States and Euratom[27] as far back as 1958 and since then several other formal agreements were concluded.[28]

Similarly the relations with *Canada* suffered from trade policy measures.[29] A co-operation agreement was concluded by Euratom[30] while the relations with the EEC are governed by the Framework Agreement for commercial and economic co-operation.[31]

4. Latin America

Since most of the countries which benefit from the Community's development policy are situated in Africa, "compensations" had to be found for non-associated countries in Asia and Latin America. With regard to the latter a first trade agreement was concluded with Brazil[32] in 1973, later replaced by a Framework Agreement[33] providing for wide-ranging commercial and economic co-operation. A similar agreement was concluded with Mexico[34] in 1975. Specific agreements were concluded with

---

[25] Eighteenth General Report (1984), 244.
[26] See the arrangement concerning trade in certain steel products between the European Coal and Steel Community and the United States (O.J. 1982, L. 307/1 and 11 and 1983, C. 334/2).
[27] J.O. 1959, 312/59.
[28] See publication of the Commission's Treaties Office.
[29] Eighteenth General Report (1984), 257.
[30] J.O. 1959, 1165. Amended in 1984, Eighteenth General Report (1984), 258.
[31] J.O. 1976, L. 260/1.
[32] O.J. 1974, L. 102/24. All these agreements are based upon EEC, Art. 113.
[33] O.J. 1982, L. 281/1.
[34] O.J. 1975, L. 247/10.

Argentina,[35] Colombia,[36] Guatemala,[37] Peru,[38] Haiti[39] and Uruguay.[40]

Contacts are also maintained with the Permanent Secretariat of the General Treaty of Central-American Economic Integration and the Central-American Common Market, the Special Committee on Latin-American Co-ordination[41] and the Andean Group (Bolivia, Colombia, Ecuador, Peru and Venezuela).[42] The "renewed dialogue" between the EEC and Latin America never materialised *inter alia* because of the Falklands conflict.[43]

5. Asia

When the United Kingdom joined the European Communities a Joint Declaration of Intent on the development of trade relations with Ceylon, India, Malaysia, Pakistan and Singapore was annexed to the accession treaty. It states that the Community is ready to examine with the developing independent Commonwealth countries in Asia such problems as may arise in the field of trade with a view to seeking appropriate solutions, taking into account the effect of the generalised tariff preference scheme and the situation of other developing countries in the same geographical area.

Consequently agreements were signed with India in 1973,[44] Sri Lanka in 1975,[45] Pakistan[46] and Bangladesh[47] in 1976. A series of agreements on trade in textile products was concluded with

---

[35] They concern textiles, nuclear energy, mutton and lamb; *e.g.* O.J. 1979, L. 298/2.
[36] Textiles (O.J. 1981, L. 273/1).
[37] *Id.* (O.J. 1979, L. 350/1).
[38] *Ibid.* at 59.
[39] *Id.* (O.J. 1980, L. 70/67).
[40] Trade agreement (O.J. 1973, L. 333/1) and specific agreement concerning textiles, mutton and lamb (O.J. 1980, L. 70/38).
[41] See Ninth General Report 1975, 269.
[42] Sixteenth General Report 1982, 260.
[43] *Ibid.*
[44] Non preferential framework agreement; sets up a joint committee to seek means of promoting genuine economic and commercial co-operation. Replaced in 1981 with new agreement (O.J. 1981, L. 328/5). Other specific agreements where also concluded (textiles, cane sugar, coir and jute).
[45] On commercial co-operation (O.J. 1975, L. 247/1).
[46] *Id.* (O.J. 1976, L. 168/1).
[47] *Id.* (O.J. 1976, L. 319/1).

Macao,[48] Korea,[49] Thailand,[50] Indonesia,[51] Singapore,[52] Hong Kong,[53] the Philippines[54] and Malaysia.[55]

A co-operation agreement was concluded with the ASEAN Group[56]; it provides a framework for commercial, economic and development co-operation.[57]

As regards Japan, only one formal agreement was concluded in 1977 concerning co-operation in environmental matters[58]; however, the importance of that country for the Community's trade is quite obvious. The relations with Japan have been a matter of serious concern for many years due to the EEC's trade deficit. Consequently the Council decided on a comprehensive common strategy aimed at improving Japan's import propensity, obtaining effective curbs on exports to the Community, implementing a Community policy to make European firms able to develop positive strategies to meet Japanese competition and achieving a balanced scientific and technological co-operation.[59]

6. Australia and New Zealand

Relations with Australia continue to be somewhat strained since Australia complains that the CAP is hitting its export trade, and the Community for its part is concerned at Australia's industrial protectionism.[60]

As far as New Zealand is concerned its trade with the Community is of great importance and this is generally recognised.[61]

---

[48] O.J. 1979, L. 298/107.
[49] O.J. 1979, L. 298/67.
[50] *Ibid.* at 224. A co-operation agreement on manioc production, marketing and trade was concluded in 1982 (O.J. 1982, 219/52).
[51] O.J. 1979, L. 350/27.
[52] *Ibid.* at 99.
[53] O.J. 1980, L. 332/1.
[54] O.J. 1980, L. 371/1.
[55] O.J. 1981, L. 332/1.
[56] Indonesia, Malaysia, Philippines, Singapore, Thailand.
[57] O.J. 1980, L. 144/1.
[58] Not published; see Eleventh General Report (1977), 148.
[59] Sixteenth General Report (1982), 248, and Eighteenth (1984), para. 673.
[60] A trade agreement was signed in 1980; it concerns voluntary restraint regarding Australia's export of mutton, lamb and goatmeat (O.J. 1980, L. 275/20).
[61] Sixteenth General Report (1982), 251.

V. *Development Policy*

The main feature of the Community policy towards developing countries is the ACP-EEC agreement,[62] which establishes commercial, industrial and financial relations with 65 African, Caribean and Pacific countries[63] on the one hand and the Community and the ten Member States on the other. This relationship grew out of a quite different set of links, which existed at the time of signature of the EEC Treaty, between most of those ACP countries and several Member States. The Treaty provides for the association of the overseas countries and territories in order to increase trade and to promote jointly economic and social development.[64] Consequently the Member States decided to associate with the Community the non-European countries and territories which have special relations with Belgium, France, Italy and the Netherlands.[65] This was of course extended to the United Kingdom after enlargement.[66] These countries and territories are listed in Annex IV of the Treaty.[67] Drafted at a time when most of these countries and territories were dependent, the principle of a special association was maintained after they gained independence.

For a first period of five years, the details and the procedure for the association were determined by an implementing conven-

---

[62] In its latest form, *i.e.* Lomé III, the agreement was signed on December 8, 1984 (Bull. 11–1984, 7). Eighteenth General Report (1984), 275.

[63] Antigua and Barbuda, Bahamas, Barbados, Belize, Benin, Bostwana, Burkina-fasso, Burundi, Cameroun, Cape Verde, Central African Republic, Chad, Comoros, Congo, Djibouti, Dominica, Equatorial Guinea, Ethiopia, Fiji, Gabon, Gambia, Ghana, Grenada, Guinea-Bissau, Guinea-Konakry, Guyana, Ivory Coast, Jamaica, Kenya, Kiribati, Lesotho, Liberia, Madagascar, Malawi, Mali, Mauritania, Mauritius, Mozambique, Niger, Nigeria, Papua-New Guinea, Rwanda, St. Christopher and Nevis, St. Lucia, St. Vincent and Grenadine, Sao Tome and Principe, Senegal, Seychelles, Sierra-Leone, Solomon Islands, Somalia, Sudan, Surinam, Swaziland, Tanzania, Togo, Tonga, Trinidad and Tobago, Tuvaly, Uganda, Vanuatu, Western Samoa, Zaire, Zambia, Zimbabwe. The first Lomé Convention was signed by 46 ACP countries; the second one by 57 and the third one by 65.

[64] EEC, Art. 3(*k*). See also Preamble to the Treaty (seventh indent) "intending to confirm the solidarity which binds Europe and the overseas countries and desiring to ensure the development of their prosperity, in accordance with the principles of the Charter of the United Nations."

[65] EEC, Art. 131.

[66] Act of Accession, Art. 23 (1).

[67] This list was modified by Act of Accession, Art. 24 (2).

tion[68] annexed to the Treaty.[69] This convention was replaced by an agreement negotiated between the Community and the emerging African and Malagasy states. This first agreement, known as the Yaoundé I Convention[70] still bears the marks of the paternalistic approach of most European countries towards their former colonies. A second Yaoundé Convention, similar to the former came into force on January 1, 1971[71]; it did not apply to the United Kingdom, Ireland and Denmark until January 31, 1975.[72]

An entirely new agreement was signed at Lomé (Togo) on February 28, 1975, between the European Community and 46 countries situated in Africa, the Caribean and the Pacific.[73] It came into force on April 1, 1976,[74] and expired on March 1, 1980.

The Lomé II Convention expires on February 28, 1985 and Lomé III was signed on December 8, 1984. The Lomé Conventions differ from the Yaoundé Conventions in that they aim to establish a kind of partnership between the developing countries and the Community. It will be noted that although there are 75 signatories, the Lomé Convention is legally speaking a bilateral agreement between the ACP States on the one hand and the Community and the Member States on the other. The Convention provides for three institutions, a Council of Ministers, a Committee of Ambassadors and a Consultative Assembly.

In respect of trade co-operation the ACP countries enjoy, without reciprocity for the Member States, free entry into the Community for most of their agricultural products and for all industrial products originating in ACP countries. The Member States only have the guarantee that they will not be treated less favourably than any other industrialised country and that all of them will be treated equally.

An entirely new feature of the Lomé Convention is the stabilisation of export earnings (STABEX) and SYSMIN systems. The former is a mechanism assuring those ACP countries whose revenues derive mainly from a single product a certain level of

---

[68] This was of course a Convention concluded between the Member States, not with the overseas countries and territories.
[69] EEC, Art. 136.
[70] J.O. 1964, 1431 and J.O. 1964, 1490.
[71] J.O. 1970, L. 282/1 and O.J. Sp. ed. Sec. Ser. I (2) 7.
[72] Act of Accession, Arts. 109 and 115 (1).
[73] O.J. 1976, L. 25/1.
[74] O.J. 1976, L. 85/1. Since it expired before the Lomé II Agreement became effective (Jan. 1, 1981), transitional measures were adopted (O.J. 1980, L. 55/1). For Lomé III see Bull 11–1984, 7 and Eighteenth General Report (1984), 275.

export earnings by protecting them from income fluctuations due to the play of the markets or production hazards,[75] the latter, in the form of special loans, aims at remedying the harmful effects to the national economy of the situation in the mining sector. The agreement also provides for an undertaking by the Community to purchase from certain ACP countries at guaranteed prices cane sugar for an indefinite period and an undertaking from these countries to supply specific quantities annually.

Another important element is the place assumed by industrial co-operation, with its industrial co-operation committee and industrial development centre. The purpose is to integrate firms and entrepreneurs into the ACP-EEC co-operation.

The Lomé Convention is accompanied by an Internal Agreement on the measures and procedures required for implementation[76] and an Internal Agreement on the financing and administration of Community aid.[77]

Finally the Lomé III Convention provides for financial co-operation to the sum of 8,500[78] million units of account for five years, *i.e.* 7,400 million for the European Development Fund (Grants 4,860, special loans: 600, risk capital: 600, Stabex: 925, Sysmin: 415) and 1,100 from the European Investment Bank as commercial loans.[79] Notwithstanding the relative modesty of the financial support, the Community, through its special relationship with the ACP countries, plays an important role in the development of the Third World. It should be noted that besides their contribution to the Development Fund, most Member States of the Community provide important aid bilaterally to a large number of the ACP countries.

The Community also contributes to the development of *non associated* third countries: India has been the main recipient of the allocated financial aid. This aid programme is intended mainly for the most under-privileged sections of the population in the

---

[75] For details see, *e.g.* Eighteenth General Report (1984), 285: the total amount of payments under this heading in 1984 was more than 50 million ECU.

[76] O.J. 1980, L. 347/206.

[77] O.J. 1980, L. 349/36 amended: O.J. 1982, L. 247/30.

[78] In the Lomé I Convention the amount was 3,466 million EUA and 5,227 million ECU in the second.

[79] See Bull, 9–1979, 11.

poorest countries. It has been running since 1976; the emphasis is on the rural sector and improving supplies of foodstuffs.[80]

While the Lomé Convention provides preferences to a particular group of developing countries, the Community also offers world-wide help to developing countries in the form of *generalized preferences,*[81] *i.e.* non-reciprocal and non-discriminatory tariff preferences for the import of manufactures and semi-manufactures and processed agricultural products from developing countries.[82]

Mention should also be made of *Food Aid*[83] and *Emergency Aid.* These aids are granted either directly to the beneficiaries or through international organisations like the United Nations Relief and Work Agency (UNRWA). Emergency aid is usually granted following situations arising from political events.[84]

VI. *The Community's Right of Passive and Active Legation*

With regard to *diplomatic representation,* the only relevant Treaty provision is to be found in the Merger Treaty's Protocol on the privileges and immunities of the European Communities: Member States in whose territory the Communities have their seat shall accord the customary diplomatic immunities and privileges to missions of third countries accredited to the Communities.[85] Reference could also be made to the statements issued after the extraordinary Council session of January 28 and 29, 1966, held in Luxembourg, where it is provided that creden-

---

[80] See Council regulation governing the implementation of the programme (O.J. 1981, L. 48/8).

[81] The decision to offer these tariff preferences was taken on the basis of an UNCTAD resolution and, as first among all the developed nations, initiated by the Community in 1971. See J.O. 1971, L. 142 for a first series of implementing regulations and decisions. A scheme for 1981–1985 was adopted by the Council in 1980 (O.J. 1980), L. 354/202, Bull. 5–1971, 25 and Fourteenth General Report (1980), 247). For the preferential tariff treatment applied as at January 1, 1984, see O.J. 1984, C. 22/1.

[82] The scheme started in 1971, for 77 beneficiaries; there were 123 in 1981.

[83] See, *e.g.* O.J. 1982, L. 120/27, for the 1982 food aid programmes. Generally speaking these programmes cover cereal and other products (O.J. 1982, L. 31/1). See also Fifteenth (1981), 239, Sixteenth (1982), 266 and Eighteenth General Report (1984), 282.

[84] For details see the annual General Report and the Bull.

[85] Protocol, Art. 17. For a list of the missions accredited to the Community see "Corps diplomatique accrédité auprès des Communautés européennes," D.G. External Relations.

tials of Heads of Missions of non-Member States accredited to the Community will be submitted jointly to the President of the Council and to the President of the Commission, meeting together for this purpose.[86]

The representatives of the Commission in various third countries enjoy the same diplomatic immunities and privileges; this is the case also for the delegations to certain international organisations, *e.g.* the Commission delegations to the ACP countries, to the Southern Mediterranean countries, to the United Nations, and the OECD.[87] Without it being more explicitly provided for in the Treaty, the Community thus exercises the right of active and passive legation.

VII. *Political Co-operation*

In the final communiqué of the Conference of Heads of State or Government on December 1 and 2, 1969, at the Hague, the Ministers of Foreign Affairs were instructed to study the best way of achieving progress in the matter of political unification within the context of enlargement.[88] At the request of the Ministers, the Davignon Report was submitted[89] and accepted by the Ministers of Foreign Affairs in 1970. The aim is to further political unification by co-operating in the field of foreign affairs.[90] In 1974, the Heads of State or Government adopted a second report on European political co-operation[91] and approved, *inter alia*, the following measures: Foreign Ministers will meet four times a year; if the circumstances are sufficiently grave or the subject matter sufficiently important, a ministerial meeting may be replaced by a conference of Heads of State or Government. The Political Directors of the Foreign Ministries meet in the Political Committee with a view to preparing ministerial meetings

---

[86] For text, see Sweet and Maxwell, *European Community Treaties* (4th ed.), p. 249.
[87] For a list of Commission delegations see Directory of the Commission.
[88] Third General Report (1969), 489 (15).
[89] See Bull. 11–1979.
[90] The objectives of that co-operation are:
  –to ensure by means of regular consultations and exchanges of information, improved mutual understanding as regards the main problems of international relations;
  –to strengthen solidarity between governments by promoting harmonisation of their views, and the alignment of their positions and, whenever it appears possible and desirable, joint action.
[91] See Seventh General Report (1973), 502.

and carrying out tasks entrusted to them by the Ministers.[92] The Commission is represented at all the meetings, and twice a year the Ministers meet with the Political Affairs Committee of the European Parliament.

It is important to note that the political co-operation machinery, which deals on the inter-governmental level with problems of international politics, is distinct from and additional to the activities of the institutions of the Community which are based on the commitments undertaken by the Member States in the EEC Treaty, although both sets of machinery have the aim of contributing to the development of European unification.

There exist, therefore, two parallel systems in connection with activities of the European Communities: one is "communautaire;" the other is "inter-governmental." Obviously there is a danger of lack of co-ordination, if not of conflict. An attempt to prevent this is undertaken in the form of close contacts with the institutions of the Community.[93] The Commission thus plays an increasing role and is fully involved in almost all the political co-operation work being carried out. With regard to Parliament, it was agreed to associate it closely with the work of the President's office, *inter alia*, through replies to questions on political co-operation put by members.[94]

At the December 1974 Paris meeting of Heads of States or Governments, it was decided that the President of the Council would be the spokesman for the Nine and would set out their views on international diplomacy. The Community is getting more and more involved in several areas of international political co-operation, an area which strictly speaking does not come under the provisions of the European treaties.[95]

---

[92] Other measures concern a "group of correspondents" with the task to follow the implementation of the political co-operation, working parties, medium and long term studies, the role of embassies in the ten capitals and in third countries.

[93] For further details, see Seventh General Report (1973), 508.

[94] See, *e.g.* Thirteenth General Report (1979), 333.

[95] The Final Act of the Conference on Security and Co-operation in Europe (Helsinki, on August 11, 1975) was signed by the President of the Council; the Community as such took part in the 1978–1979 meeting of Belgrade (Twelfth General Report (1978), 264) and 1982–1983 of Madrid (Sixteenth General Report (1982), 294).

A section on political co-operation is to be found in the annual General Report of the Community and often in the monthly Bull.

Particularly dramatic for the Community was the invasion by Argentina of the Falkland Islands, a United Kingdom dependency which is also associated with the EEC. The Ten, as they are now called, immediately expressed their solidarity with the United Kingdom in a statement dated April 2, 1982.[96] To back up its statement, the Community and the Member States imposed an embargo on imports of all products originating in Argentina for the purpose of putting them into free circulation in the Community.[97] The economic measures were lifted on June 21.[98]

Other joint statements of the Ten Member States were made on Poland, Afghanistan,[99] the Israeli invasion of Lebanon, the Iran-Iraq conflict and Surinam.[1]

VIII. *Enlargement*

More than six years ago Portugal[2] and Spain[3] made their application for membership of the Community.[4]

With regard to *Portugal* the Commission in its opinion,[5] took the view that the Community should agree promptly and unequivocally to the Portugese request for the early opening of accession negotiations. The direct economic impact of Portugal's accession to the Community will be limited given the relative weight of Portugal's economy. Problems might arise, however, primarily as a result of the appreciable disparities in development levels, which will accentuate the Community's heterogeneity and will hinder progress towards increased convergence. For Portugal itself, the prospect of integration into Europe makes it essential to consolidate its economy and remedy certain structural shortcomings.

On June 6, 1978, the Council gave a favourable response and negotiations were officially opened on October 17 of the same

[96] Bull. 4–1982, 7.
[97] Council Reg. 877/82 (O.J. 1982, L. 102/1). This Reg. refers to EEC, Art. 224 and is based on EEC, Art. 113. See also Decision of the Representatives of the Member States of the ECSC meeting in Council (*Ibid.* at 3).
[98] O.J. 1982, L. 177/1.
[99] Bull. 1–1980, 7.
[1] For details see annual General Reports.
[2] Portugal made its application on March 28, 1977; Bull. 3–1977, 8.
[3] Spain applied on July 28, 1977; Bull. 7/8–1977, 6.
[4] EEC, Art. 237.
[5] May 19, 1978; Bull. Supp. 5/78.

year. In 1983 the Commission reported that "considerable progress was made on the accession negotiations."[6]

The Community concluded an Agreement with Portugal on pre-accession aid[7] under which co-operation projects and programmes are being financed.[8]

The application of *Spain* was reviewed in the Commission's Opinion of November 29, 1978.[9] In it the Commission welcomes the prospect of seeing a democratic Spain become part of Europe and participate in its construction; it considered that the negotiations should start as soon as possible.

The Commission considered that the integration of Spain into the Community will not be straight-forward, and it is therefore necessary for the sake of both the Community and Spain to take the necessary measures and precautions to ensure that the enterprise is successful. An effort must be made to ensure the maximum degree of convergence of the objectives pursued by the Community and Spain. The measures for restructuring industry or strengthening agriculture and the regional schemes and social redeployment programmes that need to be carried out require the mobilisation of large resources and will take time to bear fruit. The Commission recommended an adequate transitional period of no more than ten years, during which the movement of persons, goods and services will be progressively liberalised.

On December 19, 1978 the Council decided to open accession negotiations with Spain and this was formally done on February 5, 1979.[10] Agreement on all subjects was reached, after lengthy and difficult negotiation during the European Council meeting of March 1985 in Brussels. Until the last minute divergences existed both among the Member States and between them and Spain and Portugal mainly on agriculture, fisheries and free movement of persons.

It is to be expected that the third enlargement will take place, as provided for, on January 1, 1986.

Further Reading

External Relations

K. Wellens, "The second Lomé Convention: some aspects of its first year of application (1983) 8 E.L. Rev. 255, 369 and 477.

---

[6] Sixteenth General Report (1982) 230.   [7] Fifteenth General Report (1981), 226.
[8] Eighteenth General Report (1984), para. 612.   [9] Bull. Supp. 9/78.
[10] See also Eighteenth General Report (1984), 238.

Chapter 7

COMMUNITY LAW

As was pointed out at the beginning of this book, the Treaties establishing the European Communities are more than agreements which merely create mutual obligations between Member States. Generally speaking, this conclusion was reached on the basis of the following facts. The Treaties have created quasi-governmental bodies—the institutions—independent from the national public authorities and endowed with legislative, administrative and judicial sovereign rights which were transferred to them by the Member States. Furthermore the Treaties lay down basic principles which are either worked out in the Treaties themselves or implemented by the acts of the institutions. These fundamental principles impose obligations upon, and consequently create rights for both the Member States and the citizens of the Community. The Treaties thus present many analogies with national constitutions: it can be said therefore that, although they started as international treaties, these texts have become together with the revising treaties the "constitution" of the European Communities.

As has been shown, the law embodied in these texts—primary European law—is constantly being expanded, made specific, implemented and applied by the various acts and measures of the Community institutions—secondary community law. The Treaties have, therefore, as the Court of Justice found, established a legal order of their own and indeed,

> "by creating a Community of unlimited duration, having its own institutions, its own personality, its own legal capacity and capacity of representation on the international plane and, more particularly, real powers stemming from a limitation of sovereignty or a transfer of powers from the states to the Community, the Member States have limited their sovereign rights, albeit within limited fields, and have thus

created a body of law which binds both their nationals and themselves."[1]

This view is shared as will be seen by many national courts such as the German Supreme Administrative Court, which stated that Community law constitutes "a separate legal order, whose provisions belong neither to international law nor to the municipal law of the Member States."[2]

1. Direct applicability

Community law being separate from national law is also independent from it, which means that rights can be conferred and obligations imposed directly by Community provisions, *i.e.* without interference or intervention, upon the national authorities and upon the citizens of the Member States. There is indeed no necessity for Member States to intervene in order that the provisions have a binding effect[3] or, as Article 189 expresses it, are "applicable"; furthermore, Member States are committed not to interfere with the application of Community law. This latter obligation follows from Article 5 of the Treaty which provides, *inter alia*, that Member States "shall abstain from any measure which could jeopardise the attainment of the objectives of this treaty."

More important than the acceptance of this "legal autonomy" of the Community legal system in regard to national law is the understanding of its *raison d'être*. The European Treaties, it will be remembered, aim at establishing within the territories of the Member States a single market characterised by the basic freedoms and constituting a geographical area wherein Com-

---

[1] Case 6/64 *Costa* v. *ENEL* [1964] E.C.R. 585 at 593. It should be pointed out that the "unlimited duration" only applies to the EEC and Euratom Treaties; the ECSC Treaty has a duration of 50 years (Art. 97).

[2] C.M.L. Rev. 1967, 483.

[3] This is what is meant by s.2(1) of the European Community Act 1972: these provisions "are without further enactment to be given legal effect or use in the United Kingdom." In other words "reception" of Community law into the national sphere is and cannot be required. Anyway reception is only required by those who adhere to the dualist theory and furthermore "if one accepts, as is logical and in one view inevitable, that Community law is *sui generis* then in strictness the monist/dualist argument is excluded, since it is an argument properly limited to international law strictly so called," which is not the case with Community law. See Mitchell, "British law and British Membership" *Europarecht*, April-June 1971, 109.

munity rules apply with the same force and with exactly the same meaning and effect to all who operate therein.[4] Therefore, the very nature of the law created by the European Treaties implies uniform interpretation and application; without those characteristics there can be no Community. Community law is either uniform in all the Member States or it is not. This does not mean that Community rules should not take into account the specificities of the Member States or of their various regions; as long as the fundamental principles are safeguarded the implementation must be adapted since applying the same rule to different situations constitutes a discrimination just as much as applying different rules to identical situations.[5]

2. Direct effect

If the consequence of direct applicability for the Member States is non-interference, for the citizens it means the possibility of invoking the Community rules in their national courts in order to protect the rights which those rules confer upon them.[6] Applicability of Community law must indeed be understood in two ways: on the one hand the prohibitions (*i.e.* obligations to abstain) or obligations imposed upon national authorities, institutions and persons; and on the other the rights of those, in favour of whom these obligations have been provided. In law, every obligation has a right as its corollary although this right is seldom clearly specified. It is of course the same in Community law, *e.g.* the obligations imposed upon the Member States generally speaking have as their corollary rights for the citizens of the Community. It is those rights which the national courts and tribunals must uphold, in pursuance of Article 5 of the Treaty.[7] It is thus not only regulations which, because they are "directly applicable,"[8] are as such suited "to grant to the citizens rights

---

[4] Case 6/64 see n. 1, at 594.

[5] See Case 279/80 *Webb* [1981] E.C.R. 3305 at 3324 (16) and Case 52/79 *Procureur du Roi* v. *Debauve* [1980] E.C.R. 833 at 858 (21).

[6] This was clearly stated by the Court in Case 43/75 *Defrenne* v. *Sabena* [1976] E.C.R. 455 at 474 (24).
The same position of the Court became already apparent in Case 2/74 *Reyners* v. *Belgium* [1974] E.C.R. 631 at 651 (25) although less clearly stated.

[7] EEC, Art. 5 refers to the "Member States" and this expression covers all the national authorities whether legislative, administrative or judicial. See *e.g.* Case 33/76 *Rewe* v. *Landwirtschaftskammer Saarland* [1976] E.C.R. 1989 at 1997 (5).

[8] EEC, Art. 189.

which the national tribunals are under obligation to protect,"[9] but all binding Community acts whatever their nature or form.[10] Consequently, the question arises: which provisions of Community law, which impose a clear and unconditional obligation upon a Member State, an institution or a person, do *not* have "direct effect."[11] The answer is: only those which leave, to the addressee of the obligation, a discretionary latitude. For instance, with regard to Article 90(2), the Court stated that:

> "Its application involves an appraisal of the requirements, on the one hand, of the particular task entrusted to the undertaking concerned and, on the other hand, the protection of the interests of the Community. This appraisal depends on the objectives of general economic policy pursued by the states under the supervision of the Commission. Consequently;... Article 90 (2) cannot at the present stage create individual rights which the national courts must protect."[12]

In other words, the obligation is not unconditional and cannot therefore have direct effect.

However, the Court made it clear that in cases where the latitude is limited in time, the expiration of the time-limit suffices to give direct effect to Community rules, notwithstanding the absence of implementing provisions which were to be adopted by the institutions or by the national authorities. The Court also found that even in the absence of any express reference to the possible action to be taken by the institutions, the Community provisions cannot be interpreted as reserving to the national legislature exclusive power to implement those rules, since such implementation may be relieved by a combination of Community and national measures.[13]

---

[9] Case 93/71 *Leonesio* v. *Italian Ministry for agriculture* [1972] E.C.R. 287 at 293 (5).

[10] *e.g.* provisions of directives, decisions and agreements; for directives, see Case 21/78 *Delkvist* v. *Anklagemyndigheden* [1978] E.C.R. 2327 at 2340 (21). For decisions see also Case 33/76, above, n.7 and for agreements see joined Cases 21–24/72 *International Fruit Company* v. *Produktschap voor Groenten en Fruit* [1972] E.C.R. 1219 at 1227.

[11] Originally, the question was put the other way round: see Case 28/67 *Molkerei-Zentrale* v. *Hauptzollant Paderborn* [1968] E.C.R. 143 at 153. See however Case 43/75 *Defrenne* v. *Sabena* [1976] E.C.R. 455 at 471 *et seq.*

[12] Case 10/71 *Ministère Public Luxembourgeois* v. *Muller* [1971] E.C.R. 723 at 730 (14–16).

[13] See, *e.g.* Case 43/75 n. 6 above (*Defrenne*) at 480 (68).

The fact that the European Treaties have created a new legal order, directly applicable and conferring upon citizens rights which national courts must uphold, was not only ascertained by the Court of Justice, but also recognised by national courts and tribunals. In the first place, the judiciary of all the Member States has implicitly recognised this for many years by making extensive use of the possibility offered by Article 177 to request the Court to give preliminary rulings on questions concerning Community law raised before them. By doing so they accepted that Community rules do apply within the territory of their jurisdiction and may confer rights which they must uphold. In the second place the fact that Community law constitutes a new legal order has nearly always been explicitly recognised by several national courts and tribunals. This was the case, *inter alia*, for the Italian Corte Costituzionale, the German Bundesverfassungsgericht[14] and the Belgian Cour de Cassation.[15] All the implications of the autonomy of the Community legal order did not always become immediately clear: it was often a lengthy process of adaptation and learning in which the Court of Justice played an important role. But even as early as 1967 the Commission could refer to the growing penetration of domestic legal systems by Community law and the steadily improving comprehension of the new situation by those working in this field as shown by the pattern of cases dealt with by the national courts.[16]

3. Precedence

In retrospect it might seem evident that the autonomy of the Community legal order, the necessity for its uniform interpretation and application in all the Member States automatically implies that the Community provisions have precedence over national legislation in case of conflict. Since the national courts and tribunals are under an obligation, as was just seen, to apply Community rules, besides the provisions of national law, it is not unlikely that conflicts will result from this simultaneous application. The European treaties contain no explicit provisions

---

[14] Judgment of October 18, 1967 ((1967–1968) 5 C.M.L.Rev. 483).
[15] *Minister for Economic Affairs* v. *Fromagerie Franco-Suisse "Le Ski"* [1972] C.M.L.R. 330. This decision will be examined below under precedence of Community law.
[16] First General Report (1976), 563.

regarding the solution to be applied in such cases[17] and therefore attempts were made at first to solve such conflict in accordance with the provisions of national law. Few national legal systems, however, provide for conflict rules of this nature.

In the United Kingdom, for example, the European Communities Act 1972 provides the necessary precedence, by accepting the "legal effect" of Community provisions in the United Kingdom[18] and also of the decisions of the European Court regarding the meaning or effect of any of the treaties, or the validity, meaning or effect of any Community instrument.[19] In relation to statute law, this means that the directly applicable Community provisions must prevail over future Acts of Parliament, in so far as they might be inconsistent with those instruments. In practice, this also means that it is implied in the acceptance of the treaties that the United Kingdom like any other Member State must refrain from enacting legislation inconsistent with Community law.[20]

In the Netherlands, the Basic Law (Constitution) not only provides that the provisions of international treaties have precedence over existing national laws and regulations; it also specifies that the same applies to the measures enacted by the institutions set up under these treaties and adds that this precedence applies in case of conflict between an existing Community rule and subsequent national law.[21]

The French Constitution provides in general terms that treaties or agreements, duly ratified or approved, shall, upon their publication, have an authority superior to that of laws, subject,

---

[17] Although very general, EEC, Art. 5 constitutes a firm legal ground on which to base this precedence.

[18] 1972 European Communities Act, s.2(1).

[19] *Ibid.* s.3(1).

[20] *Ibid.* s.2(4) provides therefore that present and future enactment shall be construed and have effect subject to s.2. See *Hansard*, February 15, 1972, Vol. 831. This basic principle derives not only from the obligations explicitly accepted by the Member States when they became members of the European Community (see, *e.g.* EEC, Art. 5) but, as was explained, from the very nature of the Community and Community law. The very existence of the Community depends upon simultaneous and uniform application throughout the Community of all the provisions of the treaties and the acts of the institutions. This was clearly stated over and over again by the Court of Justice. See, *e.g.* Case 83/78 *Pigs Marketing Board* v. *Redmond* [1978] E.C.R. 2347 at 2371 (56) and Case 128/78 *Commission* v. *United Kingdom* [1979] E.C.R. 419 at 428 (9).

[21] Dutch Constitution, Arts. 66 and 67; these were incorporated in the Constitution in 1953.

however, for each agreement or treaty, to its application by the other party.[22]

The German Constitution provides that the Federal Republic may, by legislation, transfer sovereign powers to inter-governmental institutions[23] and refers to the precedence of the general rules of public international law.[24] It is only with difficulty that one can equate Community measures with the latter.

The Italian Constitution is even less precise. It only provides that "Italy's legal system conforms with the general principles recognised by international law."[25]

These German and Italian texts and even the French Constitution form a rather meagre legal basis for the obligation that national courts should give precedence to Community law over national law in cases of conflict between the two, to say nothing of those Member States whose constitution contains no provisions in this respect. Furthermore, in certain cases, the above-mentioned constitutional provisions were not accepted by national judges as obliging them to give precedence to Community measures over national rules.[26] But even in the case of the

---

[22] French Constitution of 1958, Art. 55. In a judgment of 1962, the French Cour de Cassation held that a contested action had been carried out under an EEC decision and regulation which are "acts regularly published and having acquired force of international treaties" (*Gazette du Palais*, December 9 to 11, 1970, 6–7). See however, decision of the Conseil d'Etat, *Syndicat Général des Fabricants de Semoules* v. *Direction des Industries agricoles* [1970] C.M.L.R. 395. See also French Cour de Cassation 1975, *Administration des Douanes* v. *Jacques Vabre* [1975] 2 C.M.L.R. 336, where the French Supreme Court clearly stated that the Treaty has an authority greater than that of national acts and is binding on the national courts.

[23] Art. 24 (1).

[24] Art. 25.

[25] Art. 10 (1).

[26] By a ruling of March 1, 1968 (*Recueil Dalloz-Sirey*, 1968, jurisprudence 286) the French Conseil d'Etat ruled that a French court is bound to ensure the application of the *lex posteriori* whatever the meaning and scope of existing Community law (Second General Report (1968), 453). The Commission considered this ruling incompatible with the legal obligations deriving from the Treaty (J.O. 1968, C. 71). *Syndicat Général des Fabricants de Semoules de France*, above. See, however, Cour de Cassation, October 22, 1970, *Contributions indirectes* v. *Ramel* [1971] C.M.L.R. 315.

In a ruling of July 10, 1968, the German Bundesfinanzhof took the view that in certain cases the German constitutional provisions guaranteeing fundamental rights might be a bar to the application of Community law (Aussenwirtschafts dienst der Betriebsberater, 1968, 354, quoted in Second General Report).

Dutch Constitution, which is so explicit about this precedence, doubts might subsist as to the precise consequences. Furthermore if the sole justification for supremacy of Community law over national law were national law itself, this supremacy would be at the mercy of the next constitutional amendment. Other grounds had therefore to be found which would be accepted by all national jurisdictions without reference to their particular national legal orders. This ground was obviously the Community legal order itself, which was accepted by all the Member States which "have adhered to the Treaty on the same conditions, definitively and without any reservations other than those set out in the supplementary protocols."[27] The Court has always considered that the provisions of Community law were integrated into the legal systems applicable in the Member States and that the terms and the spirit of the Treaty make it impossible for the Member States, as a corollary, to accord precedence to a unilateral and subsequent measure over a legal system accepted by them on the basis of reciprocity. The Court added that "the executive force of Community law cannot vary from one State to another in deference to subsequent domestic laws, without jeopardizing the attainment of the objectives of the Treaty set out in Article 5 (2) and giving rise to the discrimination prohibited by Article 7."[28]

Therefore, "the law stemming from the Treaty, an independent source of law, could not, because of its special and original nature, be overriden by domestic legal provisions, however framed without being deprived of its character as Community law and without the legal basis of the Community itself being called into question."[29] To put it simply: either

---

[27] Joined Cases 9 and 58/65 *San Michèle* v. *High Authority* [1967] E.C.R. 1 at 30.

[28] Case 6/64 *Costa* v. *ENEL* [1964] E.C.R. at 594. This was once again emphasised by the Court in Case 128/78 *Commission* v. *United Kingdom* ("Tachographs") [1979] E.C.R. at 429.

[29] *Ibid.* See also Case 11/70 *Internationale Handelsgesellschaft* v. *Einfuhr-und Vorratsstelle Getreide* [1970] E.C.R. 1125 at 1134 (3). Mention must be made in this connection of a decision of the German Bundesverfassungsgericht (Federal Constitutional Court) of May 29, 1974 [1974] 2 C.M.L.R. 540, same parties, where the German Court held that it never rules on the validity of a rule of Community law; it added however that it can hold that such a rule cannot be applied by the authorities or courts of the Federal Republic of Germany in so far as it conflicts with a rule of the German Constitution relating to fundamental rights. This view was rejected by the Court of Jusice clearly stating that the effect of a Community measure within a Member State cannot be affected by

Community law stands by itself, is uniformly applied and has precedence over domestic law or it does not exist. This view now seems to be generally recognised in the Member States, although with varying degrees of conviction and acceptance. Some of the earliest and most important rulings of national courts and tribunals should be mentioned here, since they constitute essential steps towards recognition of the Community legal order and its implications. In Belgium reference must be made to a decision of 1971 of the Cour de Cassation in the Case *Belgian State* v. *Formagerie Franco-Suisse*;[30] in France, the Cour de Cassation, 1975, *Administration des Douanes* v. *Jacques Vabre et al.*[31] and for Italy mention must be made of a judgment of the Corte di Cassazione of 1972, although recent developments seem much less promising.[32]

The general principle of precedence of Community law over national law having been established, it is necessary to examine some of its more concrete consequences. As far as any national court is concerned, the Court of Justice has described its obligations as follows. Directly applicable rules of Community

allegations that it runs counter to fundamental rights as formulated by the Constitution of that State (see Case 11/70, above). See also Case 4/73 *Nold* v. *Commission* [1974] E.C.R. 491.

[30] See [1972] C.M.L.R. 330 at 373. The Cour de Cassation considered that "In the event of a conflict between a norm of domestic law and a norm of international law which produces direct effects in the internal legal system the rule established by the Treaty shall prevail. The primacy of the Treaty results from the very nature of international treaty law."

[31] The French Cour de Cassation considered that the EEC Treaty, which by virtue of Art. 55 of the Constitution has an authority greater than that of statutes, institutes a separate legal order integrated with that of the Member States [1975] C.M.L.R. 336. However, the situation in France is far from satisfactory, since the Conseil d'Etat, although it referred two cases to the Court of Justice for a preliminary ruling (Cases 11/74 *Union des Minoteries de la Champagne* v. *France* [1974] E.C.R. 877 and 48/74 *Charmasson* v. *Minister for Economic Affairs and Finance* [1974] E.C.R. 1383) does not seem ready yet to accept the unconditional precedence of Community law: see judgment of the Conseil d'Etat of December 22, 1978, in the Case *Cohn-Bendit* (1979) C.M.L.R. 701. See also Sixteenth General Report (1982), 306.

[32] Corte di Cassazione *Schiavello* v. *Nesci* [1975] 2 C.M.L.R. 198 at 202). See, however, Corte Costituzionale *Frontini* v. *Ministero delle Finanze* (C.M.L.R. 1974, 372); see also Court of Justice, Case 106/77 *Amministrazione delle Finanze dello Stato* v. *Simmenthal* [1978] E.C.R. 629, from which it clearly appears that there is a reluctance to accept all the consequences of the precedence of Community law.

law are a direct source of rights and duties for all those affected thereby, including any national court whose task it is, as an organ of a Member State, to protect, in a case within its jurisdiction, the rights conferred upon individuals by Community law. In accordance with the principle of precedence of Community law, the relationship between provisions of the Treaty and the directly applicable measures of the institutions on the one hand and the national laws of the Member States on the other is such that, those provisions and measures, by their coming into force, automatically render any conflicting provision of current national law inapplicable. Any recognition that national legislative measures, which are incompatible with provisions of Community law, have any legal effect would amount to a corresponding denial of the effectiveness of obligations undertaken unconditionally and irrevocably by Member States pursuant to the Treaty and would consequently endanger the very foundations of the Community. It follows that every national court in a case within its jurisdiction must apply Community law in its entirety and protect rights which the latter confers on individuals. Accordingly it must set aside any provision of national law which may conflict with it, whether prior or subsequent to the Community rule. It is not necessary for the national court to request or await the prior setting aside of such provision by legislative or other constitutional means.[33]

With regard to legislative bodies, the Court indicated that the principle of the precedence of provisions of Community law—in so far as it is an integral part of, and takes precedence in, the legal order applicable to the territory of each of the Member States—precludes the valid adoption of new national legislative measures to the extent to which they would be incompatible with Community provisions.[34]

As far as other national authorities are concerned, it is clear that the respect for Community law's precedence and the obligations for the Member States under Article 5 not only prevent them from enacting measures which are incompatible with Community provisions, but also impose upon them the obligation to abolish all existing contrary measures, whatever their nature. Although these measures are inapplicable, their maintenance gives rise to

---

[33] Case 106/77 above (*Simmenthal*), at 643–644 (14–18 and 21, 22, 24).
[34] *Ibid*. (at 17). See also Case 230/78 *Eridania* v. *Minister of Agriculture and Forestry* [1979] E.C.R. 2749.

an ambiguous situation by maintaining a state of uncertainty as to the possibilities available to the beneficiaries of the Community rule of relying on them.[35] It follows from the above that autonomy of the Community legal order, direct effect and precedence of Community rules over national measures are all aspects of one and the same thing: the particular nature of Community law.

A more recent development in this respect is the Court's reference to the usefulness[36] or effectiveness[37] of Community acts to justify the right of individuals to rely, before their national courts, on the obligations imposed by the act. It concerns cases where Community authorities have imposed on Member States, by means of directives, the obligation to pursue a particular course of conduct. These acts are not directly applicable, since the choice is left to the national authorities as to the form and method of implementing the directive. The implementation is left, within limits, to their discretion. As has been seen, according to the direct effect theory, the right of individuals to invoke Community acts before their national courts does not exist when the obligation provided for in the act leaves to the addressee a discretionary latitude. However, the Court admits as was also seen before[38] that provisions of directives can have direct effect especially after the time-limit set for their implementation has changed. Similarly, interested parties have the right to rely on such acts in order to have the national court determine whether the competent national authority, in exercising the choice which is left to it, has kept within the limits of its discretion as set out in the directive.[39] However whether or not the national authorities have exercised their discretionary power cannot be subject to legal review; neither can the material content of the measures which the national authorities have taken within their margin of discretion. "It is the duty of the national court before which the directive is

---

[35] Case 167/73 *Commission* v. *France* [1974] E.C.R. 359 at 372 (41); see also Case 159/78 *Commission* v. *Italy* [1979] E.C.R. 3247 and Case 61/77 *Commission* v. *Ireland* [1978] E.C.R. 417 at 442.

[36] Case 51/76 *Nederlandse Ondernemingen* v. *Inspecteur der Invoerrechten en Accijzen* [1977] E.C.R. 113 at 127 (29).

[37] Case 38/77 *ENKA* v. *Inspecteur der Invoerrechten en Accijzen* [1977] E.C.R. 2203 at 2211 (9).

[38] See above: Acts provided in Art 189, p. 89.

[39] Case 38/77, above (*ENKA*), at 2212 (10).

invoked to determine whether the disputed national measure falls outside the margin of the discretion of the Member State."[40]

4. Sources of Community law

As was previously indicated, the Community legal order has its own sources, which consist, not only of the European treaties and the acts of the institutions issued in pursuance of the powers conferred upon them (regulations, directives, decisions and agreements),[41] but also the rules relating to the application of primary and secondary Community law. These rules comprise international law, insofar as applicable,[42] and the general principles of law[43] including fundamental rights. The latter play an important role as the Court pointed out: "respect for fundamental rights forms an integral part of the general principles of law protected by the Court of Justice," and added that "the protection of such rights, whilst inspired by the constitutional traditions common to Member States, must be ensured within the framework . . . and objectives of the Community."[44] Formula-

---

[40] Case 51/76, above, n.36 (*Nederlandse Ondernemingen*), at 127 (29).

[41] See above: Community Acts, p. 88.

[42] Agreements concluded by the Community with third States or international organisations (EEC, Art. 228) are, of course, governed by the rules of international law. On the other hand, as the Court pointed out: when exercising their rights to lay down Community rules, the institutions are not bound by provisions of international law unless the Community itself has assumed the rights and obligations resulting for the Member States from international agreements to which they are parties, and unless the provisions of those agreements have direct effect within the Community: joined Cases 21 to 24/72 *International Fruit Company* v. *Produktschap voor Groenten en Fruit* [1972] E.C.R. 1219 at 1227. See also Arts. 37 (5) and *ibid.* at 1227 (18).

As for Treaty precedence over conventions concluded between Member States before its entrance into force, see Case 10/61 *Commission* v. *Italy* [1962] E.C.R. at 10, see also EEC Art. 219.

The precedence of Community law over all other applicable provisions, including international law, is recognised by the European Community Act 1972, ss.2(1) and (4).

[43] See Case 159/82 *Verli-Wallace* v. *Commission* [1983] E.C.R. 2711 at 2718 (8) and above: The Court of Justice, Grounds for annulment, p. 62.

[44] Case 11/70, *Internationale Handelsgesellschaft* v. *Einfuhr-und Vorratsstelle Getreide* [1970] E.C.R. 1125 at 1134 (4). See also Case 25/70 *Einfuhr-und Vorratsstelle* v. *Köster* [1970] E.C.R. 1161 at 1176 (36) where the Court found that a system of licences for import and export, involving a deposit, did not violate any right of a fundamental nature and Case 44/79 *Hauer* v. *Land Rheinland-Pfalz* [1979] E.C.R. 3727 where the Court examined whether a Community regulation violated the right of property and of the free exercise of a professional activity.

tion of fundamental rights is to be found, *inter alia*, in the Convention for the protection of Human Rights and Fundamental Freedoms,[45] ratified by all the Member States, to which the Court has referred in interpreting a Community provision concerning equality of treatment as regards membership of trade unions and the exercise of rights attached thereto.[46] Another formulation to be found in the Joint Declaration by the European Parliament, the Council and the Commission of April 5, 1977 on fundamental rights.[47]

Twenty-eight years ago I drafted an Article to be inserted in the Treaty Chapter on the Court of Justice which would indicate the sources of law to be applied. Although different words would be used today its basic indications still seem to be applicable today:

"1. The Court whose function it is to ensure the rule of law in the execution of this Treaty, shall apply:
   (a) the provisions of this Treaty and of the judicial acts issued by the institutions;
   (b) the conventions to which the Community is a party or which are undertaken on its behalf;
   (c) the customary law of the Community;
   (d) the general principles of the law of the Community;
   (e) the municipal law of the Member States in case of explicit or tacit reference.
2. In case of reference to international law, the Court shall apply Article 38, paragraph 1, of the Statute of the International Court of Justice.
3. As auxiliary means for the determination of the applicable law, the Court shall apply the decisions of international tribunals, those of the Community and the doctrine."[48]

---

[45] Signed in Rome on November 4, 1950, it entered into force on September 3, 1953. In April 1979, the Commission adopted a memorandum on the accession of the European Communities to the Convention; this accession would bind the Community institutions and would imply recognition of the competence of the European Court of Human Rights (Bull. 4–1979, 16). See Case 4/73 *Nold* v. *Commission* [1974] E.C.R. 491 at 507 (13).

[46] Case 36/75 *Rutili* v. *Minister for the Interior* [1975] E.C.R. 1219 at 1232 (31–32).

[47] O.J. 1977, C. 103 and Bull. 3–1977, preliminary chap. See also the European Council Declaration of April 8, 1978 on democracy (Bull. 3–1978, preliminary chap.).

[48] P.S.R.F. Mathijsen *Le Droit de la Communauté Européenne du Charbon et de l'Acier; une étude des sources*, Martinus Nijhoff, 's-Gravenhage (1957) 193.

5. Application of domestic law by the European Court

The question of applicability of national law by the Community institutions was raised on several occasions before the Court of Justice, but the Court decided that it lacked the competence to apply the internal law of the Member States;[49] consequently it cannot examine a claim that by taking a decision an institution has violated national law; neither can the Court decide on the interpretation of a national provision.[50] Application of national law by the European Court, however, does take place where the Treaty refers explicitly to national concepts.[51] This is the case, for instance, under Article 58 of the Treaty, which refers to companies and firms formed in accordance with the law of a Member States,[52] and under Article 215, which provides that in the case of non-contractual liability the Community shall make good any damage caused by its institutions or servants "in accordance with the general principles common to the laws of the Member States." Similarly, when the Court is called upon to solve a question for which there are no Treaty provisions, it must solve the problem "by reference to the rules acknowledged by the legislation, the learned writings and the case-law of the member countries".[53]

6. Conclusions

As is shown by the foregoing considerations, the Community legal order grew and developed mainly at the hands of the Community judges.[54] Over the years the Court has played an essential role in consolidating its autonomy *vis-à-vis* municipal

---

[49] See *e.g.* Case 1/58 *Stork* v. *High Authority* [1959] E.C.R. 17; joined Cases 36–40/59 *Geitling* v. *High Authority* [1960] E.C.R. 423. See, however, joined Cases 17 and 20/61 *Klökner* v. *High Authority* [1962] E.C.R. 325 and more recently Case 159/78 *Commission* v. *Italy* [1979] E.C.R. 3247.

[50] Case 78/70 *Deutsche Grammophon* v. *Metro* [1971] E.C.R. 487 at 498 (3).

[51] See Case 50/71 *Wünsche* v. *Einfuhr-und Vorratsstelle Getreide* [1972] E.C.R. 53 at 64 (6).

[52] See, *e.g.* Case 18/57 *Nold* v. *High Authority* [1959] E.C.R. 41 at 48.

[53] Joined Cases 7/56 and 3 to 7/57 *Algera* v. *Common Assembly* [1957–58] E.C.R. 39 at 55. Another example is the definition of "misuse of power" (EEC, Art. 173) based on a comparative study by the Advocate-General of this concept in the municipal law of the Member States (Case 3/54 *ASSIDER* v. *High Authority* [1954–56] E.C.R. 63 at 74).

[54] The Member States did also contribute to the consolidation and development of community law; see *e.g.* the Convention on the Law applicable to Contractual Obligations (O.J. 1980, L. 266/1).

and international law, in emphasising its originality and in imposing its precedence. It goes without saying that this task would have been impossible without the co-operation, understanding and adaptibility of the national judges, but the Community Court was and still is the driving force. It should be clear also that the task of this Court is not limited to applying, developing and interpreting Community law *stricto sensu*. According to the Treaty,[55] the Court shall ensure that "the law" is observed. Law in this provision and as it is understood by the Court refers to the concept of what is "right," much more so than to anything that has been described and analysed in the foregoing pages of this book. Seen in this light, the European Communities appear beyond all the limitations, ambiguities, hesitations and conflicts as a legal, political, social and economic system which, thanks to its balanced institutional structure and inherent potential, constitutes the only possible solution for Europe's problems and the only hope for its development.

Further Reading

Chap. 7–Community Law

Pierre Pescatore, "The doctrine of 'Direct Effect': An Infant Disease" (1983) 8 E.L. Rev. 155.

[55] EEC, Art. 164.

INDEX

(References are also made to footnotes)